WHITE AUSTRALIA HAS A BLACK HISTORY:

William Cooper and First Nations Peoples' Political Activism

William Cooper Gentle Warrior Series No 1

By

Barbara Miller

Copyright © 2019 by Barbara Miller.

All rights reserved. No part of this publication may be reproduced, distributed or transmitted in any form or by any means, including photocopying, recording, or other electronic or mechanical methods, without the prior written permission of the publisher, except in the case of brief quotations embodied in critical reviews and certain other noncommercial uses permitted by copyright law. For permission requests, write to the publisher, addressed "Attention: Permissions Coordinator," at the address below.

Barbara Miller /Barbara Miller Books

PO Box 425 Westcourt

Cairns, Australia 4870

www.barbara-miller-books.com

Ordering Information:

Quantity sales. Special discounts are available on quantity purchases by corporations, associations, and others. For details, contact the "Special Sales Department" at the address above.

Name of book /Barbara Miller
—1st ed.

ISBN-13: 978-0-6484722-1-6 KINDLE

ISBN-13: 978-0-6484722-2-3 EPUB

ISBN-13: 978-0-6484722-3-0 PAPERBACK

DOWNLOAD FREE GIFT NOW

Just to thank you for buying my book, I would like to give you a 14-page PDF of the hidden history of the first contact of Europeans with Australian Aborigines. It is the untold story that is not in your school text books. Hear from Aborigines who have had the story passed down through generations and from the explorers.

For information on my other books go to – www.barbara-miller-books.com

TO DOWNLOAD GO TO

http://eepurl.com/dn69ab

I'd love a review on Amazon and/or Goodreads. Here is the amazon link to this book - https://www.amazon.com/dp/B07X1MYCDX/

And the link to my Goodreads page - https://www.goodreads.com/author/show/17901589.Barbara_Miller

You can also email me feedback. I'd love to hear from you –

bmiller-books@bigpond.com or contact me on facebook - https://www.facebook.com/Barbara-Miller-Books-479991872149265/

Website: www.barbara-miller-books.com

Check the following books out at the end of this book

Check these books out at the end of this book

or on www.barbara-miller-books.com

Reviews

As the CEO of the Aboriginal organisation servicing the very suburbs where Uncle William Cooper spent his Melbourne years as an activist for our people, I am proud to always try my best to promote his legacy to this day - with the annual William Cooper Cup in National Aborigines and Islanders Day Observance Committee (NAIDOC) Week, the William Cooper Walk, hosting a Gala Dinner in his name – and even accompanying Uncle Boydie and family to Israel in 2010 in Uncle William's honour.

After nominating him successfully for the Inaugural Victorian Indigenous Honour Roll, I am so pleased to see this wonderful book Barbara has written continue to tell the story of this hero of our people. Well done Barbara!

Colleen Marrion, Founder/CEO, Gathering Place Health Service Ltd, Maidstone, Victoria

Miller's book about William Cooper "narrates the amazing story of an Aboriginal man's fight against racial injustice, despite his not having any legal rights ...

Miller's moving historical account fills in missing gaps in the story of Indigenous activism in Australia, including her own participation in the 1970s and 1980s. Moreover, the book adds a significant new dimension to our understandings of Indigenous politics on a global scale both pre and post-World War Two. And perhaps, most importantly, as discussed below, the account points to the intersections between Australia's Indigenous and immigration policies or, to put it another way, its internal and external racial strategies. As Miller suggests, these issues are deeply connected. This insight underscores the book's current relevance in thinking about problems on both internal and external fronts facing Australia – and other countries – in the early decades of the 21st century.

William Cooper was a stoic fighter and determined to speak out against the discrimination of his own people. Despite his family suffering enormous deprivation under white Australia's colonial policies that included explicit policies of genocide, protectionism and assimilation, Cooper set out at an early age to bring attention to the plight of Australian Aborigines…

Barbara Miller's account of William Cooper and these turbulent years of emerging Aboriginal activism in the 1920s and 1930s is truly fascinating and offers what I see as three important insights. First, apart from reminding the reader of the commitment and agency of Indigenous leaders dedicated to fighting the deeply racist policies of the period, Miller's narrative is a welcome reminder that black activism started well before the civil rights era of the 1960s and 1970s. In short, contrary to popular belief, the Australian black movement did not start with the 1962 amendments to the Commonwealth Electoral Act of 1918, 1967 Referendum, or 1972 Aboriginal Tent Embassy in Canberra and related black mobilisation centered in Sydney's suburb of Redfern. Rather, the civil rights movement in Australia was prefigured by earlier campaigns and protests that had long historical connections to British and United States anti-slavery movements…

Secondly, the William Cooper book underscores the global influences on domestic Indigenous politics in Australia … The FCAA (Federal Council for the Advancement of Aborigines), like the National Association for the Advancement of Colored People (NAACP) and the American Indian Movement (AIM) in the United States, had learnt to aggressively seek international oversight over oppressive national policies. Specifically, these organisations turned to the laws of other countries as well as the collective authority of the United Nations as leverage for domestic legislative reform. (see Darian-Smith 2012)

Thirdly, and this is what I see as truly innovative in this historical account, are the parallels and connections William Cooper made over 80 years ago between Australia's policies toward immigrant refugees and its policies toward its domestic native communities. As Miller provocatively notes, 'The White Australia Policy is usually thought of in terms of immigration but it also affected policy towards Aborigines. Why go to all that trouble to keep "coloured" races out of Australia and then have a growing group of mixed race within your own borders? This line of argument resists conventional sensibilities and offers an insightful historical lesson. So often indigenous politics – and indigenous studies in general – are contained within national borders and classified as domestic issues. … analysts and academics of both indigenous and immigrant issues seem curiously determined to keep these arenas separated.

Eve Darian-Smith, PhD LLB,

Professor and Departmental Chair Global & International Studies, USA

This book adds to the history of Aboriginal people in Australia and in particular tells the story of one man, William Cooper, who not only fought for his own people but stood up for the Jewish people who were being persecuted by Hitler. I recommend this book as important reading for all Australians to learn about the depth of the struggle for Aboriginal people in Australia and the collective leadership who were prepared to continue to fight for the rights of Aboriginal people. It documents the legacy of leaders like William Cooper who hand down the baton to the next generation to continue the struggle.

Dr Esme Bamblett,

CEO, Victorian Aborigines Advancement League, Melbourne

This book is more than just the story of one man's life. It extends to his influence on political and social activism in Australia, taking the story on after his death to the 1967 Referendum that finally accepted that Aborigines are citizens of this nation, to the watershed Mabo High Court decision on indigenous land rights, and the Rudd Apology for the 'Stolen Generations'. It is a book that includes the author's own involvement in the struggles and action on behalf of indigenous Australians. Barbara knows her subject and has thoroughly researched the story, including the lots of details of who was involved and what was done in many places. ...This is a very significant book that reveals so much that is unknown by most of the nation, and is a real challenge to all of us.

John Blacket
Khesed Indigenous Ministries, Khesed Education and Khesed Productions, Perth

A powerful book has been written by Barbara Miller, a book that doesn't shy away from the difficult issues of the time, a book that should be read by all. It's the story of how one person can make a difference and teach us about humanity, the story of William Cooper. Thank you, Barbara Miller, you have brought the story of the Aboriginal People and William Cooper into our home and into our hearts.

Your own personal journey is remarkable and brave, and you tell my story, the story of the Jewish people with great understanding and compassion. I thank your husband Pastor Norman, who, together with you, has made such a difference through your enormous devotion and energy. My parents arrived in Australia in January 1939, refugees from Nazi Europe. Their exhaustive attempt to get visas for my mother's German family failed and 29 members of the family were killed in the Shoah, the Nazi Holocaust.

My mother had a little mantra which she would keep on repeating to me, "Do you know how lucky we are to be alive?" Till one day I heard her say this in front of my 15-year-old daughter, and I realised that her feeling of guilt, which had passed onto me, was being perpetuated. I still see her in my lounge room as I said, "Mum, do you realise what you have been saying to me for so many years? Please stop, you are not right, we are entitled to be alive, we all are entitled to be alive. Blame the perpetrators, and the bystanders." Mum never used those words again.

And in the words of Eddie Mabo: “Persist and keep fighting the fight. If you give up, they win. So, don’t give up.”

Josie Lacey OAM
Life Member of the Executive Council of Australian Jewry, Sydney

Dedication and Acknowledgements

I would like to dedicate this book to the God of Abraham, Isaac and Jacob and His Messiah who has given me the vision, inspiration and strength to write this book. I would also like to dedicate this book to my beloved husband Norman for without his encouragement, belief in me and helping me to have time to write, this book would not have been completed. I would also like to dedicate this book to my son Michael and my granddaughter Jaydah, who I dearly love, and wish that this will be an inheritance for them and that they will achieve their dreams as I have achieved mine.

It is a privilege to dedicate this book to the Aboriginal and Jewish communities who have suffered so much but also achieved so much and stand out as a beacon to our common humanity. In particular I dedicate this book to William Cooper's family, especially Alf (Uncle Boydie) Turner who has done so much to promote the Cooper legacy along with friends Avraham (Abe) Schwarz and David Jack.

Special thanks go to David and Carol Jack and David's mother Betty who provide us with a home away from home in Melbourne and help us with transport. David's work on the photographs in the book is critical to its presentation and he spent many hours on the photos.

Also, thanks to the following for photos – the Australian Institute of Aboriginal and Torres Strait Islander Studies, the Mitchell Library or State Library of New South Wales (NSW), the Fryer Library of the University of Queensland and the National Library of Australia and Yad Vashem Holocaust Museum, Israel. The State Library of Victoria was a useful place for me to read the *Argus* newspaper in 1938 to see what William Cooper would have been reading at the time.

I want to acknowledge the editing advice of Abe Schwarz who has extensive knowledge of the honouring of William Cooper and Dr Sue Taffe and Dr Esme Bamblett for comments on the Cairns and Victorian Aborigines Advancement Leagues.

Foreword

As the proud grandson of Uncle William Cooper, I am honoured to have been asked by my friend Barbara Miller to write a few words in a Foreword to this publication you are now holding.

Pastors Norman and Barbara Miller have demonstrated continuous support in putting the name of my grandfather, William Cooper, out there in the world. I appreciate that Pastors Norman and Barbara specially flew back to Israel in December 2010 to support the legacy of my grandfather when he was honoured at the Yad Vashem Holocaust Museum in Jerusalem.

On reading the draft of this book, I am pleased that Barbara has so carefully researched and painstakingly recorded so many details of my grandfather's life, and not just his political activism. She has also given you an appreciation of his personal side – what the man was really like with whom I lived from when I was a baby growing up to be a 9-year-old boy.

My recollections of grandfather were that he was a quiet man until it came to the plight of his people - then he would speak up, their plight was constantly on his mind and he wouldn't talk much about anything else except the injustices his people suffered, and constantly endured.

Grandfathers' activism helped me realise that there is a greater purpose for us than just to exist for one's own life: a just and righteous act of unselfishness, a continuing fight against oppression and that he enacted one of Australia's greatest examples of living for that greater purpose.

In 1938, he was still very frustrated with the way in which things were progressing about the rights of his people, but once again this quiet man found time for others. He focused his attention on something that sickened him deeply and was very much at the heart of the matter of his *own* people and their persecution.

Grandfather had followed the constant newspaper reports about Germany under the rule of Adolf Hitler and the Nazi Party since 1933, but after the reports of the Krystallnacht atrocities in November 1938 – he could see that the singling out of the Jewish people in Europe for extermination was clearly Hitler's intent.

Grandfather could sadly recognise that same affliction of fear, desperation, bewilderment and a sense of hopelessness which the Jewish people now faced in Europe. Jewish leaders called on the world to do something to stop the atrocities.

When many countries around the world would *not* act … *he* did. After waiting a few weeks, when there was still no serious reaction from world leaders, grandfather organised and led a delegation himself to protest at the German Consulate in Melbourne.

On December 6th 1938, walking from his Footscray home, they marched on the Consulate in South Melbourne, together with other Aboriginal people, to convey a Resolution *"condemning the cruel persecution of the Jewish people by the Nazi government of Germany"* and asking *"for this persecution to be brought to an end"*.

I am proud to be the grandson of William Cooper, of this wonderful man and have tried to follow in his footsteps in the pursuit of a fair go. He was much loved, especially by his family and it is my hope that this book inspires you, the reader, as much as his family continues to be inspired and motivated by his legacy.

Uncle Boydie (Alfred Turner)

Mooroopna, Victoria

Preface

My book "William Cooper Gentle Warrior: Standing Up for Australian Aborigines and Persecuted Jews" was published in November 2012. In updating it in 2019, I have found it to be too big for one book so I have created the William Cooper Gentle Warrior Series and No 1 book is focusing on William Cooper's Aboriginal activism and No 2 book is focusing on his activism on behalf of the Jewish community. In both books, his grandson Uncle Boydie or Alf Turner and other family members have carried on his legacy and fulfilled William's unfulfilled dreams. So, the story continues.

Also, as William Cooper was a pioneer of the Aboriginal movement for human rights in Australia, much of what has happened since his passing has built on the platform he established. This means book No 1 really becomes a history of Indigenous affairs from contact till today. However, William Cooper was not alone. The stories of other key Aboriginal leaders of his time and beyond are also covered.

It is a privilege for me to bring this story to you. As you will see, I became part of the unfolding story and maybe you will too.

Table of Contents

Chapter 1

Cooper's Early Years

William Cooper, Melbourne 1935
18 December 1860 – 29 March 1941

William Cooper was born in Yorta Yorta[1] (or Joti-jota) country near Echuca, Victoria on 18 December 1860 - a colourful period that was better known for paddleboats and bushrangers. He died on 29 March 1941 and was buried with other Yorta Yorta elders in the Aboriginal community of Cummeragunja (Cummera), located near Echuca. The map below marks the position of this land.

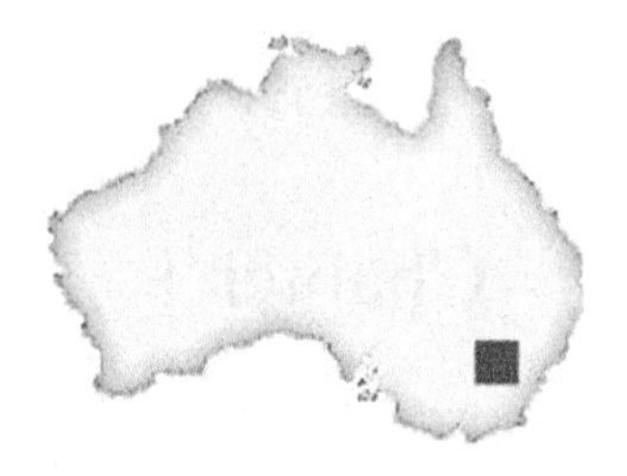

Yorta Yorta country on the map of Australia www.ausanthrop.net

When William was born, Echuca had yet to become the pivotal stop for the Murray River paddleboat trade. By 1870 when William was ten years old, the rapid growth in the wool and farming industries meant the Echuca wharf was built to make transport easier along the Murray River. The dock was to service paddle boats that came down the Murray River carrying wool from the country stations, where it would be unloaded and transported to Melbourne, the capital of Victoria.

Echuca Wharf with steamer Ulunga and barge unloading wool.
Photo Danny Matthews 1900 (Norman collection)

Paddleboats weren't the only national influence on the area William Cooper was born. Glenrowan, south of the Murray River in Victoria, was the place where Ned Kelly, the infamous Australian bushranger made his last stand before being captured and later hanged. William Cooper grew up during the time when Ned Kelly's infamous activities became part of Australian identity (1855-1880). To some, Ned Kelly was a symbol of Irish Australian resistance against the Anglo Australian ruling class and Australia's answer to Robin Hood. To others, however, he was a police killer and bank robber. His story and the issues around land selection, national identity and policing have intrigued Australians ever since.

Today, the paddleboats carrying wool and bushrangers have stopped, and Echuca is a tourist destination, where people take paddle boat trips down the picturesque Murray River.

The idyllic nature of the area around the Murray River today seems to hide the memory of the days when white settlers took land from the Yorta Yorta people, the local Aboriginal tribe. For many years, there was a famous saying: "Australia rides on the sheep's back" that described how the important the wool industry was as the source of the nation's wealth. While many Australians well know this expression, I say "Australia rode on the back of Aboriginal people" because the nation's wealth was built on their land. The government did not compensate them for this. This marginalised Aboriginal people into poverty as their hunter-gatherer economy depended on the land.

Resistance to White Settlement

With stories about the effects of white settlement filtering through, Aboriginal people around the Murray River where William Cooper was born offered more resistance to white settlement than those around Port Phillip. Despite their opposition, white settlement proved destructive to their way of life. Clark notes, "Their beliefs went first. To see white men desecrating their sacred places, violating their law and custom – yet coming to no harm – shattered their spiritual strength."[2]

This was because Aboriginal people had well-developed law and custom with the breaking of this law bringing severe punishment, even death, from spiritual forces or by the one appointed by the tribe to enforce it. I remember when I first visited Aurukun on Cape York in 1974, Violet

Yunkaporta had to put her "smell on me," i.e., her sweat. This was so that the spirits would recognise me and not harm me as we went by a small boat downstream past the "poison places" or "sacred sites" they wanted to protect from mining. Clark comments, "Instead the Aborigine was ejected from an environment in which his totemic ancestry gave him an assured place from birth to death, into an environment in which he was superfluous."[3]

It wasn't just the erosion of the spiritual strength of the Aboriginal people – their economy changed. As early settlers had their land and a cheap source of white convict labour, it was it harder for Aborigines to make the changes necessary to survive. Aboriginal people were a hunter-gatherer society, but they could no longer sustain this, so they had to find odd jobs working for the white settlers and enter the wages economy. They were no longer able to hunt and fish on their land as before as it had been taken over by gun-happy squatters' sheep and cattle. The habitat could no longer sustain native wildlife in the same way, and the settlers and their animals fouled the waterholes. At times, desperate for food, Aborigines would spear the sheep or cattle and would be shot in retaliation.

Group of Aboriginals, Chowilla Station 1886. C. Bayliss in Views of scenery on the lower Murray flood of 1886. New South Wales (NSW) Royal Commission, Conservation of Water (Mitchell Library, State Library of New South Wales (NSW) – PXE 674/1/39)

Daniel Mathews

Some Christians established missions to protect Aborigines from the squatters and to feed, clothe and school them, teaching them the Christian faith as well.

One such missionary was Daniel Mathews, whose criticism of the treatment of Aborigines made him an enemy of many. Daniel and his wife Janet faced opposition from local pastoralists who resented the loss of cheap sex and near-free labour on their properties that Aborigines had provided. Harris writes, "So opposed to slavery was Daniel that he would in times of hardship allow his farm to deteriorate rather than be accused of using Aboriginal labour without fair payment."[4]

Daniel's opposition to slavery is traced back to an interesting experience his father had. Daniel's father was Captain John Mathews of St Ives, England who was involved with the slave trade from West Africa to the sugar plantations of the West Indies during the 1830s. While on a voyage, Captain Mathews saw a ghostly figure of a man pointing to a specific latitude and longitude on the map in his ship's chart house.

Astonished, he felt the need to sail to that destination. When Captain Mathews arrived, he was even more amazed to find the man resembling the figure he had seen in his chart house, adrift on a raft. This man was lost at sea with no hope of rescue but had prayed all night that God would somehow intervene, and he would be saved. Amazingly, Captain Mathews was used to answer his prayers. This Divine intervention was a life-changing moment for the Captain, who, after heart-searching conversations with the man he rescued, became a Christian. He refused to carry any more slaves and tipped his rum overboard.[5]

As a result of his conversion and conviction, Captain Mathews lost his command of the ship and started a small business in England. This business did not succeed, causing him to migrate with his family to Australia in 1851. After the incident on the boat, John and his wife Honor had become Wesleyans and brought their family up with grace before meals, prayers twice a day, no alcohol and a strict observance of the Sabbath. Daniel Mathews was much affected by his upbringing, evidenced in his incorporating twice-daily prayers, for example, into the life of the mission he started.

Daniel and Janet Mathews and Maloga Mission

In 1864, Daniel and his brothers, John and William, set up a ships' provider business at Echuca for the Murray river-boat trade. Then in 1867, the brothers bought 800 acres of Crown land on the NSW side of the Murray River, three miles downstream from Barmah which is near Echuca. This property had a mile of beautiful river frontage, and part of it, 20 acres, was allocated to establish a mission.

The land Daniel and his brothers owned was an Aboriginal corroboree and camping site, so they used the name the Aborigines called the land - "Maloga" meaning sandhill.

The land was part of the "Moira" or "beautiful" country of lakes, lagoons, and swamps. There were red gum forests and fertile alluvial flats, the country teeming with fish, birdlife, kangaroo, emu, and possum. Food was plentiful, so there was less need for a nomadic existence compared to other tribes. As well as being hunter-gatherers, the Aboriginal people were skilled craftsmen in weaving and basketry. However, all this was changing with the encroaching of white settlement.

Maloga mission began on 26 July 1874. Daniel and Janet Mathews had tried to bring the plight of Aboriginal people to the attention of the community by talking to Members of Parliament, church leaders and writing to the media but all their attempts seemed to fall on deaf ears. It seemed many members of the community just wanted Aborigines to die out and the problem to go away. The Mathews decided they had to do something themselves, so Daniel and Janet built a schoolhouse at Maloga that formed the basis of the mission.

Janet was very devout, devoted to the mission and hardworking, with her father being in the ministry himself. He was Rev Kerr Johnstone who was chaplain at the Seamen's Bethel, Sandridge (later Port Melbourne) for 25 years.

Maloga Mission and the Cooper Family

As part of his stand for the Aborigines, Daniel got a reputation for physical and moral courage, going into the station hands and sawyers' camps to rescue Aboriginal girls and take them back to Maloga. Some of these girls, at the ages of eleven or twelve, had babies fathered by the men at the camps, and Daniel was often physically assaulted or threatened with firearms.[6]

One of the first arrivals at Maloga was Lizzie Atkinson, William Cooper's sister who arrived on 26 July 1874. She was about 14 years old and had a child Frankie, about two years old. Daniel Mathews persuaded her and another 14-year-old Aboriginal girl, Sarah with her 15-month-old son Herbert, to come, on the grounds they were in moral and physical danger and in need of care. The girls were living at Bama Mills where white men in the camp had used them.

Lizzie, Sarah Walker, Old Gracie, and Louisa at a mia-mia. (Image courtesy of Australian Institute of Aboriginal and Torres Strait Islander Studies, Alick Jackomos collection (N3743.32)

About a week later after their arrival, on 3 August Daniel decided to go and pick up Lizzie's mother, Kitty after requests from Lizzie and Sarah. In his diary he wrote:

The girls have expressed a wish several times that Kitty, Lizzie's mother, should come down from O'Shanassy's (station). As I think this would tend to settle the girls, I consented.... I started off this evening, arriving there at sundown. The few in camp welcomed me, and Kitty was ready at once to 'yam'ya'bee Maloga' ('Go along' or 'walk' Wallithica dialect) to join her daughter with Jack, her little boy 7 years old and Ada 5 years.

(4 August, Moira Station) Before the daylight was fairly in, I drew up to the camp and got Kitty, Jacky, and Ada into the cart and had them nicely covered up from the cold. Billy (William Cooper) and Bobby (Kitty's sons) each rode a horse belonging to Mr Kinnear and accompanied us all the way down to Maloga. The meeting between Kitty and the girls was affectionate.

(6 August, Maloga) The boy, Billy Cooper, shows great aptitude for learning. He has acquired a knowledge of the alphabet, capitals and small letters in three days and then taught Bobby – capitals only - in one day.[7]

William was 12 or 13 years old, and Bobby was 11 years. William was a fast learner, as were his brothers and sisters.

Kitty

William Cooper's mother Kitty lived from about 1833 to 1885. She was about 41 years of age on arriving at Maloga. The girls built a "mar-noo" or shelter for Kitty by the riverbank, and the girls slept in a bedroom at the mission nearby. Kitty loved to sit by the fireplace in the schoolroom as the children took their lessons.

Lizzie, Sarah, Billy, and Bobby were given their own Bible after a few months so they could follow Daniel in the readings. Daniel also read them Pilgrim's Progress. All seemed idyllic for a few months; then Kitty became restless. She rolled hers and Ada's blankets ready to walk back to Moira station.

Daniel offered to take all Kitty's family for a drive by buggy to Moira station. However, not only did Kitty and Ada stay, but Jack and Bobby also. As soon as station owner O'Shanassy saw Bobby "he caught hold of him, shook him and then took him into the house to frighten him into staying. Poor little Bobby was compelled to stay. Billy says he will run away down here when he gets the chance."[8]

Kitty must have gone back to Maloga at some point because, in his first Mission Report covering the year 1874-75, Mathews was disappointed that Kitty had rolled her blankets once more and left, taking her younger children. The two older girls then ran away to Barmah, perhaps missing Kitty.

A diary entry by Janet Mathews dated 17 May 1875, records her going down to the river to visit "Kitty, the sick lubra" (Aboriginal woman). Kitty had rheumatism and tuberculosis. Though Kitty was not expected to live long, she lived another ten years. When she was too ill to leave her "mia-mia," Lizzie or Ada cared for her.

Daniel educated the adults who wanted to learn to read and write, and Kitty learnt most of the alphabet while sitting in her corner by the schoolroom fire.

Kitty had three other sons, Aaron, Johnny, and Edgar Atkinson. One of the Maloga girls called Harriet married Johnny and another, Louisa, married Aaron. Lizzie Atkinson married Sampson Barber of Maloga. Louisa and Aaron had the first baby born at Maloga – Florence Atkinson. This was an exciting occasion for the mission. Later Florence was to have a child called Doug who became Pastor Doug Nicholls. Later Ps Doug became Sir Doug, the first Aboriginal Governor of South Australia and the only Aboriginal governor of any Australian state. He came a long way from his humble beginnings. Kitty then was the great grandmother of Sir Doug.

According to Clark, Doug Nicholls' biographer, Kitty lived a traditional life, "Kitty, born about 1829[9]) was a naked nomad when the early settlers from Port Phillip pushed their flocks north to the Murray in 1840. Kitty had four children to each of two white men, Atkinson and Cooper. What these men were – shepherds, shearers, settlers – cannot be traced today."[10] While Clark used the word "nomad," Aboriginal people only moved around within their tribal boundaries, following the seasonal food supply.

Kitty's Sons

Aaron was born about 1854 - seven years before William. He was good looking, stocky, with broad shoulders and a large beard. He was the second of Kitty's sons, and his surname was Atkinson. Aaron and his brother Johnny used their wages from shearing to buy and stock up on large quantities of flour, sugar, and tea which was a new thing for Aborigines at the time as their traditional lifestyle involved hunting and gathering when needed. [11]

Aaron and his wife Louisa and their three children, Willie, Henry, and Minnie, came to live at Maloga in February 1877. He had, however, much contact with Daniel before that. Louisa became the first convert to Christianity on the mission in June that year, and Aaron was converted two months later. After that, he often went with Daniel, travelling the Murray River in a native canoe or using horse and wagon to gather in Aboriginal children who they felt needed protection.

For many years, the sound of Sankey hymns and Negro spirituals wafted over the waters of the Murray River. A revival broke out at Maloga in January 1884 as some of the Aborigines returned from the Lakes. William came to Daniel after the service and said "I must give my heart to God…."[12] William was the last of his brothers and sisters to be converted.

Daniel said, "I felt melted into tenderness and tears at the prayer and meeting conversions….and rather sorry my dear wife could not enjoy it, but she had to nurse our dying child…[13] Daniel and Janet's child Vivian died the next morning. He was experiencing joy and heartbreak at the same time.

William told Daniel that his brothers were praying for him to be converted. Johnny spoke about the change in his life after becoming a Christian at a meeting on 20 January 1884, "'you all know what I was – a cattle-duffer and a very wicked man.' At the same meeting, William prayed 'Thank the Lord for saving all our family. The Lord bless our mother'."[14] Kitty was also converted in March 1884 due to the efforts of her eight children, but she did not leave the old people's camp. She died about a year later.

Johnny set up a permanent camp for him and his wife Harriet and their children to the northeast of Maloga towards Barmah. He wanted his independence from the mission, and he farmed a few acres of wheat. It proved a bit of a thorn in the side for Daniel and Janet as those who were discontent at Maloga went to Johnny's camp to live.

Gradually, by 1880, Maloga had become a small village with cottages, vegetable gardens, a ration depot, water supply, killing pens for animals as well as the school and church. Mathews was concerned that Aboriginal people were gradually being forced from their traditional life into a humiliating fringe-dwelling existence, depending on handouts, so he taught the boys and men skills like farming, ploughing, shearing, carpentry, fencing, and stock work.

Cato notes that "the generation that had grown up at Maloga, like the lads Bagot Morgan and Billy Cooper, were the first-generation half-castes who did not find much prejudice in the white settlements around. They were fine-looking men, tall and well-proportioned, with natural ability as runners and cricketers and a knack for training horses."

Daniel took William and the others as often as possible to Echuca and Moama to political meetings, to see a circus or go to a concert or to listen to visiting preachers. This contact with white people gave them confidence when they went away to work. The young men would use their wages from working at Maloga to pay their own way and buy presents for family.

The Maloga men were known as good workers as the Mathews' had instilled the Protestant work ethic in their charges. The Maloga men were at home in the white man's world and could command an adequate wage, buying themselves horses and buggies and dinghies so they could be independent of mission transport.

Daniel Mathews encouraged independence in Maloga mission people but also had strict rules, which meant the men were disgruntled from time to time. "Ironically, it was his very success with this group of educated and independent men, which led to Daniel's undoing. He had taught them self-confidence and to assert their individuality but could not reconcile this new attitude with his own ingrained paternalism and disciplinarian."[15]

They had to ask Superintendent Mathews permission to travel and were expected to attend prayers and work regular hours. The men dreamt of having individual farms they could work and then leave to their children. They felt the land should be given to them for this purpose. So, at times, resentment smouldered.

William had married Annie Clarendon Murri. Daniel records that on 6 May 1885, William came to Maloga from Johnny's camp to see his wife Annie as she had run away from their camp that morning. She was in Eliza's hut, in the family way, and in pain. Just over a week later, William and Alowidgee went away to O'Shanassy's hunting rabbits for a living and Annie went back to Johnny's camp.[16]

On 26 May, Johnny and Harriet's little son David died despite the efforts of the doctor from Echuca and the prayers of the mission. Aaron made the coffin, and Daniel led the burial ceremony. Later Johnny moved back to the mission, and his job was to attend to the horses and the feed paddocks. Many of the men owned their own horses and buggies so much feed was needed.

Influences on William

Early formative influences on William were:

1. The mission schooling as he was to become a prolific letter writer to the government on behalf of his people
2. His Christian faith
3. Mathews' championing of Aboriginal rights
4. William's time working for a politician
5. His time as a union organiser
6. The influence of Thomas James and his son Shadrach James

While William worked as a shearer and agricultural labourer for most of his life, he spent some of his early adult life employed as a coachman for Sir John O'Shanassy a prominent Melbourne politician, businessman and station owner. William's curiosity led him to learn from O'Shanassy how the political system worked. He learned petition writing from Daniel Mathews and some organising from his time as a union representative.

Another significant influence was from Thomas James, a highly educated Mauritian Indian (some accounts say Tamil), who Daniel Mathews brought to Maloga as a school teacher in August 1881. He did this as soon as the school became a recognised public school and attracted a government salary for a teacher. Thomas married Ada Cooper, William's sister and a star pupil at Maloga, and became a close friend of the Mathews family. He remained at Maloga (and later Cummeragunja) many years as there is a photo of him with the schoolchildren in 1913. [17] William was 20 years old when Thomas arrived at Maloga. Thomas and

Ada's son, Shadrach, was also an influence on William later on as he was an activist for Aboriginal advancement in Melbourne.

On 5 July 1881, the members of the Moira and Ulupna tribes, with Daniels' encouragement, petitioned Lord Augustus Loftus, Governor of the Colony of NSW, for a small part of the country which was once theirs. [18] There were forty-two names on the petition, including some of William's brothers. See Appendices 1 and 2. William was not at Maloga at the time. The government rejected the petition, though it made headlines in the papers. The petition read in part:

> *That all the land within our tribal boundaries has been taken possession of by the government and white settlers; our hunting grounds are used for sheep pasturage and the game reduced and, in many places, exterminated, rendering our means of subsistence extremely precarious, and often reducing us and our wives and children to beggary.*
>
> *We, the men of our several tribes, are desirous of honestly maintaining our young and infirm, who are in many cases the subject of extreme want and semi-starvation, and we believe we could, in a few years support ourselves by our own industry, were a sufficient area of land granted to us to cultivate and raise stock.*
>
> *We have been under training for some years and feel that our old mode of life is not in keeping with the instructions we have received, and we are earnestly desirous of settling down to more orderly habits of industry, that we may form homes for our families...*

The petition showed that the Moira and Ulupna people were trying to adapt to the colonisation which had impoverished them by making a way for themselves in the new economy which had overtaken their way of life. Until the petition, the government had been content to leave mission work to private interests, but now public opinion meant that the government had to accept responsibility. A commission of enquiry into

Aboriginal affairs was set up in 1882, and the following year, the Aborigines Protection Board of NSW was formed. The government began setting aside reserves, the first of which was Cummeragunja about three miles upstream from Maloga and about 1800 acres. While it was not the land grant they petitioned for, it created the impression among the people that Cummeragunja was a gift to them from Queen Victoria.

The petition may have failed, but it meant that the government now had to take up responsibility for Aboriginal people and Maloga's days were numbered.

It was the end of an era. Kitty died at the end of 1885 from tuberculosis. She had more than sixty grandchildren. On 2 May 1886, King Johnnie of the Moira tribe died of bronchitis, aged 82 years. Daniel said he would miss him as they were very attached, Daniel calling him "kia" (father) and him calling Daniel "maa-win" (son). [19] Old Gracie died a year later, of old age.

Daniel and Janet often took the families from Maloga mission to Brighton Beach for a Christmas holiday. However, the Christmas camp of 1888 had disastrous consequences with many contracting typhoid fever, and ten of them died. William Cooper's wife Annie was one of them, and she died in Sandhurst (Bendigo) hospital. [20] William was heartbroken with his young wife taken from him so soon. Another infant son of Johnny Atkinson also died.

Setting out from Maloga for a holiday at Moira Lakes Camp 1883. Daniel Mathews is at left, beside the horse. (Norman collection)

Chapter 2

Maloga and Cummeragunja

As there have been no grants of land made to our tribe...I do trust that you will be successful in securing this small portion of a vast territory which is ours by Divine Right.

— William Cooper, 1887

After returning to Maloga in 1884 from working with O'Shanassy, William, about 23 years old, became active in lobbying for land grants for his people.

100 Years After White Settlement in Australia

William and other Aboriginal people from Maloga Aboriginal Mission Station decided that the occasion of the centenary of the colony of NSW in 1888 and the jubilee year of the reign of Queen Victoria would be two important events which could be celebrated by granting some land to Aboriginal people for farming. William might have been familiar with the Biblical teaching that in every 50th or jubilee year, property is returned to its original owners even if it had been sold in the meantime.

So, on 20 July 1887, a group of Aborigines from southern NSW petitioned the Governor, Hon. Baron Carrington that ".... Those among us, who so desires, should be granted sections of land of not less than 100 acres per family in fee simple or else at a small nominal rental annual, with the option of purchase at such prices as shall be deemed reasonable for them under the circumstances, always bearing in mind that the Aborigines were the former occupiers of the land. Such a provision would enable them to earn their own livelihood, and thus partially relieve the State from the burden of their maintenance."[21] They thought this would be a "fitting memorial" for the centenary. The petitioners were – William Cooper, Robert Cooper, John Cooper, Aaron Atkinson, Edgar Atkinson, John Atkinson, Samson Barber, Hughy Anderson, Whyman McLean, George Middleton and Edward Joachim.

In William's earliest surviving letter, William had this to say to his local Member of Parliament: "As there have been no grants of land made to our tribe…I do trust that you will be successful in securing this small portion of a vast territory which is ours by Divine Right."[22]

While the government rejected William's appeal and the petition, nearly a decade later, blocks within what had become Cummeragunja reserve were allocated to some Aboriginal families. However, in a devastating blow, they were repossessed again in 1907.[23] William worked as a shearer and agricultural labourer for the rest of his working life, working on land that his people had owned before white settlement.

Maloga

Mathews' friend, John Brown Gribble, established a nearby mission at Warangesda on the Murrumbidgee River. They became the "virtual conscience" of the State of NSW as regards the treatment of Aborigines. Harris writes: "Maloga became a household word. Aboriginal people from far afield - Sydney and Maitland, for example – found refuge there. Maloga, and later Gribble's Warangesda, both the creation of dedicated and compassionate individuals, were the only places in NSW at that time to which Aborigines seeking a safe home could go. By 1880, there were seventy or eighty permanent Aboriginal residents at Maloga and 153 by 1887."[24]

Though Maloga was just across the border into NSW, many Aboriginal residents were from the Victorian side of the border with tribal boundaries more salient to Aborigines than state government boundaries.

Mathews was very critical of government policies in both NSW and Victoria. Mathews' efforts eventually led to the formation of the NSW Aborigines Protection Association in 1881. This was a voluntary body promoting missions, seeking funds and lobbying government.

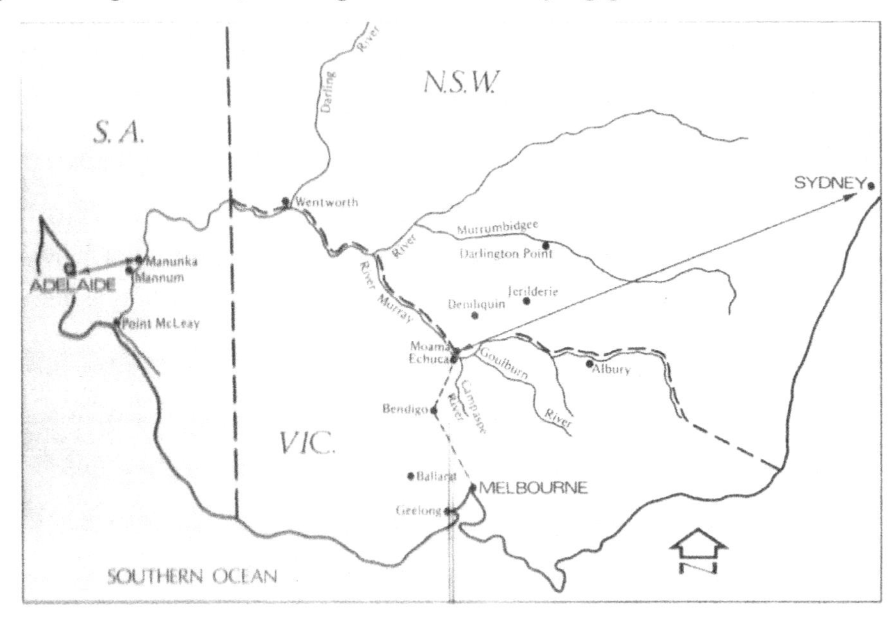

Murray River Basin (Cato 1976)

The Aboriginal people of Maloga had long wanted their own land, so Cummeragunja (called Cummera by the people themselves) was set up in 1883, next to Maloga. The government set aside 1800 acres adjoining Maloga for their use, but they did not have freehold title over it. This was the result of an 1882 government enquiry into Maloga and Warangesda which was relatively favourable and recommended the purchase of further land for the use of Aborigines.

NSW Aborigines Protection Board and Secularisation

Daniel Mathews saw NSW the Aborigines Protection Board as the "crowning achievement of his life", but he didn't realise he had "created a monster that would destroy him". [25] The first Protector of Aborigines, George Thornton, put in train a policy of secularising the missions into

Aboriginal reserves run by the state government. The secular and religious activities at Maloga were separated in 1887, reducing Daniel's responsibilities to a religious teacher. The following year, the Board moved all the buildings from Maloga to Cummera, even though the Mathews family owned all of them. Daniel and Janet resigned.

It appears there had been a government decision to close Maloga and force the Mathews family out. A difficult choice faced the Aboriginal people. Though Daniel Mathews was reportedly paternalistic and discouraged aspects of Aboriginal culture, he did not agree with, the Aboriginal people regarded Daniel and Janet with much favour.[26] Most moved to Cummera, but a few stayed on with the Mathews. Thomas James moved to Cummera with the school.

Public school, Maloga Mission c.1884, Thomas James on the right by blackboard (Norman collection)

Cummeragunja

Life was reportedly harsh under the new superintendent, George Bellenger, who was strict and lacked compassion, particularly for the sick and dying. Bellenger was furious with the Aborigines who wept and asked if they could live with the Mathews and he denied them food rations as a punishment. He refused to allow the Mathews to visit Cummera. Persevering on, the Mathews moved to the Victorian side of the border and continued their private mission.

By 1899, 12 years later, Bellenger was gone and was replaced by George Harris who had been at Warangesda. It became a happier, almost self-supporting village and the Mathews were allowed back to visit, seeing the fulfilment of their dream. Later, the Mathews founded another mission at Mannum on the South Australian section of the Murray River where Daniel died and was buried in 1902. After they left the Cummera area, Thomas James became the spiritual leader of the people, leading the unaligned church, which eventually became part of the Church of Christ.

Cummera is in NSW and is about 20 miles from Echuca and directly across the river from the Victorian township of Barmah. Cummera was laid out with two levelled, and gravelled streets, George and Cooper Streets, and a pump was supplied to each cottage with water from the Murray River. The Aboriginal men were good carpenters, and by World War 1, there were "forty-six cottages, a school, a church, a dispensary and the manager's and the teacher's residences.... (and) by 1900 the reserve had increased to 2,600 acres and the farm developed around the settlement."[27] The men were paid just a few shillings a week and given rations, with profits going to the Board.

Eighteen families received forty-acre blocks of land in 1898, but these were permissive occupancy, not ownership. Aaron Atkinson had one of them. It was heartbreaking to have these blocks revoked ten years later, after all their hard work and plans of passing the land on to their children.

A few people had not worked the land well, and some had leased it to Indian hawkers. Also, there were issues with grubs and floods, so the Board decided the land would yield better results if worked as a whole. However, many had been faithfully producing enough to provide independently for their families and were very disappointed. They felt they had been cheated, and they lost their incentive to work. It was the start of a long-term grievance between the people and authority.

Assimilation Policy

The NSW Parliament passed the Aborigines Protection Act in 1909 which gave the Protection Board broad powers over the lives of NSW Aborigines. It was the beginning of their assimilation policy with the aim that Aborigines who were half-castes or less would be removed from reserves and work in the white community. This Act would further remove them from their land and their people.

In 1915, the Act enabled the Board to take Aboriginal children and place them in training homes and apprentice them with "suitable" employers. When they built the Cootamundra Training Home for Girls, the Board decided to take the children without their parents' consent, beginning the stolen generations discussed in chapter 10.

They removed William Cooper's great-niece, Doug Nicholls' sister Hilda under this policy. The removals caused great distress and would haunt the people who feared when it would happen next. Clarke records the event:

The day came at Cummeragunja when police arrived in cars from Moama and took, with other girls, Doug's sister, sixteen-year-old Hilda. The police came without warning, except for the precaution of ensuring that the men had been sent over the sandhills to cut timber. Some of the girls eluded the police by swimming the Murray. The police forced children into the cars, with mothers wailing and threatening the officers with any weapon at hand. Doug saw his mother chase the police with a crowbar. She and other mothers scrambled into the cars with the children and refused to get out. They went as far as Moama with them, and they were forced out.[28]

After that, the children rushed to hide under the floor of the schoolhouse when the police cars arrived. After a few months training at Cootamundra, the girls were apprenticed out and received one shilling a week pocket money, with two shillings and sixpence being paid into the Board weekly to be handed out at their discretion.

There was an announcement by the NSW Aborigines Protection Board in 1919 that farming activities on Aboriginal stations would end. The authorities announced the enforcement of the 1909 clause that able-bodied Aborigines and all half-castes and less must leave the station and find work outside. This assimilation policy was to get lighter Aborigines to merge into the white community. Another aim was to put a stop to separate Aboriginal communities that were close to self-supporting. The policy had moved from protection or "smooth the dying pillow" to losing their identity in the white community. The thought seemed to be – "if they won't die out, we'll breed them out."

Many of the Cummera men travelled far and wide to get work, but often when they returned home, they found their houses had been cruelly pulled down by the authorities. Makeshift shelters of flour bags and flattened kerosene tins began to appear. The government marginalised Aboriginal people again. Another wave of dispossession was occurring.

Of the 2,600 acres at Cummera, the government leased 2,000 to white men. The Aboriginal people left couldn't stomach the profits of their cheap labour going to the Board, so apathy started to creep into the elders and rebellion into the young. The manager at Cummera had complete control. Drunkenness and obscene language were punishable by expulsion. The manager expelled more and more people. Hopelessness was taking over.

Move to Melbourne

Thomas James (now known as Grandpa James) retired in 1922 after forty years' service. He moved to the opposite side of the Murray River in Victoria and then later moved with his family to Melbourne where he set up as a herbalist. He had been the mainstay of Cummera for so long. Now he was gone. Eddy Atkinson, who had been mentored by Grandpa, took over the spiritual leadership of his people, interspersed with his seasonal work and football.

After two years in Melbourne during which time he encouraged William Cooper and Doug Nicholls, Grandpa James moved to Mooroopna where some of the Cummera people were living on the banks of the Goulburn River. He felt they needed him, and he shared their poverty and poured out his love to them until he died at age 92 years.

William retired to Cummera in about 1929 when he was about 68 years old and found the petty interference in Aboriginal people's lives by government administrators oppressive after the free life he had experienced as a shearer. Horner[29] said that because William had some European blood, he could not get the pension if he remained on the government station. William objected to conditions at Cummera and left.

William was six-foot-tall, with white hair and beard, an impressive looking old gentleman. With his wife Sarah, he rented an old cottage without gas or electricity in the Melbourne suburb of Footscray. The depression meant that white men were tramping the country looking for work and children were hungry. There was little work for Aborigines.

In Footscray, about a hundred Aborigines were living in poverty, many of them from Cummera. William heard about actions by Aboriginal people in other states to bring social change. Two Aboriginal men working for the betterment of the lives of Aborigines were Norman Harris and William Harris in Western Australia.

News of their work influenced William. Supported by like-minded family members such as his brother-in-law, Thomas James and nephew,

Shadrach James, who had been speaking up for Aboriginal rights for some years, William gradually emerged as the leader and spokesperson for Victorian Aborigines and lobbied nationally for all Aboriginal people.

William would hold meetings in the front room of his cottage with two candles flickering on the mantelpiece. As well as Shadrach James, people like Margaret Tucker and Caleb and Anne Morgan, ex Cummera Aborigines, regularly came to meetings. Margaret was one of the girls stolen by the police and sent to Cootamundra Training Home for Girls.

Cummera Reduced to a Reserve

There was a succession of managers at Cummera, and by the 1930's it was again an oppressive place. In 1939, there was a strike or mass walkout of the Cummera people who crossed the river and camped at Barmah on the Victorian side of the Murray River. They were concerned about malnutrition, disease and lack of education of their children. William Cooper was very supportive of this strike and provided much-needed support, including food and lobbying.

The population at Cummera continued to decline with the 1939 strike and people choosing freedom living on the river banks. Cummera continued to go downhill with good and bad management until the government withdrew the last manager in 1953. They reduced the station to the status of a reserve and leased all but 200 acres to non-Indigenous people.

Clark writes of Ps Doug Nicholls return after Cummera had been reduced to the status of a reserve:

He could not believe what he saw. The little settlement had vanished. There was not a splinter of the imposing ornamental posts at the entrance to the reserve, which his grandfather, Aaron Atkinson, had helped to erect. There were not more than five scattered houses and as many humpies left. The church had been removed, though the school remained with about fifteen pupils – bright-eyed, good looking children. The manager's residence had been sold to a farmer across the river. The two stores had gone. The well-formed gravel streets, even the trees along their length – all gone. A boggy track now led in from the punt. The water tanks still stood, but only an exposed bit of water pipe in the paddock bore witness to their useful past.

On the block where Doug's old home had been were a couple of peppercorn trees, a box-thorn and clumps of jonquils – but no sign of a house.[30]

Like many others, Doug had had a difficult but secure and happy childhood at Cummera. Though the people had had harsh managers, they had also had good ones. Despite living in relative poverty, many times, there was plenty of food. Most importantly, this was their land, the land of their forefathers, a land that told them stories of themselves, who they were, their place in the world and held out hope of a future. This was where their ancestors were buried, where they grew up and married, and their children were born. This was the community that they were part of. This was the community they loved. Now it was almost gone. A forlorn place – as if it was not loved.

Doug, whose grandfather Aaron was William Cooper's brother, mourned that even the little he had been given of the law and way of life of his people of the Murray River, could be lost to generations to come. He started to feel guilty. If he had not been so devoted to sport, so involved with his white friends, could he have made a difference to the fate of Cummera? The thought that he had left his people kept haunting him. Could he even have saved it for the benefit of future generations? [31]

Doug was later to do just that, as he cast a vision of Cummera as he knew it to his people and fired their imaginations to see it re-established. It was not till 1964 that Cummera became an Aboriginal-managed community after 25 years of lobbying led by Sir Doug Nicholls, Kerin Atkinson, Colin Walker and others. It flourishes today.

Cummera had been like a place of refuge, a place for the Aboriginal people to lay down their head and rest from the fray of having to come to terms with the white world on the white world's terms. Cummera was also a place of love and laughter. But they had been hunted out to fend as best they could. Against the odds of racism, contempt, indifference, misunderstanding and suspicion, they had to try to make their way in a foreign culture and maintain whatever human dignity they could.

William, a Maloga and then a Cummera man, beat the odds stacked against him. One of the things that stood out about William was his dignity. He stood straight and tall and looked white people in the eye. No bowed head and averted eyes in deference as was the habit of many of his people. He knew from Bible teaching that all men are made of the one blood. He knew all men are equal. He had a dignified bearing, and his good character shone through and made people listen to him as he became the voice of his people.

Chapter 3

The Struggle for Equality and the Australian Aborigines League

At times I get very discouraged at the slow progress of our cause, and at other times the evidence of improvement heartens me. The fact is that there is continued improvement all the time of late years, but the rate of progress is too slow...We have suffered enough, God knows, but surely the day of our deliverance is drawing nigh. I hope to live to see it....

— William Cooper, 1936

William Cooper, centre, and the Australian Aborigines League

Australian Aborigines League

Soon after his arrival in Melbourne, William organised the group that formed around him into the Australian Aborigines League (AAL) to work for the "uplift" of Aboriginal people to be treated fairly and to the same standard as non-Aboriginal people.

The AAL was a pioneering organisation, one of the very first organisations for Aboriginal advancement run by Aborigines in Australia. There were white supporters such as Helen Baillie and Arthur Burdeau, who became President.

William formally founded the Australian Aborigines League in 1936, although he had been using the name since 1932. It had a formal structure with a constitution, office bearers and policy statement. Full membership was for Aborigines, but non-Aborigines could become associate members. The Department of Interior investigated the League in 1938 but found nothing illegal or untoward.

Helen Baille, a trained nurse, formed the Aboriginal Fellowship Group in the 1930s. She believed that her income inherited from her father was derived from land that had once belonged to Aborigines, and therefore, she should help them as best she could. She was a long-term supporter and friend to William and other League members.

William realised that his great-nephew Doug Nicholls had a profile as a talented footballer and this would help promote the Aboriginal cause. So, the old man would walk in from Footscray and be waiting outside the Fitzroy football ground when Doug finished his training at night and badger him about "wobbling his tongue" on behalf of his own people. Doug came only slowly to the cause. He said, "I used to wish I could dodge Uncle William, but he stuck at me.... It was William sticking at me – and these stories[32]- that fired me. I can see it now: William was the contact that brought me back to our people. Everything comes back to William Cooper – the hostels, the League – he fired me to follow through."[33]

Petition to the King

How could equality with white Australia be achieved William asked himself? The main strategy he had was to petition King George V, King of England, to prevent the extinction of the Aboriginal race and to grant Aborigines representation in Federal Parliament.[34] See Appendix 3.

The Melbourne Herald reported on 15 September 1933,

> Australia's native race – the Aborigines – is taking steps for the first time in its history to secure from the King representation in the Federal Parliament. This is demanded as a right in a petition which is being circulated for signatures.
>
> Some people of Aboriginal blood are interesting themselves in the move, and much of the initial work is falling to the lot of Mr William Cooper, of Footscray, who said today that the object was to place the Aborigines on the same footing as the Maoris. In New Zealand, he said, Parliamentary and Government offices were open to Maoris equally with Europeans.
>
> ... Mr Cooper will seek the signatures of Aborigines and half-castes at mission stations. Even without these, he hopes to secure about 600.

William forwarded the petition to the Commonwealth Government in October 1937, requesting that it be presented to the King, via the Prime Minister, Mr Joseph Lyons. It read:

> YOUR PETITIONERS therefore humbly pray that Your Majesty will intervene on our behalf and through the instrument of Your Majesty's Government in the Commonwealth of Australia: To prevent the extinction of the Aboriginal race and better conditions for all and grant us power to propose a Member of Parliament in the person of our own Blood, or White man known to have studied our needs and to be in sympathy with our Race to represent us in the Federal Parliament.

The petition was a cry to be involved in the nation's governance and to be able to make decisions for their own communities when the government had taken that decision-making power from them. It was also a cry not to consign Aborigines to the graveyard or the rubbish bin of life.

Despite considerable government opposition, the petition was widely circulated throughout Australia and had nearly 2,000 Aboriginal signatures by early 1935.[35] This was a remarkable achievement in those times with no computers or TV etc. and limited resources. William was living on a pension and used to catch the train or walk to gain signatures for the petition and help his people. He would get white friends to drive him to meetings or long distances to find out the needs of Aborigines.

What was also remarkable is that about 900 or half of the 1814 signatures William and the League obtained were from Queensland, mostly from Palm Island. Palm Island, off the coast of Townsville, had been established as a penal colony for Aborigines considered "troublemakers" for standing up for themselves and their families. There were over 500 signatures from Western Australia, 350 from South Australia, nine from the Northern Territory and a small number from NSW and Victoria. [36] It shows that the petition was a genuinely national one because most states were represented.

Delegation to Federal Parliament

While it was on William's heart to have an Australia-wide delegation of Aborigines to Federal Parliament in 1935 to raise their issues, he had to make do with a delegation from Victoria and NSW due to lack of finances and state government obstruction. They met Thomas Paterson, Minister for the Interior and argued that, as they were British subjects, they should have the same rights as white Australians.

Specifically, William and his group, including Doug, asked for Aboriginal representation in state and federal parliaments. They also asked for a federal Department of Native Affairs so that there would be a uniform national policy on Aboriginal affairs with a sympathetic administrator.

They lobbied for state councils consisting of a social anthropologist, medical and educational advisors, a representative of the Aboriginal race, and at least one woman. The next Premier's conference discussed these matters, but nothing came of it.

The Melbourne *Argus* quoted William as saying:

> The whites had failed to observe their commission to protect the blacks, who were being driven further and further back into the barren wastes on which it was impossible to live much longer. The race was in danger of extinction, and its members were debarred from making themselves good and useful citizens. In Mr Cooper's sixty years' experience, no industry had been provided to enable the blacks to become useful citizens. The Maoris of New Zealand had had parliamentary representation since 1867; therefore, Aborigine representation was long overdue.

The Minister for Interior, Mr Paterson responded that the Commonwealth Government had responsibility and authority only over Aborigines in the Northern Territory. Aboriginal affairs were a state matter. Setting up a Department of Aboriginal Affairs was listed for discussion at a future Premiers Conference. William and the AAL had to wait another two years.

New Deal

The government held a conference of Commonwealth and State officers charged with the protection of Aborigines in April 1937 in Canberra, and there was a move towards a uniform policy of assimilation. It was to be a "New Deal", but the Native Affairs Branch of the Department of Interior which was to institute the changes was not set up until February 1939. However, the Second World War intervened, and the New Deal was lost. No wonder William was frustrated at the slow progress.

William continued to put pressure on state and federal parliaments, though after 1936, he found it hard to maintain hope. [37] In the Annual Report for the Aborigines Advancement League in 1936, he wrote:

> Dear Fellow Members of the Dark Race,
>
> It is with mixed feelings that I report for the year. At times I get very discouraged at the slow progress of our cause, and at other times the evidence of improvement heartens me. The fact is that there is continued improvement all the time of late years, but the rate of progress is too slow…We have suffered enough, God knows, but surely the day of our deliverance is drawing nigh. I hope to live to see it….

William Discouraged but Perseveres

Australia was in a real malaise at the time in terms of Aboriginal advancement. William himself writes of his discouragement and the slow progress. But he was not one to give up. His Christian faith and the support of missionaries who were activists for Aboriginal rights and the support of unionists kept him going.

Regarding the 1937 meeting of administrators of Aboriginal affairs from all states and territories in Canberra mentioned previously, Harris writes that its resolutions were later to prove highly significant, but at the time, William was starting to despair. He wrote to Prime Minister Lyons on 26 October saying that the conference was a "confirmation of our humiliation."[38] His hopes for justice were not coming to fruition. In another letter, he wrote, "I am an old man…. My hopes are not being realized." Cooper expressed his discouragement in an interview with the Melbourne *Herald* on August 7, 1937 "We are coming to the end of our tether."

He needed a breakthrough, an end to the impasse. A glimpse of hope, to know that all his struggle had not been in vain. But while it was not visible at the time, there was progress behind the scenes. The work of William Cooper and others was denting the armour of the state.

Ernest Gribble was an Anglican missionary who had been actively supporting Aboriginal rights in Victoria and Western Australia. He was on Palm Island Aboriginal reserve in 1937 when my first husband Mick Miller was born, and when Arthur Burdeu, Cooper's loyal friend and supporter, wrote to Gribble:

> Mr Cooper does get depressed at the slow progress made and the result of the meeting of the chief Protectors... is most disheartening. These men never learn and never progress and when they adopt a resolution to consult America and South Africa for advice on the problem of the dark man (it) makes one wonder if the day will come when the dark man in Australia will have to walk off the footpath and keep off trams which contain white folk. Still, God is not dead. [39]

150th Anniversary of White Settlement/Day of Mourning

However, William was not going to give up. The new focus of the campaign was to be on citizenship rights. He had another plan up his sleeve. The 150th anniversary of white settlement in Australia was coming up on 26 January 1938. While the nation celebrated, Aboriginal people would be mourning their lack of citizenship and inequality. So why not call it a Day of Mourning and institute a commemoration service using that name? It was a clever move. He put it to a meeting on 12 November 1937.

William said to the meeting, "This is the day they remember their achievements in subduing the land – and us – in bridging rivers, in building railways, in setting up great industries. But we were doomed the day they landed. Let us have this Day of Mourning on 26 January-the whites' Australia Day."[40]

Burdeu and Cummera Aborigines agreed. Doug Nicholls said, "Aborigines are not satisfied merely to be kept alive by a weekly issue of rations. We do not want chicken feed. We are not chickens. We are eagles."

Aboriginal leader William (Bill) Ferguson from Dubbo, NSW was at the League meeting. He was organising secretary of the Aborigines Progressive Association of NSW formed in 1937. He gave NSW support for the Day of Mourning. While there would be activities in both Sydney and Melbourne, the Aboriginal leaders agreed that the main focus would be on Sydney where the first fleet re-enactment would take place. Ferguson was cutting in his comments on the treatment of Aborigines, "It would be better for the authorities to turn a machine gun on us." He felt that would be better than the slow death they were facing.[41]

There were noted academics who opposed the view that the Aborigines were a dying race. They pointed out that it was the government who hoped they would die out to get rid of the reminders of their disenfranchisement and get rid of their responsibility. One of these was Adelaide surgeon, Dr Charles Duguid, a long-term supporter of Aborigines.

Another was Professor Wood Jones, a noted anatomist, who, six days after the Aborigines decision to hold a Day of Mourning, gave his final lecture to the Anthropological Society of Victoria. He said, "It has been said recently, and by a person of eminence, that when the white man came to Australia, he found a dying and degenerate race. This is the humbug with which the white man has always gilded his extermination of native races. There is no truth in it. The Aborigines were never a dying race until we made them die … The Government point of view is something like this – they are going to die; it is better they should die and get rid of the blot a quickly as possible."[42]

Of course, the government denied this assertion. There was a heated debate in the newspapers leading up to the Day of Mourning, some of it centred on the issue of Aborigines as a dying race. The Australian

Aborigines League in Victoria, led by William Cooper and the Aborigines' Progressive Association in NSW led by William Ferguson (the two Wills as they have been dubbed) prepared for the event.

Historian and Aboriginal rights campaigner Jack Horner told the story of how the manifesto preceding the Day of Mourning came about. Bill or Will Ferguson and Jack Patten, key NSW Aboriginal activists, had come dispirited from the Select Committee Proceedings to Mick Sawtell's health food shop where they and their supporters often gathered to drink tea. There they met two Territorians, Tom Wright, who had just taken up trade union politics in Sydney and Xavier Herbert who was in town for the publication of his novel "Capricornia." The next day Patten met Herbert at his publishers Miles and Stephensen, and it was Stephensen who urged Patten to write a manifesto saying he would cover printing and publicity costs. "There is a vitality about 'Aborigines Claim Citizen Rights!' that suggests a picture of men (Patten and Ferguson) writing against time, off the top of their heads, from personal knowledge bitterly gained in their lives and assimilated in frequent argument."[43]

Patten and Ferguson in the manifesto start bluntly with:

> You are the New Australians, but we are the Old Australians. You have almost exterminated our people, but there are enough of us remaining to expose the humbug of your claims, as white Australians, to be a civilized, progressive, kindly and humane nation …
>
> We do not wish to be regarded with sentimental sympathy or 'preserved' like the koala bear, as exhibits, but we do ask for your real sympathy and understanding.
>
> We ask you to teach our people to live in a modern way, as modern citizens. Our people are quick and good at assimilating knowledge. Why do you deliberately keep us backward? Is it merely to give yourselves the pleasure of feeling superior?

> The fact that there are more than 20,000 half-castes in Australia is proof that the mixture of Aboriginal and white blood is practical. Professor A. Watson of Adelaide University has explained to you that Aborigines can be absorbed into the white race within three generations without fear of a 'throwback'. This proves that the Australian Aborigines is similar in blood to white people as regards intermarriage. We ask you to study the question and to change your whole attitude towards us to a more intelligent one...
>
> We ask you to be proud of the Australian Aborigines and not to be misled any longer by the superstition that we are a naturally a backward and low race. This is a scientific lie that has helped push our people down into the mire. At worst we are no more dirty, lazy, stupid, criminal or immoral than white people.[44]

They make the point that the purpose of Aboriginal legislation is not to protect them but to exterminate their people: "...But you dare not admit openly that you hope for our death! You hypocritically claim that you are trying to 'protect' us: but your modern policy of protection (so-called) is killing us off just as surely as the pioneer policy of giving us poisoned damper and shooting us down like dingoes!"[45]

This mirror held up to the face of white Australia was not a pleasing reflection. In other words, you are not the civilised, humane nation you think you are but a nation that has almost killed off our race even though this is our country and we were here first. You want to treat those of us who've survived like animals in a zoo. While we are quick learners, you put a lid on our education to keep us backward so you can feel superior. You don't like intermarriage, but your lust has produced 20,000 babies, mostly to white men with Aboriginal mothers. For the most part, you reject your babies and cast off their mothers, providing no protection or support, trying to hide your shame. We are those offspring, so don't push us aside or hope we die out. We are no more dirty, lazy, stupid, criminal or immoral than you are.

The Melbourne *Argus* came back with a stinging reply that reflected the views of most of its readers on 17 January 1938:

> Fair-minded Australians will welcome such an expression of opinion as that contained in the manifesto issued by the Aboriginal Progressive Association a few days ago. But … claims contained in the manifesto will not withstand critical examination. The demand for intermarriage with the white race is definitely inadmissible. From the practical viewpoint, only the dregs of the white race would consider such a union, and the inevitable result would be the breeding of a race of half-bloods and quarter-bloods who would be undesirable on grounds other than colour.
>
> One of the arguments for intermarriage – that Aborigines can be absorbed into the white race within three generations without fear of a 'throwback' is illogical. If that were so, the Aborigines would face extinction as a race, a fate which no race welcomes. The manifesto decries as a 'scientific lie' the classification of Aborigines as a naturally backward and low race. Unfortunately for the self-esteem of many worthy survivors of a dying people, it is the simple, self-evident truth. The Australian Aboriginal culture belongs to a very early stage of mankind's development. Aborigines, in spite of their occupation for untold centuries of a favoured land, had not, at the advent of the white man, advanced beyond the stage of being nomadic hunters. Their implements and weapons were most primitive. Agriculture, one of the earliest phases of civilization, was to them an unknown art …
>
> The Aborigines … cannot be treated as a modern, civilized race. They are properly regarded as a dying relic of a dead past, and as such should be treated with the broadest tolerance and humanity.

This racist response must have been a hurtful to the two Wills, Jack Patten and their organisations, as indeed all Aborigines who read it. The *Argus* reporter thought the demand of the Manifesto was for intermarriage when it was really for recognition of Aboriginal people who had mixed heritage like the writers. Marriage would have afforded more protection for the children of mixed-race liaisons. The view that Aborigines were a backward race and only the dregs of white society would want to marry them, and an inferior, undesirable progeny would result was, unfortunately, a deeply held view for many Australians at the time.

Brisbane's *The Courier Mail* and the *West Australian* newspapers were more interested in the implications of William Cooper's petition which now numbered 1800 signatures. The Perth newspaper was favourable, but the Brisbane editor said Aborigines needed to be educated to be socially equal.

Sydney was abuzz for the 150th anniversary of white settlement. There were open-air concerts, brass band recitals, surfing and sports events, a high school pageant in the Town Hall, a ball and private parties. The warships of five nations moored at Circular Quay on goodwill visits and uniformed sailors mingled with the locals on the streets. There were thousands of visitors in Sydney over the weeks leading up to the 150th anniversary while an air of celebration hung over Sydney. People took advantage of the hot, dry summer to cool off down at the harbour at night or go window shopping or visit restaurants.

The government planned to bring Aborigines from Palm Island to Sydney to act as the Aborigines that were encountered by the first white settlers. However, infantile paralysis broke out on Palm Island which had been established as a penal settlement for Aborigines.

Instead, a group of Aborigines from Menindee were trucked in and billeted at police barracks at Redfern in rough accommodations. The government would not pay them for their acting job and wanted to hide them from Sydney Aborigines.

One of Ferguson's supporters, Helen Grosvenor, revealed their location to him because her father was the tracker and horse-breaker at the Redfern station. Bill tried to get relatives of theirs to talk to them, including Hero Black, leader of the Menindee group, but security around them was too heavy.

The government planned that the first boat would come in and put the Aborigines to flight and then the next boat would come in with Governor Phillip. It would be an exercise in showing off the dominance of the settlers. Bill saw this as humiliating and wanted to talk the Menindee group out of it if he had access to them.

About a week before the big day, 20 January, a newspaper leak said that the federal cabinet could not agree to the request by William Cooper for political representation in parliament because Aborigines were not allowed to vote in national elections. This was a huge blow.

The big day had come. On 26 January 1938, key Aboriginal people came in from parts of NSW and Victoria to support Sydney Aborigines. "The irrepressible Helen Baillie drove William Cooper, Margaret Tucker and Doug Nicholls from Melbourne. Jack Patten, later to become Ferguson's rival in a leadership struggle, drove from the north coast bringing Bert Marr, the sympathetic Australian Inland Mission (AIM)[46] Missionary from Taree."[47] Other notable leaders who came were Frank Roberts of Tuncester, Jack Kinchela from Coonabarabran, Tom Peckham from Dubbo and Jack Johnson from Bateman's Bay.

Cooper was dignified and wore an old faded tweed coat while his eager disciple, Ps Doug Nicholls, by then a lay preacher for the Church of Christ, was dressed in a black suit and striped tie.

From left-Will Ferguson, Jack Kinchela, Helen Grosvenor, Mrs S. Patten, John Patten & Patten children, Article on 'Aborigines Day of Mourning, 26 January 1938', (Man magazine March 1938. Held in State Library of NSW – MLQ 059/9)

Holding placards with the words "Aborigines Claim Citizenship Rights," they watched the procession but did not go to the beach to watch the re-enactment of the arrival of the first fleet. It would have been too humiliating for them to watch a group of Aborigines, trucked in from Menindee, flee from the invaders along the beach.

Instead, they went to Sydney's Australian Hall on that sweltering day, so hot that some of the men had to remove their suit coats. Jack Patten took the chair about 1.30pm, flanked on his left by Bill Ferguson and on his right by Ps Doug Nicholls, William Cooper and Jack Kinchela. They officiated behind a table draped with a painted motto "Full Citizenship Rights". Despite two press and two policemen at the back, it was a blacks' only meeting. Helen Grosvenor kept a record of the proceedings.

Horner captured the moment:

After telegrams were read, Jack Patten launched into a loud, forceful and evocative speech setting the mood of aggressiveness and sense of injury that prevailed through the meeting. Though Patten had a stocky figure tending to stoutness, he looked like a huge League footballer in a dark suit. His mind was quick and his bearing hostile. He was a superb public speaker and was the best and most talented orator among the Aborigines. His debating points were made with a stirring and enviable flow of talk. They were called together, he said, to bring to the attention of white people of Australia 'the frightful conditions in which the native Aborigines of this continent live.' The latter were pushed further into the background, though they once owned the land. 'We refused,' he told his audience, 'to be pushed into the background. We have decided to make ourselves heard.'[48]

He read the following resolution from a printed handbill. They passed the resolution unanimously and circulated it throughout Australia:

Doug Nicholls and William Cooper, seated listen to Jack Patten read the resolution. Also pictured are Tom Foster and Jack Kinchela, partly obscured, Article on 'Aborigines Day of Mourning, 26 January 1938', (Man magazine March 1938. Held in State Library

> We, representing the Aborigines of Australia, assembled in conference at the Australia Hall, Sydney on the 26th January 1938, this being the 150th Anniversary of the white man's seizure of our country, hereby make protest against the callous treatment of our people by the white men during the past 150 years, and we appeal to the Australian nation of today to make new laws for the education and care of Aborigines, and we ask for a new policy which will raise our people to full citizen statue and equality within the community.[49]

In formally seconding the resolution, Ferguson spoke of the need to abolish the Aborigines Protection Board, proper education for Aborigines and the abolition of domestic service training for girls which he saw as slavery. He was also concerned about the effects of tuberculosis, which was affecting the health of Aborigines on reserves.

As he warmed to his topic with powerful oratory, he spoke of the need for progress:

> We are backward only because we have had no real opportunity to make progress. We have been denied the opportunity. In many parts of Australia, the white people on the land are helped by Aborigines to such an extent that they could not carry on grazing occupation without Aboriginal aid. The Aboriginal is producing wealth, but not for himself. Yet he is not even allowed money with which to buy food and clothes. If the Aboriginal can help the white man make money outback, why not give him the chance to make money for himself? We did not need government protection. [50]

We don't know from records much about what William Cooper said though he was the person whose vision it was to hold this protest meeting. He did, however, give a call to unity and for those gathered to be involved in the fight for justice. No doubt he was just as passionate as other speakers.

Ps Doug Nicholls, in his colourful and entertaining speaking style that was to make him a sought-after speaker to white audiences interested in the Aboriginal cause, declared that they were eagles, not chickens. Never a rancorous person, he spoke of the plight of the Aborigines he saw begging for food along the trans-continental railway when he went on an interstate sporting tour to Western Australia. It tugged on his heart and made a deep impression on him, contributing to his taking up the struggle for justice for his people.

There was free discussion, and other speakers were Pearl Gibbs, Tom Foster, Mr Connelly, Jack Johnson and Mrs Ardler.

The manifesto, written by Patten and Ferguson for the occasion, was circulated and supported. It was named "Aborigines Claim Citizenship Rights" and called for the following:

1. The end of the Aborigines Protection Board
2. Proper education
3. Laws to prevent the exploitation of Aboriginal labour in the outback
4. An end to domestic service by Aboriginal girls and
5. An end to all discrimination and injustice towards Aboriginal Australians

Meeting with Prime Minister Lyons

On the following Monday (31 January), a twenty-member delegation led by William Cooper met Prime Minister Joseph Lyons, Dame Enid Lyons and John McEwen, the Minister for the Interior, at Parliament House, Canberra. The delegation included Cooper, Ferguson, Patten, Tom Foster, the open-air Aboriginal preacher from La Perouse, Pearl Gibbs and Helen Grosvenor.

Prime Minister Lyons decided on a friendly, personal approach to the Aboriginal leaders with his wife present and without public servants.

This appealed to the Aboriginal delegation. After a short speech by Lyons expressing interest in their welfare, Patten gave a long speech and then handed the Prime Minister their "Ten Points" document. Patten, Cooper and Ferguson had thought a great deal about this plan while preparing it.

The Australian Abo Call published by Patten covered their representation:

> To the Right Hon. The Prime Minister of Australia, Mr J.A. Lyons, P.C.C.H.M.H.R.
>
> Sir,
>
> In respectfully placing before you the following POLICY FOR ABORIGINES. We wish to state that this policy has been endorsed by a Conference of Aborigines, held in Sydney on 26 January of this year. This policy is the only policy which has the support of the Aborigines.
>
> Before placing before you a long-range policy for Aborigines, and while the long-range policy is under consideration, we ask as a matter of urgency:
>
> That the Commonwealth Government should make a special financial grant to each of the State Governments, in proportion to the numbers of Aborigines in each State, to supplement existing grants for Aborigines. We ask that such aid should be applied to increasing the rations and improving the housing conditions of Aborigines at present under State control. **We beg** that this matter be treated urgently, as our people are being **starved to death**. (emphasis mine)

A Long-Range Policy for Aborigines (10 Point Plan)

Their 10-point plan for the advancement of Aborigines read:

1. We respectively request that there should be a National Policy for Aborigines. We advocate Commonwealth Government control of all Aboriginal affairs.
2. We suggest the appointment of a Commonwealth Ministry for Aboriginal Affairs, the Minister to have full cabinet rank.
3. We suggest the appointment of an Administrative Head of the proposed Department of Aboriginal Affairs, the Administrator to be advised by an Advisory Board, consisting of six persons, three of whom at least should be of Aboriginal blood, to be nominated by the Aborigines Progressive Association.
4. The aim of the Department of Aboriginal Affairs should be to raise all Aborigines throughout the Commonwealth to full Citizen Status and civil equality with the whites in Australia. In particular, and without delay, all Aborigines should be entitled:
    a) To receive the same educational opportunities as white people.
    b) To receive the benefits of labour legislation, including Arbitration Court Awards, on an equality with white workers.
    c) To receive the full benefits of workers compensation and insurance.
    d) To receive the benefits of old age and invalid pensions, whether living in Aboriginal settlements or not.
    e) To own land and property, and to be allowed to save money in personal banking accounts, and to come

under the same laws regarding intestacy and transmission of property as the white population.

f) To receive wages in cash, and not by orders, issue of rations, or apprenticeship systems.

5. We recommend that Aborigines and Half-castes should come under the same marriage laws as white people, and should be free to marry partners of their choice, irrespective of colour.

6. We recommend that Aborigines should be entitled to the same privileges regarding housing as are white workers.

7. We recommend that a special policy of Land Settlement for Aborigines should be put into operation, whereby Aborigines who desire to settle on the land should be given the same encouragement as that given to Immigrants or Soldier Settlers, with expert tuition in agriculture, and financial assistance to enable such settlers to become ultimately self-supporting.

8. In regard to uncivilized and semi-civilized Aborigines, we suggest that patrol officers, nurses and teachers, both men and women, of Aboriginal blood, should be specially trained by the Commonwealth Government as Aboriginal Officers, to bring the wild people into contact with civilization.

9. We recommend that all Aboriginal and Half-caste women should be entitled to maternity and free hospital treatment during confinement, and that there should be no discrimination against Aboriginal women, who should be entitled to clinical instruction on baby welfare, similar to that given to white women.

10. While opposing a policy of segregation, we urge that, during a period of transition, the present Aboriginal Reserves should be retained as a sanctuary for aged or incompetent Aborigines

> who may be unfitted to take their place in the white community, owing to the past policy of neglect.[51]

The Prime Minister told the Aboriginal delegation that their request for federal control of Aborigines would not be easy as it would require the agreement of the state governments or constitutional change.

Dame Enid Lyons told newspapers afterwards that she was most impressed with Pearl Gibbs and another woman who spoke and was very moved by their speeches and hoped her husband would change these deplorable conditions. Pearl had vigorously spoken of conditions she had recently seen at Brewarrina and the South Coast and indignantly commented, "I am more proud of my Aboriginal blood than of my white blood."[52]

To us today, references to "incompetent Aborigines" or "uncivilized or semi-civilized" or "wild" Aborigines may make us cringe. However, we need to remember the times they were in where there were still a lot of Aborigines in various parts of Australia who had little or no contact with European settlers. It was still only 150 years since the first fleet arrived from Britain and declared Australia, a British colony. Being in the south-east of Australia, William was part of a tribe that had borne the full effects of that settlement and the devastation it had brought.

Today, we may criticise the policy of assimilation because of the connotation of cultural absorption rather than the recognition and appreciation of cultural diversity. However, at that time, it was a goal of Aborigines to be assimilated as the meaning they attached to it was being treated equally to white people. What had prevailed up to that time had been a frontier situation where Aborigines were under threat of extinction, and government policy had been to "smooth the dying pillow."

Public opinion was starting to recognise that Aborigines were not going away, and they had to deal with them. However, their tiny numbers compared with the white population (even today Aborigines are about three per cent of the overall population) meant they were never a political force. The Ten Points presented by Aborigines led by Cooper, Ferguson and Patten were a well-considered plea for equal rights for Aborigines and an end to discrimination based on race. Had the Second World War not intervened, the outcome might have been very different. However, all action was shelved because of the war and Aborigines were still not citizens in their own land. That battle still had to be fought.

Unfortunately, the two NSW leaders, Patten and Ferguson were clashing more and more, having very different styles of leadership. Ferguson focused on launching the movement for the advancement of Aborigines around the common needs and desires of reserve Aborigines. Patten focused on what Europeans demanded of a movement – broad membership, a constitution, clear policy and publicity. It ended in a public clash at La Perouse at Easter 1938. However, they did patch things up and worked together before Patten joined the military, training for overseas service in north Africa.

White people were starting to take an interest in Aboriginal issues prompted in part by an election promise of Colonel Michael Bruxner, deputy Premier in the NSW government of a 'new deal for Aborigines' and a new Protection Act. The Committee for Aboriginal Citizen Rights (CACR) also stirred up support from churches, unions, welfare and women's groups at an Easter meeting.

Australia Day 1939-41 and Aborigines Sunday

William Cooper wanted to see Australia Day the following year as a Day of Hope, not another Day of Mourning.

William was sick but was pleased that at last on 25 January 1940, his earlier call for a special "Aborigines Sunday" had been taken up by the churches. On the same day, all over Australia, sermons were to be preached from every pulpit on the Aboriginal cause for advancement. This seemed to William to be the best way to reach the conscience of white Australia.

Michael Sawtell decided to hold a public meeting in Sydney that first Aboriginal Sunday. Though it was the fulfilment of William's dream, he was not one of the speakers, presumably because of his health. Speakers were William Ferguson, Pearl Gibbs, Ps Doug Nicholls, Frank Davidson, President of the Fellowship of Australian Writers and J. B. Steele, a crusader for prison reform.

They talked about Aboriginal girls in domestic slavery, receiving 1s a week and the Aborigines Welfare Board holding about 15,000 pounds in trust funds which should have been paid to the girls who often became mothers of 'half-caste' babies and then the Board sent them back to the compound.

Archdeacon Hammond held a leading place in the most conservative Anglican diocese in Australia, and he was outraged over these revelations, including that Aboriginal people were denied the vote, the old-age pension, the right to own land and citizenship rights. Reports of his public support that day for citizenship rights circulated widely. In 1943, the government abolished the system of deferred pay, and full pay came in, but it did not repay the thousands of pounds of withheld pay kept in trust to its rightful owners.

However, the first Aboriginal Sunday certainly made its mark.

Constitution and Citizenship

It was a significant setback when the government informed William on March 1938 that they could not forward the petition to the King of England on constitutional grounds.

Why? Incredibly the reason given was that the Aboriginal petitioners were all subjects of the King, but none of them was a citizen of Australia! Markus,[53] in writing of this says that the Australian government would not pass on this petition because they were not citizens of the nation of Australia that the Commonwealth parliament represented.

They were not citizens in their own land! They were non-persons, of no account! This must have been an enormous blow. Not only did they lose their sovereignty, never ceded, their land and their way of life to the newcomers, but the new settlers were citizens of this land, and the original inhabitants were not!!

Also, section 51 of the constitution meant that the Commonwealth Government had no authority to pass legislation at all for Aborigines. It could not, therefore, pass legislation giving them representation in Federal Parliament. It only had jurisdiction over the Northern Territory. It was a great disappointment to William, who was aging, and his health began to be affected by frustration and feelings of injustice.

The baton was being passed on to Ps Doug Nicholls as he went through a time of apprenticeship to William, absorbing William's hopes and dreams for his people. Ps Doug was in the papers regularly as a speaker at youth groups and churches as well as a sportsman. However, he was mainly speaking as an evangelist to white congregations. His time to be the voice of his people was still to come.

Though there was often indifference or hostility towards Aborigines from many of the white population (now Australia is much more multicultural), there were various white groups who were active in supporting the Aboriginal cause. They were the Aborigines Uplift Society, the Victorian Aboriginal Group, the Aborigines Assistance Committee and the Aborigines Fellowship Group.

Cummergunja Strike

Just days before the Federal Government announced its New Deal for Aborigines, the people of Cummera went on strike. They had had enough. Over eighty Aborigines had already left Cummera because they had found the conditions there unbearable or the manager had expelled them as he had complete control. Now another 200 of the 300 residents packed what they could onto their flat-bottomed boats and rowed from the NSW side of the border where Cummera was located to the Victorian side as the Murray River was the state boundary. It was on 3 February 1939. This exodus was called a strike.

William must have felt some responsibility for what had happened. A few months before, in October, the Cummera people had asked William what to do regarding their bad treatment by the manager. He told them to petition the NSW Aborigines Protection Board to remove him. This backfired as the Board did not remove him and the manager further victimised the petitioners. William said that conditions at Cummera had never been so bad.

Besides the cruel treatment of the Cummera people by their manager, another trigger was the visit by Jack Patten, President of the Aborigines' Progressive Association of NSW, about a week before the strike. He was making a tour of inspection of the state's reserves and stations for the Association, and he had close relations at Cummera. Because of the poor conditions, he advised them to leave the reserve to draw public attention to their plight.

The scene was very dramatic. Though presumably, Patten had a permit to be on the station, two policemen were present as he told the people what their rights were and heard their complaints. He reportedly raised their fears that the government would make the reserve into a compound and that their child endowment would cease. Fear ran through the people that the government would take their children away. Though Patten had not said that, the people remembered this happening 20 years before. The police arrested Patten in the middle of his address to the meeting for inducing the people to leave. He was later convicted but discharged.[54]

This incident reminds me of when I was arrested for trespassing on the Weipa South Aboriginal community in 1973 while visiting the Mapoon Aborigines who had invited me. I was also under house arrest at the hostel in Bamaga over Easter that year, not permitted to meet with the people even though I had a written permit. They decided I was probably a trouble maker as it was rare for a young white woman to visit a remote Aboriginal or Torres Strait Islander reserve in those days.

A few hours after Patten's arrest, the majority of the people moved, leaving the little security they had behind. Meagre as they were, there would be no more government rations.

Hour after hour, small parties gathered their belongings and rowed across the Murray River, downriver to Barmah on the Victorian side. For some hours, boats plied back and forth, picking up more families. The generous river gums provided some shade as they set up camps on the muddy banks of the Murray River, just using hessian bags and the boughs of trees. Most of the 250 or so people moved out in the mass exodus.

What were conditions like before the strike? Clark gives us some of the picture:

> The police were constantly appearing on the station searching for men under expulsion orders. In the middle of the night, they entered and searched houses, waking and terrifying the women and children. If a man was found, he was dragged out of bed and bundled off to Moama lock-up. Rations were poor and insufficient, the value still being 3/6 a week for an adult and 1/9 for a child.

Cummera shack built in the 1930s in the Depression

> There were medical facilities on the station, a well-equipped treatment room having been established in 1935, but more than fifty per cent were suffering from trachoma, and no attempt was made to isolate tuberculosis sufferers. One young girl, suffering from this disease, had been driven forty-five miles to hospital one winter's morning in the back tray of an open truck because the cabin was not considered the place for an Aborigine.
>
> The general management was so poor that none of the station's large heard of cows was giving milk, and the whole place was infested with burrs and rabbits.[55]

Jack Patten wrote to a Sydney newspaper on 30 November saying that people at Cummera told him they were being starved. He was probably getting this information by letter from relatives there. "If orders are not obeyed," Patten wrote, "food supplies were stopped…Children are allowed meat once a week, with three onions and two potatoes." He listed ten deaths since 1937 and of these, four were children as well as a number of small babies.[56]

Two or three weeks after the walk-off, the Aborigines Advancement League visited and helped with food and blankets and worked hard to gain public support and raise finances for them. While the strikers did it tough, they valued their freedom. The publicity did have some effect, and by the end of 1939, the government replaced the manager. Others believed, however, that the strike was a failure.

In the meantime, the people did it pretty tough. The manager, A.J. McQuiggan, ridiculed the stories of the people saying that they were not starving or malnourished and there were no deaths of children or substance to the charge that a compound was to be set up. He minimised the numbers on strike and persuaded his superiors he was in control.

The Cummera people were in desperate need of food, but the manager said he had supplied them well before they left. Arthur Burdeu and the AAL appealed to the Victorian government to help, but the

Victorian government said it had no authority to inquire into the NSW government's administration at Cummera and believed the manager that they had food.

Cummera people worried about how long they could last without food. This was so ironic because, before white settlement, their ancestors had lived on one of the best food supplies in the nation, but the ecology had been changed by settlement so that it could not support them as before.

The AAL and their supporters from Melbourne went to Barmah for the weekend of 25-26 February for a meeting, with Ps Doug Nicholls chairing it. Ps Eddie Atkinson reminded them about their petition, but the manager said there would be no inquiry till they moved back.

The strikers agreed that they would return to Cummera but only if given an assurance that there would be an inquiry and the government children would not steal their children. Hillus Briggs organised a school for the children, and they settled in for a long wait. And so, the strike dragged on and on through the freezing weeks.

After six weeks of holding out, the AAL advised the strikers that it was best to return and wait for an inquiry as it was hard to get enough supplies up for them from Melbourne. Some families did, and by 12 May, only twenty-five families were left at Barmah. A week later, however, seventy-seven people returned to Barmah from Cummera, after having enough of the punishing tactics of the manager. The manager had shifted them from houses they had lived in for years, and their supplies of curry and pepper were cut off. The League depended on fundraising from union sources, and this funding was drying up.

The League tried to get government support for the twenty-five children at Barmah School saying that some of the men worked fruit picking seasonally in Victoria and paid Victorian taxes entitling them to sustenance when this work was not available. However, they could only get social services during the winter and then it would stop and support for the school was not forthcoming. While there had been support from journalists and a lot of coverage of the strike, as the weeks went by, confusion as to what was the real state of events, led to the exhaustion of readers' interest.

Horner's take on it is that, "they were beaten. The humiliating thing was that nothing at the station changed. The intimidating manager, McQuiggan, was still there until August 1940…The exodus had achieved nothing in their favour…. The tradition of proud independence at this station, which had been nurtured by Daniel Mathews and 'Grandpa' James, at Maloga, was broken."[57]

In June 1940, the NSW Aborigines Protection Board was restructured and became the Aborigines Welfare Board with more finances to provide for Aboriginal welfare, particularly housing.

However, many of the families never returned, and its lack of use by these families contributed to the break-up of Cummera. It also caused division between those who stayed and those who didn't. Some of the older families who Matthews trained and who were experienced workers managed to find jobs and move into houses in nearby towns. The younger, inexperienced ones found it harder to survive. More humpies appeared on the riverbanks of towns around places such as Mooroopna and Shepparton.

Chapter 4

Who Was William Cooper the Man?

It can be done. Will you do it? The Aborigines have human affections which can respond to human treatment. Will they get it? Finally, do you intend to become as culpable as our original despoilers? Are you like the prominent Parliamentarian who, as late as 1935 said 'The nigger has got to go, the sooner the better.'

—William Cooper to Prime Minister 31/3/1938

I am a father of a soldier who gave his life for his King on the battlefield and thousands of coloured men enlisted in the AIF (Australian Imperial Force). They will doubtless do so again, though on their return last time, that is, those who survived, were pushed back to the bush to resume the status of Aboriginals...

—William Cooper to Minister for the Interior, 3/1/1939

What was William Cooper like as a person? William was a family man. He was the fifth child of eight children of Yorta Yorta Aboriginal Kitty Lewis. His father was white labourer James Cooper.

A pastoral invasion of their land in the 1830s had left the Yorta Yorta totally dispossessed by the time William was born in 1860. With the Yorta Yorta people decimated by the violence of the settlers and their introduced diseases, many of his people worked on pastoral properties in the area to survive. These included Ulupna and Moira stations, owned by Sir John O'Shanassy, a prominent businessman and politician. O'Shanassy took William with him to live at Camberwell in Melbourne when William was about seven years old. William remained there for about three years and then was sent home to the Murray to work on Moira station as a labourer where he also learnt to break in horses.

Hard times would have influenced Kitty to arrive at Maloga mission with William, then 13 years old and some of his brothers and sisters. A few years later, William and two of his brothers, Bob and Jack, moved to Warangesda, 240 km north of Maloga. Missionary John Gribble founded it in 1880.

Returning to Maloga in 1884, William, 24 years old, converted to Christianity following the steps of his brothers and sisters. In June that year, William married Yorta Yorta woman Annie Clarendon Murrie. They had two children, only one of whom survived before Anne died in 1889. So, William was married at about 24 years and widowed at about 29 years of age.

William moved to Cummeragunja, which meant "our home" in Yorta Yorta language. He married Agnes Hamilton from Coranderrk, another Victorian Aboriginal reserve, in 1893 when he was about 33 years old. William was widowed again, this time at 50 years of age. They had six children together before Agnes death in 1910. [58] One of these children was Amy, who was to become the mother of Alf Turner, or Uncle Boydie.

At the age of about 68 years, William married Sarah Nelson nee McCrae in 1928. She was also from Coranderrk, and they lived for a time at Cumeragunja before moving to Melbourne in 1931, so William could get the old-age pension. This freed him to work full time for human rights for Aborigines.

One of his children Lynch, a famous runner, worked with him for Aboriginal "uplift" at the Australian Aborigines League while another son

Dan was killed in World War 1. William also brought up a number of his grandchildren when circumstances were difficult for them and their parents. Uncle Boydie was one of them, living with grandfather William and Sarah both at Barmah and then in Melbourne.

Uncle Boydie describes that in 1929, as a very small child, he was taken by his mother Amy to live with his Puppa and Nan on the banks of the Murray River. It was a timber, and corrugated iron house lined with hessian. The house was two miles down from Barmah, opposite Cummera and they lived there for about four years. A while after William and Sarah's move to Melbourne, Alf and three other grandchildren joined them there. After a while, Alf returned to his mother in Mooroopna with fond memories of Puppa and Nan. [59]

William Cooper's family about 1900 - William's second wife Agnes with Amy on her knee. Dan is on her left, Jessie and Gillison on her right. Emma, a daughter from William's first marriage, is standing. Image courtesy of Australian Institute of Aboriginal

William Cooper's third wife Sarah, nee McRae (Norman collection)

A National Leader

William was passionate for the cause of his people, not just his own mob, the Yorta Yorta people, and not just Victorian or NSW Aborigines, living as he did on the Murray River and on both sides of the border. He had a national vision and was a national leader. William was a charismatic figure, being able to gather a group of supporters around him, both black and white. He wrote a petition to the King of England and numerous letters to government and newspapers. In one of his representations said:

> I desire to draw attention to the inhuman treatment of aborigines in Central Australia……White men who call themselves civilised, go among them with firearms, and often use them on unarmed aborigines….
>
> We read in the newspapers of 3 February 1933, of a grave charge against the police for alleged acts of brutality against aborigines. These charges were made by Mr R. S. Schenck, of the

Mount Margaret Aboriginal Mission Station, Morgan, WA (Western Australia). He stated that for no apparent reason, police shot natives down.[60]

Christian Character

William was a clean-cut character, not known for drinking, smoking or gambling and was of good character living a Christian life. He treated his wife and children well and all who knew him. He worked unfailingly to improve the lot of Aborigines in Australia.

Tenacity and Determination

Despite the challenges, William was a man of hope. It was his Christian faith that kept him going despite disappointment after disappointment, knockback after knockback, setback after setback and the sheer indifference he often faced. Though often wracked with despair towards the end of his life, William had the tenacity and perseverance to keep going to the end. He never gave up. He was doggedly determined despite bouts of depression and despair.

Politically Active as a Young Man

Even before he started the League, William, as a young man, 24 years old, began lobbying for the advancement or "uplift" as he called it, of his people. He became active in 1884 with a petition for land for his people, so his quest for Aboriginal advancement was a lifelong journey with nearly 60 years of activism, most of it in his later years.

The 1930s saw the emergence of politically active Aboriginal people and the emergence of Aboriginal organisations. For the first time, there was a pan-Aboriginal consciousness developing. The key people in these organisations were generally Christians or at least mission educated. Some missionaries were happy with this, and some weren't.

Wanted to be a Member of Parliament

On 21 August 1940, William wrote to Mrs Norman, Daniel Mathew's daughter, and outlined Aboriginal policy. He expressed disappointment that as he was approaching 80 years of age on 18 December next that he would not be able to represent his people in parliament as was his desire. William added that he had been working solidly for the cause for nine years without payment and spent 100 pounds of his own money though on a pension. He continued, "However I don't mind for it is for a good cause and I have European blood in my veins. I am endeavouring to clear myself with the Supreme Ruler from the cruelty that is being committed against the original occupants of this country. I am living in hopes of being rewarded in the end."[61]

This statement was made near the end of his life and seemed to indicate that he was not only advocating on behalf of his Aboriginal people but taking responsibility for his European heritage in putting things right.

A Pioneer

William was a pioneer. He did not act alone. His story is also the story of the Australian Aborigines League, a Victorian organisation which William founded and which became a national organisation. He wrote these letters as secretary of the League. William's son Lynch was the assistant secretary. Ps Doug Nicholls was treasurer and a vice president. Margaret Tucker (Liliarda) and Mrs N. Clark were also vice presidents. Alfred Burdeu was the only non-Aboriginal council member and was president with Helen Baillie, also non-Aboriginal, being a life member.

William, Margaret Tucker, Lynch and Sarah Cooper in the choir. Image courtesy of Australian Institute of Aboriginal and Torres Strait Islander Studies, Alick Jackomos collection (N5344.15a)

The Australian Aborigines League was one of the first Aboriginal organisations in the nation, and it has an enduring legacy. The ideas William and the League put forward in the 1930s were before their time. They were ground-breaking and were good policy, and they would set the tone for decades. I can remember Aborigines at the forefront of the movement for Aboriginal advancement in Queensland in the 1970s, quite unaware of William Cooper, but putting forward many of the same ideas which were as yet unfulfilled.

Finances Didn't Stop Him

William had scarce funds, working as a shearer, drover, horse-breaker and agricultural labourer for most of his life. He worked in Queensland, NSW, Victoria and South Australia so got around and saw a lot. Near the end of his life, William lived on a pension. Even though he couldn't afford electricity or heating in his Melbourne home, he would write his numerous letters to various state and federal governments by candlelight, even in the freezing winters. His grandson, Uncle Boydie, remembers living with him and Nan in Melbourne, along with some of the other grandchildren. He remembers how poor grandfather William was, the candles and the lack of heating. He remembers the League planning meetings in William's home and long walks William made to meetings because he couldn't afford the tram fares.

Travelled a Lot

Despite limited finances, somehow William managed to travel around Victoria and NSW and even to other states such as Queensland (Qld), South Australia (SA), WA and the Northern Territory (NT). He sometimes travelled by train and sometimes in the car of white supporters, church people or trade unionists. Some trade union supporters of William's were also Christians. He wanted to see firsthand the situation of his people so he could advocate on their behalf more effectively. He wanted to connect with them, hear their needs, organise them to sign petitions and turn the League into a national organisation. He wanted to be a voice for his people, and he was. I am reminded of Mahatma Gandhi when he got on a train and travelled throughout India so he could understand the plight of his people. However, William was part of a race who was a small minority and so powerless.

Disappointed with Government and Church

William was disappointed that little came from the Premiers' Conference that would help his people. Administrators of Aboriginal Affairs from all states and territories met in Canberra in 1937 for the first time. William and the AAL and other Aborigines had done much lobbying. However, its resolutions seemed to William to be "a confirmation of our humiliation". [62]While he didn't realise it then, these resolutions were to be highly significant in years to come. Of his disappointment, he said, "I am an old man...My hopes are not being realised."[63] He let his disillusionment be known publicly by telling the Melbourne *Herald* "We are coming to the end of our tether."[64] However, William did not let this stop him. He did not give up promoting the cause of his people.

William wrote to Ernest Gribble, an Anglican priest expressing his disappointment in the level of support he got from churches in Melbourne but drawing encouragement from his friendship with Gribble and Gribble's support for Aboriginal people:

> I did not get any sympathy from the church people here in Melbourne. The Government and our Christians are very dull on (the Aboriginal) question. I am at a loss to know why, as I am sure they know their responsibility for the Aboriginal people. The Aboriginal men, women and children (are the same as the non-Aboriginals are) in God's sight. God has made us after His own image and left with us the fear of Himself, the same as He did with the white races… If every man had the same respect as you have for the Aboriginal race, there would be no suffering for this race of people.[65]

Wanted a Day of Hope

Even though he instituted a Day of Mourning on Australia Day (26 January) in 1938, he longed for a Day of Hope. He wrote to Prime Minister of Australia Joseph Lyons on 31 March 1938, referring to a programme announced for the "uplift" of his people. "This must inspire State Administrations, and it appears we have reason to feel that the Day of Hope is already dawning. When the uplift is materially advanced, our promise of being a loyal, capable people, of which the outback is no problem, will be shown to be no vain promise. And in that day the open back door to invasion will begin to close."[66] He believed Aboriginal people were the best to keep Australia's northern borders safe and intact.

Strong Sense of Justice

William had a strong sense of justice and right and wrong. In this same stirring letter to the Australian Prime Minister, he said:

> It can be done. Will you do it? The Aborigines have human affections which can respond to human treatment. Will they get it?

> Finally, do you intend to become as culpable as our original despoilers? Are you like the prominent Parliamentarian who, as late as 1935 said 'The nigger has got to go, the sooner the better.'
>
> Will you by your apathy tacitly admit that you don't care, and thus assume the guilt of your fathers? Are you prepared to see a race of people, without whom the centre and north of Australia can never be brought under human control, die and become extinct while you stand by and do nothing?
>
> OR – Are you prepared to admit that since the Creator said in his Word all men are of "one blood," we are humans with feelings like yourselves in the eyes of Almighty God, that we have joys and our sorrows, our likes and our dislikes, that we can feel pain, degradation and humiliation just as you do. If you admit that, will, you like true men do your bit to see a great injustice at least mollified by agitating for us to get a fair deal before it is too late?[67]

Again, on 23 May, 1938, Cooper wrote to Prime Minister Lyons of his worry that Australia might go down the segregation track of the USA and South Africa because the minutes of the meeting of the Chief Protectors of Aborigines from the various states said they would seek advice from the governments of America and South Africa. "....... In the matter of the first, we trust that there will not be copying of the shocking treatment of the natives in either place. Here, if we have the money, we are able to ride in trams and walk on footpaths and, in the civilised parts, white men will treat coloured women as women."[68]

Non-violent Action

Cooper was a gentleman with respect for the King of England and British justice yet at the same time he was fearless to point out the faults of the Australian government in treating Aboriginal people. He was no freedom fighter in the sense that there was never talk or threat of taking up arms, but he was undoubtedly a thorn in the side of parliamentarians and Aborigines Protection Boards and an effective fighter and lobbyist for the freedom of his people. He was always on their case, taking grievances from his people and directing them to government.

He often argued that Aborigines should have the full protection of the law as any other citizens of the British Empire and should have the privileges of British citizenship, particularly as they were not recognised as citizens in their own land by the Australian government. He also believed that, when settling Australia, the orders or commission by the King of England was to protect Aborigines and their rights, not to take them away. He saw the Queen's proclamation for protection of Aborigines at Maloga. [69]He wrote, "This more particularly in view of the fact that history records that in the commission originally given to those who came from overseas the strict injunction was given that the Aborigines and their descendants had to be adequately cared for. This benevolent intention of his most gracious Majesty towards his primitive people was not carried out." [70]

This led to his organising a petition to King George V and his successor George VI as discussed previously.

Gave Credit Where Due

Despite his disappointment, William was prepared to give credit where credit was due. In his numerous letters, he was continually thanking the government for any small improvement and even for listening to his case. However, he still urged them to try to think black. In a letter to the federal Minister for Interior, John McEwen on 17 December 1938, Cooper says:

> .... The white man cannot think black, but I submit that our chieftain, which is your particular position, and the government, which is our Guardian, should set themselves to learn to "think black".
>
> We speak thus to you only because we know in our hearts that you personally, and the government of which you are a

> member, do want to do the right thing by us. We respect you, personally and the government, and repeat what we have told you before, and made no secret of publicly, that no government has previously shown the same interest as the present Lyons Government in the natives. It is possible for us to ask of you what we want instead of being in the position of being suppliants for mercy from unsympathetic over lords.... [71]

Interestingly, Cooper was not a man to stir for the sake of stirring, and he believed in investigating complaints from his people and verifying them before representing his people to government.

Patriotic but Disappointed

William, like many Aborigines, was very patriotic though he experienced tension in seeing his people die without recognition. He said about one thousand Aborigines fought for Australia in World War 1, a little-known fact. His son Dan went to war for a country in which he was not a citizen and was killed in action in Belgium. When the Aboriginal soldiers came back from war, they were not treated as heroes. After having experienced equality in the trenches, they came back to a land that wanted to relegate them to the backwaters again and not even provide them with the benefits of other returned soldiers like allotments of land. Worse still, Aboriginal land reserve was taken and given to the white returned soldiers.

Consequently, when World War 2 came, and Aborigines were still not citizens in their own land, William said he could not support their going to war again unless some changes were made to upgrade their status. He wrote to the Minister for the Interior 3 January 1939:[72]

> I am a father of a soldier who gave his life for his King on the battlefield and thousands of coloured men enlisted in the AIF. They will doubtless do so again, though on their return last time, that is, those who survived, were pushed back to the bush to resume the status of Aboriginals...

> the Aboriginal now has no status, no rights, no land and, though the native is more loyal to the person of the King and the throne than is the average white, he has no country and nothing to fight for but the privilege of defending the land which was taken from him by the white race without compensation or even kindness. We submit that to put us in the trenches until we have something to fight for, is not right….
>
> My point, Mr McEwen, is the enlistment of natives should be preceded by the removal of all disabilities. Then, with a country to fight for, the Aborigines would not be one whit behind the white men in value. Can you not get my point?

There is an increasing tone of frustration in this letter. Sometimes William must have wondered why his son died for a country that did not seem to care about him or his people. Was it pointless? Was it all in vain?

When William wrote to a family friend in July 1940, he gave the sad news of his brothers and sister. He said that Edgar, Lizzie, Johnny and Aaron had passed away but that Bobby, Ada and himself were all well.[73]

Later that year, his health failing, William and Sarah returned to his own country (tribal land). He died on 29 March 1941 at Mooroopna hospital near Shepparton and was buried with his people at Cummeragunja. But his story lives on; his legacy lives on, and his life still speaks to us. His story is so important, and it is still being told.

Barbara Miller

Chapter 5

VAAL, Cairns League and FCAATSI

I came here (Melbourne) in the year 1931 and have been here ever since. During all this time I have been pleading for my people throughout Australia, and only, after working seven years, I got slight results in the NT. SA is now also improving, but Queensland, with the exception of Cowal Creek, where an Aboriginal leader, Jomen Tamwoy, has gathered together three tribes, taught them about God and they have now, without outside assistance, built their own little homes with gardens in front. They are over 150 persons, they grow their own vegetables, and as there are plenty of wild cattle, they are not short of meat. As far as the government is concerned, Queensland is at a standstill. In WA and NSW, natives are still very badly treated.

— William Cooper in a letter to Mrs W. Norman, daughter of Daniel and Janet Matthews, 30 July 1940[74]

Passing on the Mantle

Following William's death in 1941, the diversion of war and Arthur Burdeau's death in 1942, the League became less active. Not only was William, the originator and vision carrier sorely missed but also Arthur, his white supporter. Arthur not only had valuable links in the white community, but he was a hard worker and the only one in the AAL with a car. "After his death, it was simply not possible to coordinate to the same degree the activities of the League members scattered around the State, to bring choirs to Melbourne for fundraising activities, or to distribute the food, clothing and, at Christmas, toys which were collected by the League for Aborigines in country areas."[75]

However, the AAL was revived by Ps Doug Nicholls and Eric and Bill Onus after the Second World War. In 1962, it became the Aboriginal branch of the Aborigines Advancement League (Victoria)[76] which formed in 1957. The Cummera people kept it alive – Ps Doug, Bill and Eric Onus, Shadrach James Jnr and Caleb and Anne Morgan. Bill was President and Ps Doug secretary.

Doug Nicholls

Pastor Doug Nicholls continued William's work. Doug was forever bringing home Aboriginal people who needed a place to stay, and his wife Gladys kindly looked after them. Doug saw the need for a Girls Hostel and with the help of friends, raised the finances for it. It began in 1958 with twelve girls and was looked after by an Aboriginal couple, Henry and Amy Charles, both born and bred at Cummera, Amy being William Cooper's daughter. Later Doug and his supporters raised the money for a Boys Hostel.

With the new Aborigines Act 1957 in Victoria, the last two barriers to full citizenship rights for Victorian Aborigines were removed. Previously the Licensing Act had prohibited the supply of liquor to an Aboriginal on licensed premises, and the Police Offences Act provided that a white person could be imprisoned if "found wandering or lodging in company with any of the Aboriginal natives of Victoria." However, Victoria was the only Australian state at this time where Aborigines had citizenship rights.

The Federal Aborigines Mission of the Churches of Christ gave Ps Doug Nicholls a base and resources to set up an Aborigines Mission in

Fitzroy, Melbourne and this became a focal point not just spiritually but for welfare work and the organising of Aboriginal people.

Victorian Aborigines Advancement League

In 1946, the British and Australian governments decided to build a rocket range in Central Australia which would fire missiles across the Great Central Reserve and the Warburton Ranges Mission. This was a large space occupied by a considerable number of Aborigines living a traditional lifestyle without the means or experience to make their protests heard. It was as if the governments decided this was unoccupied or sparsely occupied land so we can't do too much harm here. Again, it was as if the Aboriginal people were invisible or didn't matter.

Ps Doug Nicholls and Helen Baillie, a nursing sister who had long supported William Cooper, met the Governor-General, the Duke of Gloucester, at Government House to lobby on their behalf. They gave assurances re the protection of Aboriginal people, but this did not materialise. A group of concerned citizens formed the Rocket Range Protest Committee. Those involved were Doris Blackburn, an independent Member of the House of Representatives (MHR), later to be a founding member of VAAL and Dr Charles Duguid, who later became the first President of Federal Council for Aboriginal Advancement (FCAA) and others. The rocket range plan went ahead, and the issue died down, but the tragic effects of the rocket range on the lives of the Warburton Aborigines were to play a significant role in the setting up of the Victorian Aborigines Advancement League (VAAL) about ten years later.

Concerns about the effects of the testing of the atom bomb by the British at Maralinga, SA over a large area, which also affected a considerable number of Aboriginal people in WA, were raised by William Grayden. He was the WA parliamentarian representing the area. Also, with the government trying to keep them out of the rocket range area, Aboriginal use of the tribal lands to gather food etc. was affected.

Grayden's motion for a Select Committee to investigate was passed, and he headed it.

The Select Committee were shocked by what they saw in the Warburton Range area with the Aboriginal children and their parents suffering from malnutrition, dehydration and disease:

Some members of a group of Aborigines that had recently struggled into the mission from north of the Rawlinson Ranges were so dehydrated that they could not urinate for three days. The committee also saw children aged between seven and nine years weighing less than thirty pounds; a mother whose right arm was rotting away between the wrist and elbow from yaws, but who still had to search for seeds and hunt small game; many Aborigines, young and old, afflicted with trachoma, some blind.[77]

Ps Doug Nicholls had been invited by Grayden to visit the area with the Select Committee. After sitting in the red dust of the Warburton Ranges area with a tribe living so like their ancestors, Doug started to identify with the desert people as well as the fringe-dwellers[78] and the word "equality" that he heard so often from his mentor William Cooper, started to stir in him more profoundly and call him to action. Ps Doug and the League did a lot to raise support on this issue. What was happening at the Warburton Ranges was what had happened to Victorian Aborigines 120 years earlier with the ravages of colonisation.

After a shocking report on 12 December 1956 by the Select Committee, little was done by the West Australian government. However, a Save the Aborigines Committee was formed in Melbourne by white supporter Doris Blackburn and some church and other leaders including Stan Davey, a Church of Christ pastor and Ps Doug Nicholls. Gordon Bryant, the Australian Labor Party (ALP) Member for Wills, came to one of the meetings and offered his assistance. Ps Doug showed around the powerful and disgraceful images of the suffering Aborigines at Warburton Ranges. Doris Blackburn, Gordon Bryant, Stan Davey and Doug Nicholls all worked on this issue and, one month later, at the February meeting, it was decided to disband the Save the Aborigines Committee and build a longer-term organisation with broader objectives of Aboriginal advancement and the VAAL was born.

The Save the Aborigines Committee was a short-term response to the plight of the Aborigines in the Warburton Ranges area, but the VAAL was to provide a long term one. Stan Davey, a white supporter of the Aboriginal cause, asked Gordon Bryant if he would become President this new organisation, which would sponsor Doug to work full time for the Aboriginal cause as a field officer. He agreed. Gordon Bryant and Kim Beazley Snr,[79] another federal ALP parliamentarian, became watchdogs on Aboriginal issues in parliament, challenging their own as well as the Liberal Party on Aboriginal issues over many years.

VAAL was to focus on citizenship rights and anti-discrimination, working out of small rented premises in Russell St in the Central Business District (CBD) and "meeting in an unheated classroom in Fitzroy State School where hot soup had to be passed around to prevent the members' chattering teeth from interfering with discussion."[80]

While Aboriginal people like Doug Nicholls, Margaret Tucker, Geraldine Briggs and Bill and Eric Onus were involved with VAAL from the outset, there was a white majority in the VAAL's membership and a strong influence of white supporters over the next ten years. This seemed to work well, as there was still Aboriginal leadership in policy making and making important decisions. It did become a contentious issue over time however, with some Aborigines wanting Aboriginal membership only.

Cooper's AAL was the first Aboriginal organisation in Victoria, and it had a national impact. The VAAL's history of itself states, "It is worth emphasising that this forerunner to the Victorian Aborigines Advancement League, later to merge with it as its Aboriginal branch (in 1962) was an all Aboriginal organisation. Almost forty years later, virulent and hysterical reactions by the press and State government to the management committee of the Aborigines

Australian Aborigines League 12 February 1949. From left -Herbert Groves (NSW), Athol Lester (NSW), William Onus (Vic), William Ferguson (NSW) and Aussie Davies (Qld). Photo (Sunday Herald)

Advancement League becoming totally Aboriginalised suggested that such a move was radical, premature and dangerous."[81]

This was the reference to the Black Power issue and what was seen as increasing militancy of the VAAL as it sought to have black control of the movement for black rights. In William Cooper's day, this did not seem to be an issue.

Protest March, 3rd from left in front row-Bruce McGuinness (Private collection)

There were several worthwhile causes that the VAAL took up. Examples were

- the testing of the atom bomb by the British at Maralinga SA, affecting vast numbers of Aboriginal people
- the shocking conditions of Aborigines at Warburton WA
- representation for Albert Namatjira, the famous Aboriginal artist who was gaoled for six months for supplying alcohol to a relative, deemed an Aboriginal ward of the state

- supporting Yirrkala people in the NT who were not consulted about bauxite mining on their land and were due to have 140 sq. miles of their hunting grounds excised without compensation
- preventing the last land at Cummera being taken from them and rebuilding the community
- preventing the closure of Lake Tyers Aboriginal reserve in Victoria
- the re-enactment of Batman's treaty, the only treaty ever made with Aborigines which was made near Melbourne
- the major one taken up by the League and later the Federal Council - the fight to change the constitution of Australia resulting in the 1967 Referendum

Federal Council for Aboriginal Advancement

There were a number of Aboriginal organisations in each state working for Aborigines. Many were affiliated with the Council for Aboriginal Rights Victoria (CAR). Shirley Andrews mentioned the idea of a national federation of these groups in 1953 and Jessie Street in 1956, and they worked with Charles Duguid, Stan Davey and Doug Nicholls to bring it together.

Stan Davey became full-time secretary to the Victorian League in January 1958 and contacted Dr Charles Duguid, President of the SA Aborigines Advancement League who was interested in establishing a national organisation. He was an Adelaide surgeon and noted member of the Presbyterian Church. The Adelaide group agreed to host the first national meeting while Victorian group sent out invitations to the states and helped organise it.

Nine Aboriginal advancement bodies had come together in Adelaide in 1958 to form the Federal Council for Aboriginal Advancement (FCAA), realising a national pressure group would help them work for Commonwealth control of Aboriginal affairs as state-based legislation was affecting their civil rights.

They came from Victoria, NSW, Queensland and WA and met in Adelaide - representatives from nine organisations and inaugurated the FCAA. Of the twenty-five people who attended, only four were Aboriginal – Ps Doug Nicholls of Victoria, Jeff Barnes of SA, Bert Groves of NSW and also Bill Onus of Victoria as an observer. Bert was the only Aboriginal on the NSW Welfare Board, and Jeff later became the first Aboriginal on the new Welfare Board in SA.

From 14-16 February 1958, they settled on the Council's five basic principles:

- Equal citizen rights with other Australian citizens for Aborigines
- All Aborigines to have a standard of living adequate for health and wellbeing, including food, clothing, housing and medical care not less than for other Australians
- All Aborigines to receive equal pay for equal work and the same industrial protection as for other Australians
- Education for detribalized Aborigines to be free and compulsory
- The absolute retention of all remaining reserves, with native or communal or individual ownership

Ps Doug and Stan travelled extensively on lecture tours of church and various community groups to get their message across.

The first three Presidents of FCAA were – Dr Charles Duguid, Doris Blackburn and Don Dunstan, the latter later becoming Labor Premier of SA. Their experience in dealing with the government, the press and public opinion was invaluable though it meant there was a robust non-Aboriginal influence on the organisation with which some Aborigines were later to take issue.

Cairns Advancement League

In January 1960, the Cairns Aboriginal and Torres Strait Islander Advancement League (CATSIAL) formed with Gladys O'Shane as President. Joe McGinness, Ruth Wallace (now Hennings), Ruth's sisters Muriel and Etta Callope and her husband Pedro Wallace were also very involved as were Evelyn Scott, Ettie Pau, Elia Ware, Sandra McGinness, Joe's daughter and Pedro and Joe Guivarra. Alf Neal and others from the nearby Aboriginal community of Yarrabah were enthusiastic members.

There was strong union support for the Cairns League, with Joe McGinness, a key League member, being a wharfie as were other Indigenous members of the League. Gladys O'Shane's husband, Paddy or Tiger, was also a wharfie. Gladys and Tiger's children, Pat, Margaret, Terry, Danny and Tim were active in the Cairns Advancement League and FCAA with Terry and Tim being in the Seaman's Union. Pat's husband, Mick Miller, a teacher, was also very involved with the Cairns League and FCAA.

When the structure of FCAA widened in 1962 to enable other bodies besides Aboriginal advancement leagues to join, the Cairns Branch of the Waterside Workers Federation and the Queensland Trades and Labour Council were among the first unions to affiliate.

Sue Taffe[82] describes the close association the Cairns League had with members of the Communist Party of Australia (CPA) because of the support they received from people like Fred Paterson, a Townsville lawyer who did pro bono work for the League, Fred Thompson of Townsville and Dr Len Webb of Cairns. Joyce Tattersell who had been a reporter on the staff of *Tribune* in Sydney staffed a basic office for the League in Cairns. Pauline Pickford, Shirley Andrews and Dr Barrry Christophers from Melbourne were also members of the CPA who supported the Cairns League. The CPA was at the ready with logistical and financial support and preparedness to fight exploitation of Indigenous people when help from other quarters was wanting in Cairns. Some of the Aboriginal and Torres Strait Islander members of the Cairns League were also CPA members. The Cairns League was more dependent on support from the unions and the CPA than the southern states as it did not enjoy the high level of support from church, welfare and women's groups that the southern states did.

Despite this, it is important to note that Indigenous leaders ran the Cairns League.

Cairns was very much a working-class place and, of its 22,000 population in the late 1950s, Taffe[83] points out that there were over 2,000 workers in ten sugar mills in Cairns and another thousand men were employed on the Cairns wharves before bulk handling came in. This, coupled with the development of plastic buttons in the early 1960s which eroded the trochus and pearling industries, meant that Cairns attracted a movement of workers to it from Aboriginal and Torres Strait Islander communities.

The Cairns League put out a declaration of Rights at its first conference in Cairns 29-31 July 1960 decrying discrimination. While there was much to attend to with discrimination in the local picture theatre and bars of Cairns and problems with police treatment of Aborigines in Mossman and Mareeba, there were three major fights they tackled, and these have come to define the contribution of the organisation. However, as part of the Federal Council,[84]The League was very involved in the 1967 referendum struggle for recognition. These three major fights were:

- The Freddie Reys case
- The Jimmy Jacko case and
- The Mapoon people's removal from their land

Freddie Reys

In late 1959, the case of Freddie Reys prompted the formation of the Cairns League. Reys had taken a job as a taxi driver with the Blue and White Taxi Company. Being of Aboriginal and Filipino parents, the white staff decided to break his spirit, even though they had gone to school with him as they thought he was too 'cocky'. The radio operator sent Reys off on fake calls several times, making it difficult for him to earn a living. His wife had just given birth to their first child. They even arranged for a female passenger to lay a false charge of sexual harassment against him.

Depressed, he was ready to quit but Pedro Guivarra, an Aboriginal wharfie told him to hold on. They sacked Reys anyway. The matter was raised at the Trades and Labour Council just before Christmas Day, and they ran a boycott of the taxi company. The Mayor of Cairns intervened when it became public and apologised on the local radio station. Reys was reinstated, and it lifted the hopes of Aboriginal people of what could be achieved.

Jimmy Jacko

The second case of Jimmy Jacko involved a young man from Hopevale Aboriginal community near Cooktown. Lutheran missionaries ran Hopevale but under the racist Queensland Aborigines Act.[85] The missionary saw Jimmy sitting with his girlfriend at the local football game, breaking the rules against unmarried couples socialising. The punishment was two weeks work without pay. Instead, they ran away together, returning a few days later.

The usual punishment for women in missions in Queensland was to have their hair roughly cut off in front of others to shame them. They caned her as well. Pastor Kernich flogged Jacko who was then to be transported to Palm Island government settlement as further punishment, i.e. banned from his community. While en route in Cairns, Jacko gave the police the slip and told his story to Joe Guivarra who relayed it to Joe McGinness.

This situation prompted the first organised campaign by the Cairns League which had the support of left-wing unions. Cairns League members and wharfies sheltered Jacko even though, under the Act, it was a crime to harbour an Aboriginal.

The government held an enquiry at Hopevale and Pastor Kernich was found to have infringed regulation 29 of the Act. Not only did Gladys O'Shane and Joe McGinness go to the Hopevale hearing but also ALP parliamentarian Tom Uren, Fred Paterson, formerly CPA state Member for Bowen and now Jacko's legal representative, Pauline Pickford from the Council for Aboriginal Rights in Melbourne, Torres Strait Islander Fred Walters and members of the Trades and Labour Councils from Cairns and Townsville.

As well as winning the day for Jacko, they were able to achieve the broader goal of getting information out on the infamous Queensland Aborigines Act, which controlled the life and movements of Aborigines and show the harsh conditions under which Aborigines lived.

Mapoon

Thirdly the story of the Mapoon people near Weipa in Cape York which I later documented[86] as Barbara Russell was something that was first taken up by the Cairns League. I didn't come along till January 1974, at the request of Mick Miller and Keith Saunders at a meeting in Canberra attended by Charlie Perkins and Gordon Briscoe and organised by Harry Penrith. I did the fieldwork on the project, which led to the books, and we ensured that Vol 1 told the story of the people in their own words. It was *The Mapoon Story* by the Mapoon People.

In 1962, the Mapoon people started calling out to the League for help. The Presbyterian Church ran Mapoon and co-operated with the Queensland government in a proposal to close down the mission after a large mining lease covering their land was given to Comalco without the Aborigines permission.

The League produced a leaflet "They Have Made Our Rights Wrong: The Struggle for Mapoon" and publicised the plight of the people widely. Jean Jimmy, one of the key leaders of the Mapoon people, even travelled to one or two FCAATSI meetings to raise support but to no avail. In 1963, the police moved in and forcibly removed the Mapoon people from their land and burnt their houses so they would not return. The government removed everything, including the church and the store. The people were heartbroken and longed to return.

In 1974, when I visited the Mapoon people who had been scattered to Weipa South (today called Napranum) and New Mapoon near Bamaga at the tip of the Cape, I was able to rally the support for them to move back and today Mapoon is a flourishing community. I wrote about their removal and return.[87]

Nth Qld and Torres Strait Islander delegation about to board a train to Canberra 1966 for FCAATSI meeting, L-R Jack Congoo, Ettie Pau, Jean Jimmy, Joe McGinness, Peter Guivarra and Elia Ware. (FCAATSI collection)

Cairns League and FCAATSI

In 1961, Joe McGinness, secretary of the Cairns League, became President of FCAA, a position which he held till the organisation wound up in 1978. Although FCAA had its national headquarters in Melbourne, its leadership was from far north Queensland. So, there was a strong connection between Cairns and Melbourne.

It was the Torres Strait Islander members of the Cairns League who pushed for FCAA to change its name to FCAATSI to include the name of the other Indigenous group in Australia from the islands between Australia and Papua New Guinea. Islanders like Dulcie Flower, Koiko Mabo of Mabo native title court case fame, Elia Ware, Ettie Pau, Jacob Abednego, Fred Walters and Wees Nawia and others represented Islander interests in the Cairns and later Townsville Leagues or at FCAATSI.

Mick and Pat Miller, involved with the Cairns League in the 1960s, also attended FCAATSI meetings and held positions. Mick was Vice President of FCAATSI in 1971-72 and Pat was General Secretary briefly in 1973. Gordon Briscoe remembers first meeting Mick and Pat in Sydney in 1969, where they had travelled to campaign for civil rights.

Black Self-determination

VAAL's assessment was that FCAA's objectives were not in the direction of black self-determination that William Cooper's now-defunct Australian Aborigines League had been operating and that its goal outlined at its formation in Adelaide in 1958 reflected the preoccupations of its predominately white founders. VAAL comments, “Although wholly admirable in their concern to ensure that the civil and human rights and material wellbeing of Australia’s Aborigines were developed and maintained, FCAA’s objectives did not, and could not, contain the moves for black self-determination and vehement anti-assimilationism which marked the stance of the by-then defunct Australian Aborigines League, which were to preoccupy black activists in the late 1960's and early 1970's and which are now accepted as basic tenets by most Victorian Aborigines."[88]

Those objectives were largely achieved over time but not solely through the work of FCAA/FCAATSI. Today there is still a considerable gap between Aboriginal and non-Aboriginal people on most socio-economic indices so much so that there is a special government program called "Closing the Gap" which is having limited success.

Interestingly, there was also a Jewish-Aboriginal connection around this time with Emil and Hannah Witton and Rosie Guiterman being involved with the Australian Aboriginal Fellowship (Sydney) and Lorna Lippman and Colin Tatz giving a great deal of support to the VAAL and FCAATSI.

Chapter 6

The 1967 Referendum

1. The petition to His Majesty, seeking representation in the Commonwealth Parliament for aborigines. As you know, our Maori brothers have four members, including one minister of the Crown....

2. The new policy "the Aboriginal Magna Carta", and its full implementation in the areas controlled by the Federal Parliament. Also, the effect of the State Control of aborigines by the new policy. We have urged that the Federal Parliament should take over the State rights in this matter and we have been advised by certain State Administrations that they are not opposed to this....

— William Cooper, AAL to Prime Minister Robert Menzies, 5 October 1939[89]

Gordon Bryant worked with the VAAL to prepare a petition to the Federal Parliament to secure a referendum to change the constitution so that the Commonwealth could take control of Aboriginal affairs. Amazingly, 25,988 signatures were collected in three months so that they presented the petition on 17 September 1958.

FCAATSI Meet Prime Minister Menzies

A historic meeting was held in Canberra when a deputation from the Federal Council met Liberal Prime Minister, Sir Robert Menzies on 27 September 1963. They were asking for a referendum on two sections of the constitution – Sections 51 and 127. Section 51 gave the Federal Government power to frame laws for "people of any race other than the Aboriginal race in any State for whom it is deemed necessary to make special laws."

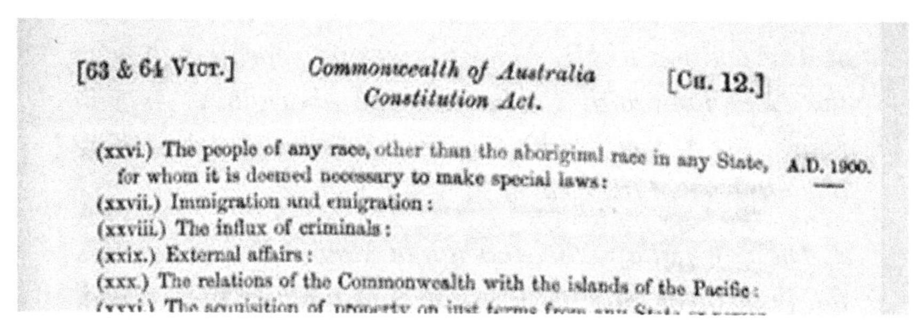

[63 & 64 VICT.] *Commonwealth of Australia Constitution Act.* [CH. 12.]

(xxvi.) The people of any race, other than the aboriginal race in any State, for whom it is deemed necessary to make special laws: A.D. 1900.
(xxvii.) Immigration and emigration:
(xxviii.) The influx of criminals:
(xxix.) External affairs:
(xxx.) The relations of the Commonwealth with the islands of the Pacific:

Section 127 read: "In reckoning the numbers of people of the Commonwealth, or of a State or other part of the Commonwealth, Aboriginal natives shall not be counted." This denied them equality. It was a grave denial of their humanity and existence. It was as if Aboriginal people did not exist, that they were invisible, that they were not worthy of being counted.

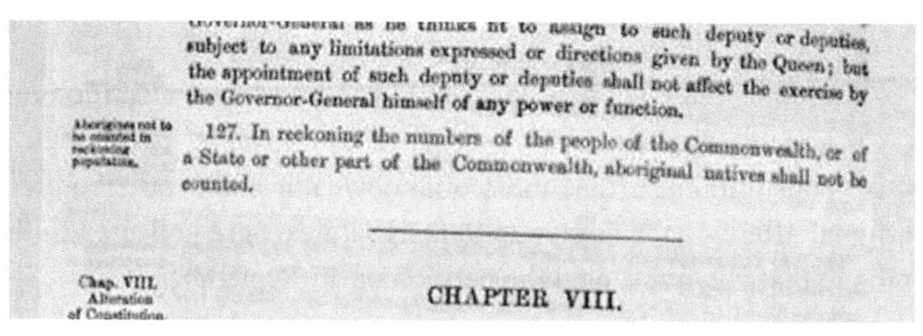

Governor-General as he thinks fit to assign to such deputy or deputies, subject to any limitations expressed or directions given by the Queen; but the appointment of such deputy or deputies shall not affect the exercise by the Governor-General himself of any power or function.

Aborigines not to be counted in reckoning population. 127. In reckoning the numbers of the people of the Commonwealth, or of a State or other part of the Commonwealth, aboriginal natives shall not be counted.

Chap. VIII. Alteration of Constitution. CHAPTER VIII.

It is interesting that when the white settlers came to take over the land in Australia, the legal fiction of "Terra Nullius" or that Australia was an empty land was touted. Because Aborigines had not fenced off their land as white people do, they were considered not to own the land. However, they knew their tribal boundaries very well, marked by rivers, mountains and other natural features. And to trespass on another tribe's land without asking permission meant death. The settlers pointed to the fact that Aborigines did not farm or build permanent homes and were nomadic hunter-gatherers as another reason they did not own the land. But the Aborigines moved around seasonally following the food supply and moved within defined boundaries, returning to their shelters and favourite camping spots regularly. The more fertile the territory, e.g. in places like the Murray River, the less movement there was.

So somehow, Aborigines were invisible to the white settlers though their black skins stood out from the rainforest, the cleared farmland or the desert scenery. The sheer numbers of white Australians compared to Aboriginal people, particularly after the massacres and deaths of Aborigines from introduced diseases helped perpetuate this myth.

The concept of "Terra Nullius" was not put to death till the Mabo High Court decision on 3 June 1992 which recognised that Aborigines indeed inhabited Australia before white settlement and that they had native title to the land except where it had been already alienated by development. The ALP government of Prime Minister Paul Keating enacted native title legislation in 1993 to put this decision into effect so cases would not have to be taken to court and decided on a case by case basis. Native title applicants would have to prove continuing association with the land which was difficult as government policies over the years had forcibly moved them off their land.

So, the Federal Council eagerly and hopefully put their case to the Prime Minister of the day. Can we have a referendum to get rid of discrimination from the constitution? They also wanted State Acts for Aborigines abolished and all Aborigines to be brought under federal law and bauxite royalties for the Yirrkala people.

The six Aborigines in the delegation were Ps Doug Nicholls from Victoria, Kath Walker and Joe McGinness from Queensland, Malcolm

Cooper from SA, Ted Penny from WA and Phillip Roberts [90]from the NT. Faith Bandler, a Pacific Islander who threw her lot in with the Aborigines, represented NSW. There was no delegate from Tasmania. Gordon Bryant, who had previously approached Sir Robert Menzies on their behalf, introduced them.

Phillip Roberts asked the Prime Minister why Aborigines were not allowed to build houses on reserves. He said he didn't know. Ted Penny raised the issue of white people not being allowed to visit Aboriginal reserves, not even a white man with an Aboriginal wife. Joe McGinness brought up the need for training centres and training programs for developing the north's Aboriginal labour force. Doug emphasised the need for equality for Aborigines in all walks of life – living standards, education, opportunity etc. The Prime Minister said he was impressed by their presentation and that they had managed to bring such a big group from different states. He promised to consider their case for the referendum. [91]

FCAA mounted an extensive public campaign for the referendum, and on April 1965 the Federal Government announced its decision to have one on section 127 of the constitution.

At the Easter 1964 FCAA meeting in Canberra, their seventh conference, there were 110 delegates, forty of whom were Aborigines and Torres Strait Islanders. They represented sixty affiliated organisations from around Australia. There were also eighty observers, half of whom were Aboriginal. Among the observers were representatives from the embassies of the USA, Canada, the Soviet Union, Indonesia, Brazil, Burma and the Irish Republic.

Some of the key figures were Joe McGinness, a waterside worker from Cairns who was elected president for the third year in a row. The famous poet, Kath Walker, State Secretary for Queensland, grew up on Stradbroke Is and had been enlisted as a switchboard operator during the war. Charles Perkins, born in Alice Springs, was in 1964 studying an arts course at Sydney University. Charlie led a Freedom Ride in NSW similar to those in the USA where he travelled by bus through country NSW towns with university students challenging the segregation of facilities. He later became head of the Department of Aboriginal Affairs in Canberra.

Elia Ware from St Paul Island in the Torres Strait was a volunteer in the Torres Strait Island Light Infantry Battalion in World War 2, and at, the 1964 meeting, he proposed that they add Torres Strait Islanders to the name of the organisation. It became FCAATSI through his persuasiveness.

Alick Jackomos, while an Australian born Greek, was married to Kitty Cooper's granddaughter Merle and had immersed himself in the Fitzroy Aboriginal community since he was a child, following Ps Doug around and helping him. It was now decided that he would take over Ps Doug's role as field officer of the League as Ps Doug had resigned.

FCAATSI Canberra conference Easter 1966, Joe McGinness front row centre and Doug Nicholls front row right. (FCAATSI collection)

There was a massive campaign for a yes vote in the 1967 referendum, and just over 90% of the population said yes. For the Indigenous people and their supporters who had worked so hard, it was like a dream come true. It was very unusual for the Australian population to vote yes at a referendum, and this was a resounding result. Faith Bandler led the NSW campaign, and Kath Walker (later known as Oodgeroo Noonuccal) led the Queensland campaign. Faith said, "People in Australia have to register their dogs and cattle, but we don't know how many Aborigines there are." [92]

It is essential to be clear that the 1967 referendum did not give Aboriginal and Torres Strait Islander people the right to vote. That came for all states except Queensland in 1962. From 1829 (first settlement in Australia was 1788) Australia was considered part of the Dominions of the Crown which meant that all inhabitants of Australia, including Aborigines, were British citizens. It was the passing of the Commonwealth Franchise Act 1902 and the Commonwealth of Australia Constitution Act 1900 which meant that Indigenous people were not included as citizens of Australia and thus could not vote. Aborigines were stripped of their rights at the point of nationhood for Australia when the states joined together to form the Commonwealth. Queensland followed the other states and gave Aborigines voting rights in 1965.

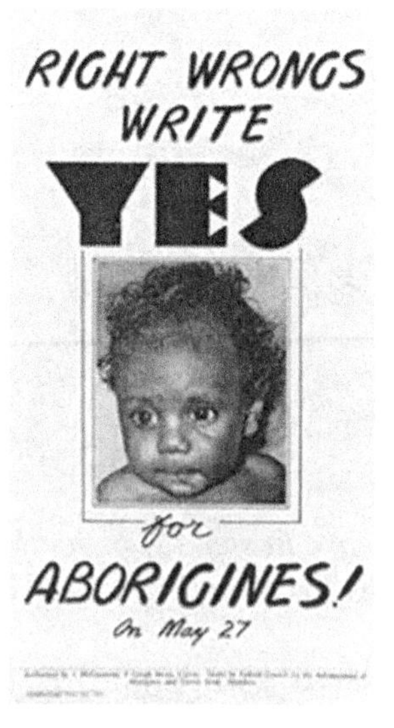

Poster and flier used for referendum campaign (Aboriginal-Australian Fellowship records. Mitchell Library, State Library of NSW MLMSS 4057/7)

What the 1967 referendum was about was counting Aborigines in the census. It was finally recognition of their humanity, shocking as this is that this recognition still needed to happen as late as 1967. Just before the 1967 referendum, Charles (Chicka) Dixon, manager of the Foundation for Aboriginal Affairs, explained how he felt that the referendum would bring acceptance to Aborigines as people. Up until the referendum, government policy suggested Aborigines were not human beings.[93]

There were several developments that brought Australia to this point. While the FCAATSI was in a sense the mother organisation that birthed the constitutional change that came from the 1967 referendum, international developments were a key mover and Aboriginal organisations before FCAATSI prepared the way.

What were these international developments?

After World War 1, the creation of the League of Nations and the International Labour Organisation meant that there was now international monitoring of human rights

After World War 2, Australia was one of the founding members of the United Nations, and on 10 December 1948 the UN General Assembly agreed on the Universal Declaration of Human Rights

The London Anti-Slavery Society planned to approach the UN to promote the Aboriginal cause and Lady Jessie Street visited Australia to gather information. In 1957, she campaigned for a referendum for Aborigines to be included in the Australian census and her petition was read in Federal Parliament on 14 May.

Harold Holt succeeded Robert Menzies as Prime Minister of Australia in January 1966 and signed the UN International Accord for the Elimination of All Forms of Racial Discrimination, meaning that he had to do something about the "White Australia" policy

On 16 December 1966, the UN General Assembly passed two covenants, the International Covenant on Civil and Political Rights and the International Covenant on Economic, Social and Cultural Rights

As international pressure on Australia mounted, the war effort of Aborigines and Torres Strait Islanders in both wars broke down some barriers. Key Aboriginal people and the organisations they founded played their part in building momentum towards the counting of Indigenous people in the census and the Federal Government's ability to make legislation for Indigenous people and even take control of Indigenous affairs. They were:

- Fred Maynard started the Aborigines Progressive Association (APA) in 1924 to work for the recognition of Aboriginal rights but, after continual police persecution, he disbanded it in 1927
- William Cooper set up the Australian Aborigines League in 1932 in Melbourne to work for the uplift of his people
- In 1937 in Dubbo, NSW, William Ferguson and Jack Patten with the help of Pearl Gibbs and Jack Kinchela re-launched the APA and, with William Cooper, organised the Day of Mourning in Sydney on 26 January 1938
- In 1965 Charlie Perkins, who was to become a key person in Aboriginal affairs, organised Freedom Rides in NSW where Aboriginal and non-Aboriginal students from Sydney drove around country towns to break segregation. This was following the example of freedom rides in the southern USA. They received international as well as local media attention
- The Gurindji people of Wave Hill station in the NT went on strike in 1966 rather than work for almost slave labour for Vesteys pastoral company. This started a push for land rights

Norman Miller with his painting for 40th anniversary of the referendum (photo Barbara Miller)

From October 1962 to October 1963, supporters of the petition, working voluntarily, set up tables in the streets of all capital cities and country towns urging people to sign the petition. They obtained about 100,000 signatures. The Melbourne-based national campaign committee got the maximum benefit out of it by sorting over 6,000 forms into electorates and then tabling these petitions by electorate in parliament every sitting day over seven weeks. They became so regular that it was like the prayer with which parliament commenced commented one Parliamentarian.[94]

Prime Minister Robert Menzies introduced the Constitution Alteration (Repeal of Section 127) Bill as he said that section 127 was completely out of harmony with our national attitudes, but he did not include amendment of section 51 (xxvi). He argued that the words "other than the Aboriginal race in any state" were protection against discrimination by the Commonwealth Parliament. This point appeared academic and unconnected to the public debate.[95] Parliament passed the Bill and set a date for a referendum.

After Menzies' retirement in January 1966, the new Prime Minister, Harold Holt announced that he would put the planned referendum to repeal s127 on the back burner and he would reopen debate as to whether the amendment to s51 (XXVI) should be included in the referendum. In March the same year, Liberal William Wentworth introduced a Private Member's Bill for the whole of s51 (xxvi) to be deleted, and a new section added, s117A, preventing discrimination against any person because of race. It was defeated. Attorney-General Nigel Bowen, in a February 1967 cabinet meeting, reviewed the arguments and made a recommendation that they have the referendum on s127 and s51 (XXVI) in the form that went to the people. Parliament agreed, and so the historic referendum was held.

Referendum delegation. L-R: Gordon Bryant, Faith Bandler, Prime Minister Harold Holt, Ps Doug Nicholls, Harry Penrith, Win Branson and William Wentworth. FCAATSI newsletter may-June 1967 (FCAATSI collection)

Considering this had been a ten year plus struggle, the referendum was welcomed with much anticipation by the Indigenous community, and earnest campaigning ensued. The churches came out strongly for a "yes" vote. One slogan was "Count us together, make us one people". Another slogan on a poster with an Aboriginal child's face read "Right wrongs, Write yes for Aborigines." FCAATSI appointed Gordon Bryant and Joe McGinness to run the national campaign and state directors to campaign for a "yes" vote.

On a historic day, 27 May 1967, 90.77% of voting Australians voted "yes", and a gigantic shift took place in Indigenous Affairs in Australia. What is interesting is that the "no" case for the 1967 referendum was never really put to the people as the "yes" case had the support of the majority of parliamentarians across party lines.

While the Commonwealth was slow to use its new powers, the effect of this decision was to reverberate down through the years and have significant consequences. As part of Reconciliation Week, 27 May is celebrated each year as Recognition Day.

Referendum celebration party Tranby College 1967. (FCAATSI collection)

Charlie Perkins was by then vice president of FCAATSI and recommended to Prime Minister Harold Holt the formation of a federal Aboriginal Affairs Bureau which could concentrate on employment and education but also look at the status of Aborigines as the original owners of the land.

Parliamentary discussion centred on the government policy of assimilation and NT parliamentarians privately expressed concerns they might lose their seats with an organised Aboriginal vote. The Prime Minister announced that Herbert (Nugget) Coombs, the governor of the Reserve Bank would head up a new Council for Aboriginal Affairs which would provide policy advice to the Federal Government. This might seem a strange appointment, but he was well respected and made a point of listening to Aboriginal voices.

The key outcomes were that it was an enormously important symbolic victory for Aborigines. Despite its racist past, at this moment, white Australia embraced Aborigines and Torres Strait Islanders. It was a forerunner of the public opinion that led to the massive marches for reconciliation across bridges many years later.

What was also important was that the Federal Government could now override racist state legislation. The government enacted the Racial Discrimination Act 1975, and, while the Queensland government resisted it for some time with a big federal-state struggle, eventually the racist Queensland Aborigines Acts were repealed. In 1984, the Community Services Acts took their place, giving a measure of local government to Queensland Indigenous communities.[96]

The government passed other significant legislation, one example being the native title act in 1993 after the historic Mabo court case[97] in 1992 found in favour of native title rights. Mabo Day, 3 June each year is now also part of Reconciliation Week.

The victory of the 1967 referendum was behind them. The Victorian government granted land rights to Aborigines over the two existing Victorian reserves, Lake Tyers and Framlingham. Cummera is under NSW authority, but most of the 1500 or more Aborigines living in the Goulburn Valley of Victoria are descendants of the Cummera people. Land rights are so much a part of the spiritual and economic base for which Aboriginal people have lobbied hard.

But the winds of change were blowing and with the advent of Black Power in 1971, much of the sympathy and financial support from the white population which had kept the Aborigines Advancement League going, dried up. Ps Doug resigned from the committee because of tensions and ill health.

Much of what William Cooper had worked for had borne fruit, but there was still much more to be realised. As mentioned earlier, the Australian Aborigines League that William had started and that had lapsed during the war years was revived again by Ps Doug Nicholls, Bill and Eric Onus and others and in 1962 became the Aboriginal branch of the VAAL. There were about twenty-eight branches state-wide. Bruce McGuinness, a Yorta Yorta man, was to become secretary of the Aboriginal branch and he would become a central figure in the transfer of power in VAAL to Aborigines.

The Aboriginal branch was interested in black self-management and more political issues than welfare so that tensions between it and white-run sections of the League started to show. The Aboriginal branch even lobbied that VAAL's hostels be given to the state government to run because the government should be responsible for welfare and that would free the League for more political activities. The move was defeated.[98] A lot of work and fundraising had gone into these hostels by the Aboriginal people, so this would have been a big step.

A visit by black Caribbean activist, Dr Roosevelt Brown to Melbourne on 24 March 1969 had a dramatic effect. He met with Bruce McGuinness and Bob Maza, a member of the Aboriginal Branch and VAAL President. Ps Doug Nicholls and Dr Brown publicly clashed at a press conference and concerns about Black Power were raised in the press. Ps Doug decided to resign from VAAL on 2 October 1969 over philosophical differences with emerging leaders. The newspapers revealed the next day that a secret meeting of Aborigines on 17 September had decided to ask for the resignation of all white members of the management committee and white staff. At extraordinary meetings of VAAL mid-

October, they rescinded the motion. It appears that the split was not on racial lines as some Aboriginal people wanted to keep it multi-racial and some non-Aboriginal people like clergyman Bruce Silverwood, co-director of VAAL, advocated that Aborigines fill all positions. [99] However, there appeared to be some resistance by white position holders like Silverwood as to suddenness of the moves. When Bruce McGuinness replaced Silverwood as VAAL director, the League had an all Aboriginal staff for the first time.

The public infighting in the VAAL led to the government withholding a grant for a time, and it became difficult to raise funds from community donations from where most of VAAL's support had come. Not only that, the white volunteer support and membership dropped off. This made it difficult for VAAL to continue all the excellent welfare work it had been doing. However, under Bruce McGuinness' leadership over the next three years, it worked on land rights, compensation and black management of black affairs, all areas that needed attention.

Similar moves in FCAATSI were afoot. When a motion by non-Aboriginal Barrie Pittock for the Aboriginalisation of membership and policy-making positions was lost on a tied vote at the 1970 conference, this was seen as paternalistic, and a new body – National Tribal Council – led by Kath Walker and Ps Doug Nicholls formed as a breakaway group which lasted 3-4 years.

FCAATSI did become an Indigenous run organisation in 1973, but things were changing. The numbers of Indigenous grassroots organisations were expanding, and there was now a Department of Aboriginal Affairs and a National Aboriginal Consultative Committee. This meant FCAATSI found it hard to be a genuinely umbrella body for Aboriginal organisations. The final blow came when the Federal Government suddenly cut its funding in 1978 and FCAATSI had to close down its activities.

What is a real achievement is that VAAL continues to this day, probably the oldest existing Aboriginal organisation in Australia. Though its role has diversified over the years, it is still filling a critical need. Rather than band-aid welfare, it has moved to more preventative and community development type programs. It plays a coordinating and liaison role in the Aboriginal community so that lobby groups can be more productive.

A building appeal raised sufficient finances that the VAAL owns its own building, completed in 1982, which is a real success story and a symbol of land rights in Victoria.

Visit to VAAL

Norman and I visited the Aborigines Advancement League in Melbourne the day Barack Obama was inaugurated as the first African-American president of the USA, 20 January 2009. We met with Dr Esme Bamblett, who was then and is currently CEO. Esme has been an Aboriginal pastor of Barak Christian Ministries which she founded in 2000. She named her ministry after William Barak (1824-1903), a respected Aboriginal spokesman and Christian, also called 'King William, last chief of the Yarra Yarra tribe' or 'Beruk'. He belonged to the Wurundjeri Willum horde whose country lay along the Yarra and Plenty Rivers. Her church meets at the League's offices on Sundays. While we were visiting, we stopped to watch Obama's inauguration on TV for a few minutes, a historic moment of world importance. We were moved to see a mural of William Cooper on the wall at the League.

Barbara and Norman Miller outside Aborigines Advancement League, Melbourne (photo David Jack)

Howard and Randi Bass, Messianic Jewish pastors from Israel, were able to see the mural of William Cooper as well and meet Esme. In 2010, Norman and I hosted Howard and Randi on a speaking tour in Sydney and Melbourne. As part of this, Howard and Norman spoke at the church service at the League. Norman and I then took them to Parliament House Canberra where Howard was a key speaker at a Christian conference we organised.

Barbara Miller

Chapter 7

National Aborigines Day and NAIDOC

And He has made from one blood every nation of men to dwell on all the face of the earth and has determined their pre-appointed times and the boundaries of their dwellings."

— Acts 17:26 (NKJV)

I did not know William Cooper personally. He died a decade before I was born. I didn't even grow up with stories of him to inspire me, though no doubt many Aboriginal people in Victoria and NSW did. As a Queenslander, it was not until I had been an activist lobbying for Aboriginal human rights for over 20 years that I heard about William Cooper. But since then, his story has inspired me. So much so that I am writing about it today. I'd like to say that I'm a lady of leisure now who has the time to write and reflect on my life and others of significance to me, but that is not so.

Nevertheless, I feel compelled to write his story. And as I've been writing, I've found a little of my story woven in. In the process, much of the story of the Aboriginal movement in Australia has woven its way into the book as well.

The William Cooper story began for me in the 1990s when I read the book "One Blood" by John Harris in my Cairns home. It is a substantial volume about the history of Aboriginal missions in Australia. But I avidly read all of it. While very interested in the Queensland missions because I had visited a number of them and knew people living there, even written about them[100] and lobbied extensively on behalf of these communities, another story gripped my attention.

It was about an Aboriginal man called William Cooper. Why out of all the stories of Aboriginal people from around Australia did it stand out? I had been attending NAIDOC [101]celebrations and marches since 1974 when I moved to Cairns. These days were opportunities for the Indigenous community and their supporters to find some recognition for Indigenous people in a country slow to recognise their rights, assemble to discuss issues, rally support for their cause and socialise. It turned out we owed it all to William Cooper, a Christian, who started it all by initiating Aboriginal Sunday throughout Australia, a day the churches could recognise and pray for Aboriginal people.

William had felt for some time that there should be some permanent Aborigines Day and he and Arthur Burdeu and members of the Australian Aborigines' League often discussed the matter. Arthur thought the churches should do more for Aborigines and in 1936 he had submitted a motion to the Federal Conference of the Churches of Christ for the formation of a federal Committee on Aborigines. This was accepted, and the Churches of Christ set up a Federal Missionaries Board in 1941 and began active missionary work.

The League decided to lobby for an Aborigines Day. William wrote to the National Missionary Council of Australia (NMCA) on 31 January 1939 asking for the assistance of the Council in promoting a permanent Aborigines Day.

The Convenor of the NMCA Aborigines Advisory Committee was the Anglican, Canon Needham, a friend of the Aborigines and the Committee was in favour of the idea and requested churches to observe Aboriginal Sunday though not connected with any Aboriginal Day of Mourning. Most of the churches agreed and the first Aboriginal Sunday was 28 January 1940 (the Sunday preceding the Australia Day holiday).

Although William lived to see only two Aboriginal Sundays, it was observed for the next fifteen years in the churches on the Sunday preceding Australia Day.

However, the date was changed in 1955 to the first Sunday in July. Why was this? The NMCA wanted to make it a national day and involve the federal and state governments and other organisations in its observance and change it from a time for churches to remember and give welfare to Aborigines to a day when Aborigines were recognised and the rest of the population educated about Aboriginal issues. The Minister for Territories, Paul Hasluck agreed to Federal Government cooperation with the date change.

But why the date change? Ps Doug Nicholls is one of the ones that asked that question. "Did they think that such painful memories took from the pride of Australia Day? Did they think the reminder was too much? We didn't argue about the change to the July date – but we should have. There is so much that has not changed. On Australia Day, the whites – rejoicing – hold out their hands to the immigrants, the New Australians, make them citizens, give them jobs. But they haven't yet bridged the gulf to the Old Australians. It's still our Day of Mourning."[102] Doug could not help but think back to the Day of Mourning that William Cooper had organised. The images of that day kept playing in his mind.

In 1955, the date changed to the first Sunday in July and became known as National Aborigines Day. Then, in 1957, the National Aborigines Day Observance Committee (NADOC) [103] was formed whose goal was to promote awareness of Aboriginal people, their cultures and their plight. In 1989, the title changed to NAIDOC Week to include Torres Strait Islanders in the national celebrations. This event is of considerable significance to Aboriginal and Torres Strait Islander people all over Australia, so I was excited to hear the story of its founder. Not only that, he was way ahead of his time in lobbying for the rights of Aboriginal people.

Chapter 8

William's Dream of Land Rights Finally Realised, at Least in the NT

Ningla –A-Na which means Hungry for our Land

A catch cry of the Aboriginal land rights movement and the name of a documentary of the Aboriginal tent embassy.

In 1972, I again visited friends in Sydney and Melbourne and on my way home to Brisbane, I stopped in Canberra. I headed to the Australian National University (ANU)[104] and met a Christian girl with whom I struck up a friendship. She put me up in her room at Uni with permission of the authorities for a couple of weeks and paid for a stretcher bed for me.

Eventually, a group of students and I rented a house, and we called ourselves the Canberra Christian community. I was the main one behind it, and I spent time sharing the gospel. I had a close communication with the Lord. Looking back, I see the main flaw with this is that I was not grounded in a local congregation where I could get teaching, mentoring and prayer covering.

Arrested During the Vietnam War

Two key things happened to me in Canberra before I moved back to Brisbane. One incident was during the days of the Vietnam War. I handed out anti-draft leaflets in Canberra in July 1971 during a period of registration for the draft and became one of the few women in Australia ever arrested on a national service charge. The charge read "Inciting young men not to register for national service". I was put in the Canberra watch house overnight. I refused to make a plea in court as I didn't recognise the charge, and I didn't have legal representation. As I was not married, my name was still Barbara Russell.

I was found guilty and refused to pay the fine, as I didn't recognise the charge. As there were no jails in Canberra, the police flew me to Sydney on 12 September 1972 handcuffed to a policewoman. The *Sydney Morning Herald* interviewed me at Sydney airport on my way to Silverwater prison. [105]There was a demonstration for me outside Silverwater, and it made the papers. About a week later, Dick Klugman, an ALP parliamentarian from Sydney who was driving to Canberra came and paid my fine, got me out of jail and drove me back in Canberra.

Barbara Russell under arrest arriving at Sydney airport 12.9.72 (photo Sydney Morning Herald)

A group of mostly middle-aged middle-class mothers formed the Save Our Sons (SOS) group in Sydney in 1965 to protest their sons being conscripted and forced to fight in the Vietnam War. This had a radicalising effect on the women, especially those who were Liberal voters. In April 1971 five SOS women were arrested on a charge of trespass and sentenced to 14 days in Fairlea Women's Prison for handing out anti-conscription leaflets to men registering for national service. The case created a lot of media attention, and the state released the women after 11 days. I was not aware of this at the time and only found out about it when researching this book.[106]

Aboriginal Tent Embassy Canberra

The other incident revolved around the Aboriginal Embassy demonstrations. It was not only a bad decision but a poorly timed one that the government chose Australia Day 1972 to announce that there would be no Aboriginal title to land. It was reinforcing this as the day of defeat for Aboriginal people. Instead, Aborigines in the NT could apply for 50-year general purpose leases with the proviso that they put the land to reasonable 'economic' or social use. It was 34 years since William Cooper, Will Ferguson, Jack Patten and other Aboriginal leaders had had their National Day of Mourning in Sydney.

First Aboriginal Tent Embassy under umbrella 26 January 1972 (Tribune SEARCH Foundation. State Library of NSW – ON 161/680/34)

Four young Aboriginal men quickly responded to Prime Minister Billy McMahon's statement - Michael Anderson, Billy Craigie, Bertie Williams and Tony Coorey. They set up a protest under a beach umbrella on the lawns of Parliament House, Canberra and proclaimed themselves the 'Aboriginal Embassy'.

Aborigines came on buses from all over Australia to support the Aboriginal Tent Embassy as it became known and several tents sprung up as people camped on the lawns of Parliament House. Its name is changed to Old Parliament House as a new one was built and opened in 1988.

A large group of Aborigines came down from Brisbane, and I remember talking to them in Brisbane before they went down. I had given away all my possessions except a few clothes as I'd taken a vow of poverty (probably from the Catholic influence) as I thought this was what a committed Christian did. We enjoyed having some of the people from the Aboriginal Embassy people (like Pat Eatock, Bobby McLeod and Ambrose Golden Brown) stay over at our community house.

The police kept pulling the tents down. Women leaders like Aboriginal Femmi Bostock and black American Carol Johnstone suggested that the women surround the men to protect them. So, we did.

We encircled the men, and there were a few rows deep of men and women. The idea was that the police would not attack the women. We were wrong. The police charged us, batons and all, punching into the women with their fists. I don't know how many times the police punched me! I remember that every time I got pulled out by the police, I just kept running back in again. No doubt others did the same. We were trying to prevent the tents being pulled down and protect the embassy, a symbol of the call for Aborigines to be heard.

I was wandering around a bit stunned afterwards, and someone took me to the Canberra hospital as I was injured. I was diagnosed with internal muscle sprain of the chest and neck and did not need to be admitted. Some Aboriginal leaders like Paul Coe had more severe injuries. The DVD "Ningla –A-Na" which means" Hungry for our Land" captures the event. I am on the unedited version in a striped jumper and with short light brown hair, looking a bit dazed from the fray.

Background to the Aboriginal Embassy

But why were we there? The movement to return some land to Aboriginal people was gathering momentum. Aboriginal people had roamed this continent within their various tribal boundaries undisturbed for generations upon generations. Then in 1778, the British planted their flag, declared it was theirs and set up a penal colony. They needed a place to send their convicts as the gaols in Britain were overflowing with the poor. Young men were transported to Australia for things like stealing a loaf of bread or stealing money to buy medicine for their family.

Some Aboriginal people were killed in frontier wars, and some died of introduced diseases. As Aborigines were forced to move off their land, their lives became more difficult to sustain. Introduced cattle and sheep used their waterholes. The hunting and gathering lifestyle of Aborigines became more difficult as native wildlife was marginalised, and the landscape changed. In their hunger, Aboriginal people sometimes killed cattle or sheep to survive and were then hunted by the white settlers and killed as pests. Some settlers gave or would leave out flour laced with arsenic or infected blankets for the Aborigines so that more were killed off. This was an excruciating death.

In a colony with far more men (soldiers and convicts) than women, rape and relationships of convenience occurred. Aboriginal people could no longer be self-governing, and they had no say in white society. It became difficult to practice their spirituality and culture in traditional ways as it was tied to the land where they were born and its sacred sites.

William Cooper and the Aboriginal Advancement League and other Aboriginal organisations in Australia realised that land was needed for Aboriginal people as an economic base and the continuance of their lifestyle and culture.

NT Moves for Land Rights

It was in the NT that two significant moves towards land rights started to take place – the efforts of the Yirrkala people and the Gurindji people.

The Yirrkala Aboriginal people took mining company Nabalco and the Australian government to court. They wanted to have their interests in the land they had occupied for thousands of years recognised. On 27 April 1971, Mr Justice Blackburn handed down his judgment, shocking the Yirrkala people and disappointing many Aboriginal Australians:

> … the relationship between clan and land did not amount to proprietorship as that is understood in our law; and that the clans had not sustained the burden of proof that they were linked with the same land in 1788 as now; that no doctrine of the common law ever required or now requires a British government to recognise land rights under Aboriginal law such as may have existed prior to the 1788 occupation; that Aboriginal land rights in Australia were never expressly recognised; and that if the clans had had any rights they would have been effectually terminated by the mining (Gove Peninsula Nabalco Agreement) Ordinance 1968.[107]

Stunned by the knockback, the Yirrkala sent representatives to Canberra to present a statement to Prime Minister William McMahon. McMahon assured them that a Ministerial Committee would look at how to protect their reserves for their recreational, ceremonial and religious use and how to give them tenure for commercial enterprises, buy land etc.

At the same time, the Gurindji people were still fighting for their traditional lands at Wattie Creek in the NT. They had walked off Wave Hill station 600km south of Darwin in strike action in 1966. British pastoral company Vesteys owned wave Hill station and working conditions were intolerable. They were working for board – a tin shed with no sanitation and flour, sugar and tea.

Vincent Lingiari, a gentle stockman, inspired his people to go on strike and 200 Aboriginal workers and their families walked off the station and set up camp at Wattie Creek which they renamed Daguragu or “a place for us”[108]. For some time, the Gurindji had helplessly watched their land fenced off by pastoralists who spoiled their waterholes and food supplies. The pastoral company had virtually reduced them to slave labour for those who had taken their land without giving any compensation.

Now they had some dignity back, and they inspired a protest movement around the nation as they began the long struggle to have their land ownership recognised. The song "From Little Things Big Things Grow," a rock protest song, was written by Paul Kelly and Kev Carmody. First recorded in 1991, it told the story of the Gurindji's struggle for land rights.

It showed political ineptitude that, after nine months of considering the options in the Yirrkala case, the government chose Australia Day 1972 to announce that there would be no Aboriginal title to land.

Petition

The Aboriginal Tent Embassy sounded to the government like a claim to sovereignty, and they saw it as apartheid, so they opposed it. However, it was a "powerful symbol as the original owners of the land had set up an embassy opposite the parliament, as if they were foreigners. This act showed the strength of their sense of alienation compellingly. They were landless. Their embassy was a tent – a well-understood image of poverty and impermanence. Their camp attracted unprecedented support from people across the country who recognised their sense of grievance and made their views known to the government."[109]

The Aboriginal Tent Embassy grew in numbers and drew up a petition to present to parliament. It outlined a five-point plan for land rights:

Control of the NT as a state within the Commonwealth of Australia; the parliament in the NT to be predominantly Aboriginal with title and mining rights to all land within the Territory.

- Legal title and mining rights to all other presently existing reserve lands and settlements throughout Australia.
- The preservation of all sacred sites throughout Australia.
- Legal title and mining rights to areas in and around all Australian capital cities.

- Compensation monies for lands not returnable to take the form of a down-payment of six billion dollars and an annual percentage of the gross national income.[110]

Leader of the Opposition, Mr Gough Whitlam, visited the Aboriginal Tent Embassy, discussed the petition and promised that a Labor Government would reverse the government's policy on land rights, allowing ownership of land by tribal communities. He also promised the introduction of a civil rights bill, overruling state laws that discriminated against Aborigines, a fully elected Legislative Assembly in the NT with a non-discrimination charter and free legal representation for Aborigines to test their rights in court.[111]

National Aborigines Day 1972

Abschol was set up to support university scholarships for Aboriginal students and was a committee of the National Union of Australian University Students. In the 1960s, it affiliated with FCAATSI. Abschol organised a national moratorium for "Black Rights' for 14 July, National Aborigines Day 1972. Unionists stopped work and workers, students and Aborigines marched in capital cities. Tension was mounting.

Clashes with Police

Aboriginal Tent Embassy supporters and police outside Parliament House 1972
(photo Ken Middleton, National Library of Australia)

As I gathered with others around the tents on the lawns of Parliament House to support the Aboriginal people and their cause on Thursday 20 July, a police force of 150 marched towards the embassy. We linked arms around the tents and sang "We Shall Not Be Moved". As the police charged us, we were getting punched by police, shoved and pushed and forcibly removed. The police arrested several people. The tents were pulled down. The television cameras beamed it across the evening news.

President of the Australian Council of Churches, Bishop Garnsey immediately sent a telegram to the government protesting the removal of the Aboriginal Tent Embassy and supporting Aboriginal land rights legislation.

The following Sunday, 23 July, Aboriginal Tent Embassy representatives met with Department of Interior officials at which the

Department refused permission to re-erect tents. Following the meeting, I was part of a group of 200 demonstrators who tried to re-establish the embassy, and eighteen people were arrested. Gary Williams addressed us, and also, Len Watson, Michael Anderson, Chicka Dixon, Paul Coe, Bobbi Sykes, Shirley Smith and Dennis Walker. Gary Foley later described the day as 'one of the most violent confrontations in the history of Canberra' and Chicka Dixon as 'the most violent event he had witnessed.'[112]

Support was swelling. On 30 July, 2000 people marched to Parliament House and re-erected the Aboriginal Embassy. Instead of violent confrontations like before, there was a stand-off, and the police allowed peaceful protest before removing the tent embassy.[113]

When a court ruled the trespass ordinance under which charges were laid against demonstrators had legal problems, the Aboriginal Tent Embassy was re-erected on 12 September by Bobby McLeod, Tiga Bayles, Bob Bellear and Ambrose Golden Brown who were due to appear in court on charges arising out of earlier demonstrations.

Embassy Pulled Down Illegally, and Author Gaoled Illegally

It wasn't till I was researching this book that I found out I was gaoled illegally over handing out anti-conscription leaflets and that there was a debate in parliament about me. Also, as I researched this book, I found out an amazing coincidence! During my first night in jail in Sydney, the government had rushed through an ordinance in the middle of the night between parliamentary sessions and without debate to make my jailing legal and to make the pulling down of the tent embassy legal.

The Hansard record of the federal parliamentary debate on 13 September 1972[114] records the debate about the inappropriateness of this action. The ordinance enabled the police to pull down the embassy on the night of 12 September in the freezing cold and remove occupants while they were sleeping.

It is interesting that Gordon Bryant, the Member for Wills, compared the ordinance rushed through to remove peaceful Aborigines as reminiscent of the Eureka Stockade which occurred because of the objectionable way the licence system was administered. He complained that this ordinance which enabled the police to remove the embassy was not written or passed through parliament but produced administratively and the Minister for Interior, Ralph Hunt and the Attorney-General, Senator Greenwood signed it.

It appears that previous removals of the tent embassy were illegal, and the Court of Petty Sessions in Canberra which dealt with me did not have the authority to jail me. A court decision of 12 September made this clear which was why an ordinance was gazetted in a big rush to make further such removals valid.

Gordon Bryant continued:

> I saw what happened to the victims of the events of 20 July.[115] .... I saw the people manhandled over there. I saw them with arms wrenched up behind their backs. I saw the indignity being foisted on them of being thrown into the police wagons. I saw the blood upon their faces.[116]
>
> The acts of 20 July were invalid. They were illegal and, within the limits of the attitude of civilised communities, they were totally brutal. I believe that the time has come for us to find a new way of establishing rapport between the government and the citizens. Somehow, we must find a better way of dealing with recalcitrant citizens instead of beating them up, throwing them into prison and dragging them into court, particularly when those people are operating, in a peaceful, inoffensive and symbolic way.
>
> It is a serious reflection on the whole society and particularly on this government that, in the dealings with one of the least offensive and least violent people on this planet, we had to descend to the final brutality of assault by the Australian Capital

Territory police. I regret that the Australian Capital Territory police, for whom I have a great respect and who on the whole carry out their duties as one of the most civilised sections of the constabulary in Australia, were dragged into this operation.[117]

Dr Dick Klugman, the Member for Prospect, who was to come and collect me from Silverwater prison in Sydney a few days later and drive me back to Canberra on his way to the next sitting of parliament, said on 13/9/72:

> I would like to deal with one specific case that has arisen from this mess-up. It is the case of Miss Barbara Joyce Russell, an unemployed nursing aide, aged 22, of Strzelecki Crescent, Narrabundah, who was fined $40 by Mr Dobson, SM, in the Canberra Court of Petty Sessions on Monday. She was found guilty of encouraging the commission of an offence by distributing a leaflet on 28 July encouraging people not to register for national service. She is to be incarcerated, with light labour, at Silverwater Detention Centre in Auburn, Sydney. The *Sydney Morning Herald* today said:
>
> 'Looking pale and nervous at Sydney airport yesterday, Miss Barbara Joyce Russell, an unemployed nursing aide, said the sentence would not deter her from her cause. I think the National Service Act is an immoral and unjust law, and I won't comply with it in any regard because I feel it is my Christian duty.'
>
> She was found guilty of handing out a leaflet entitled 'Don't Register for National Service'. As it happens, I don't feel strongly one way or another about national service. I can see arguments either way on the question of national service as distinct from forcing people to go to Vietnam and fight there. But surely a person is entitled to distribute those sorts of leaflets. That, however, is irrelevant to this case as it exists at present.

> The point is that looking at it in retrospect, Mr Dobson, SM, was not acting legally last Monday when he fined her $40 or sentenced her to 20 days gaol in lieu of the fine. The Court of Petty Sessions Ordinance is one of the ordinances that were found to be invalid yesterday by the Australian Capital Territory Supreme Court. Therefore, until this validating legislation is passed, Miss Russell is being detained illegally. It seems obvious to me that she should be released until such time as both Houses of the Parliament decide that the validating legislation should be passed. I approached the Attorney-General (Senator Greenwood) and asked him to release her as she was being held illegally. He told me that I was right on that point but that she should brief counsel to take legal action. She is an unemployed nursing aide. The Commonwealth is going to use Government money – the people's money – to fight this case and postpone it until such time as the validating legislation is passed. I think that this is shocking behaviour.
>
> … Here is a girl who, because of her Christian beliefs, feels that she should distribute certain leaflets. She is put in gaol for 20 days. What happened was illegal. The Court of Petty Sessions was not a proper court to deal with her. Another ordinance was gazetted during the night to change that, and this legislation (that we are debating now) will retrospectively validate the situation. I realise that. But the point is, the Attorney-General should not keep people in gaol on the basis of legislation which **may** be passed by the parliament in the near future. He should agree to release the lady. When she appeared in court previously, she said she was prepared to go to gaol if she had broken the law. So, there is no reason to fear that she will not return if she is required to do so.[118]

It was amazing to me to read that the debate in the Australian parliament on the Ordinances and Regulations (Notification) Bill intertwined these two key events I was involved in during my time in

Canberra, the Aboriginal Embassy and my protest at young Australian men being conscripted to fight in the Vietnam War. However, the illegality of the government and court actions brought the two together.

Despite the orderly and peaceful nature of embassy members and their visitors, the government reacted out of embarrassment to remove the people violently to the protestations of the Labor Opposition. Bryant, Cameron, Klugman and Foster were all Labor (ALP) parliamentarians.

Mr Foster, the Member for Sturt, weighed into the debate:

> … Why were people camped on the lawns in front of Parliament House in the first place? I shall answer that question by referring to the judgment of the Full Court of the Supreme Court of the Australian Capital Territory, which reads:
>
> These persons, encamped, as mentioned, constituted what has come to be known as the Aboriginal Embassy. The purpose of the embassy was to bring to the attention of members of parliament and others, matters of complaint concerning the welfare of the Aboriginal race and in particular their land rights. Apparently, no attempt was made during the period mentioned by anyone in authority to remove the tents; it is not suggested that the behaviour of embassy members or their visitors was other than orderly.

Mr Foster[119] continued:

> … The marauders at Munich [120] at midnight last week drew blood. The marauders in front of this House at midnight last night did not draw blood, but they may well have drawn blood because of their failure to appreciate the meaning of the basic principle of land rights to the Aborigines. The government has also failed to appreciate it. What caused the Minister for the Interior to run frantically through the corridors of Parliament House last night and to come into this chamber at midnight and bring before the House in the manner in which he did a measure which enabled the removal of people from the lawns in front of Parliament House at

> a time when it was raining, when snow was falling on the hills surrounding this city and when it was as cold as blazes, if I may use that term. The Minister went outside with not one thought of compassion in his mind and said: 'We can now pull down the tent'. Basic to the human race is food and shelter, but the Minister denied these people shelter last night.
>
> .... No supporter of the government has ever said that the government would be prepared to meet the councils of these people in proper conference and under proper circumstances, to listen to them, to talk to them and to find out their requirements.

More amazing is that there was another reason I should not have been in gaol. Not only did the court not have the power to do it, but the legislation I was supposed to have infringed was no longer operative.

Clyde Cameron, the Member for Hindmarsh, advised of further information coming to parliament that my arrest was illegal because the national service regulations were also inoperative. He said:

> I now learn from the Leader of the Opposition (Mr Gough Whitlam) that he has confirmed that the national service regulations are themselves inoperative. Is the government going to allow this young woman who is in gaol because she handed out leaflets advising not to observe an inoperative law – this person who was put into gaol by a person who had no right to impose a penalty on her – to spend tonight in prison? It will be a disgrace and a national scandal if this young woman is allowed to stay in prison tonight. It is high time that the government took stock of itself. The government needs to realise that this is not a dictatorship; this is not a police state; we are not living under a government of Hitlerite Germany; we are not living in the Soviet Union...

Cameron continued:

> …. God, what sort of a setup are we living under? Just where do the rights of man end or begin, if this is the way you are going to treat this young woman? I say to the Government: If it can act as quickly as it acted last night to correct the defect in the law which made it an offence to have an embassy on the lawns opposite, to get the printing presses going after midnight and to get police storming the countryside in the early hours of the morning, then why in the name of God can it not act with the same alacrity to ensure that this young woman is not kept in gaol tonight against her will? It is a scandal. [121]

I must admit I am amazed that they spent this much time talking about me and I am amazed at the fervency of the comments. Despite the passionate pleas of a number of Members of Parliament, I spent about a week in gaol. While I was there, some held demonstrations outside the prison on my behalf. The authorities put in the prison hospital with the excuse it was for my protection. They tried to force me to take sleeping pills at night, but I refused. The government did not act to rectify my unlawful imprisonment by releasing me. Dr Klugman paid my fine and collected me. I was willing to go with him as I felt I had made my point. I had not planned to be arrested and go to court, but when it happened, I was prepared to accept the consequences of breaking a law in which I did not believe. I had a general anti-war stance and did not believe in forcing young men to go and fight a war that they may or may not have believed in.

Government Member, Mr Sinclair responded that though there were a large number of ordinances that needed to be revalidated in the House of Representatives that night, most of the debate had centred around one of them. He said, "The genesis of this debate was the inoperativeness as determined by the full Bench of the Supreme Court of the Australian Capital Territory, of the Trespass of Commonwealth Lands Ordinance 1972 within the terms of the Seat of Government (Administration) Act."

How much the Aboriginal Embassy protests and the government's reaction to it had to do with their losing the election, we don't know, but it did have some influence. On the theme of "It's time for a change," a Labor Government was elected on 2 December 1972 and Prime Minister Gough Whitlam reaffirmed land rights as part of the government's legislative program. The Commonwealth Government took more control of Aboriginal Affairs through the creation of the Department of Aboriginal Affairs, and Gordon Bryant was appointed Minister for Aboriginal Affairs.

Prominent Aboriginal people associated with the tent embassy were co-founders Michael Anderson, Billy Craigie, Tony Coorey and Bertie Williams and others Gary Foley, Paul Coe, Isobelle Coe, Chicka Dickson, Roberta Sykes, Femmi Bostock, Leicester Bostock, Pat Eatock, Dennis Walker, Len Watson, Cheryl Buchanan, Pearl Gibbs, Kevin Gilbert, Mum Shirl Smith, John Newfong, Neville Williams, Ambrose Golden Brown, Bobby McLeod, Tiga Bayles, Bob Bellear and Kevin Buzzacot.

The tent embassy was raised again and again over the years and still stood on the lawns outside Old Parliament House for its 40th anniversary on 26 January 2012, a reminder of what happened in 1972 and that there are still issues to be addressed.

William Cooper's Dreams of and Work for Land Rights Come True for the NT

The Gurindji had many land claims rejected and suffered economic sanctions. However, a breakthrough came in 1972 with the ALP back in power. Gough Whitlam, the new Prime Minister, visited Wattie Creek and handed Vincent Lingiari the deed to the Gurindji land. As a sign of ownership, Whitlam poured the soil into Lingiari's hand. Vincent said, "We all friendly now. We're all mates. We're all mates."[122]

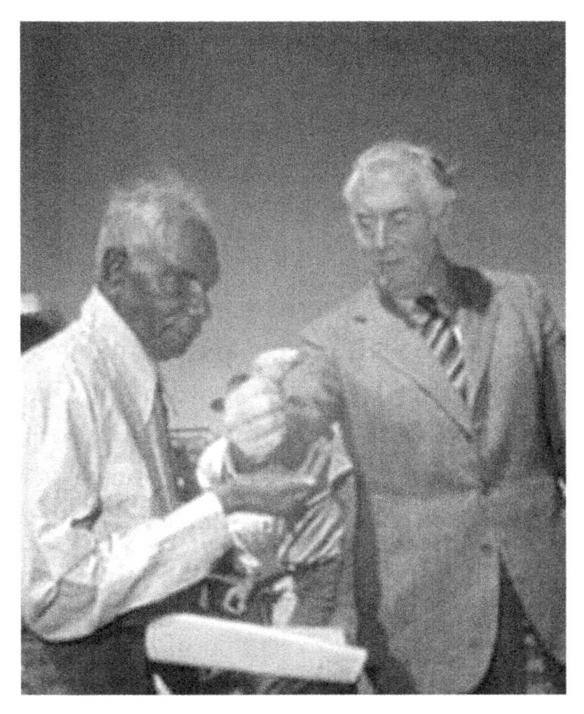

Prime Minister (PM) Gough Whitlam pouring the soil symbolically into Vincent Lingiari's hand

The protests eventually led to the Commonwealth *Land Rights Act (NT) 1976*. This Act gave Indigenous Australians freehold title to traditional lands in the NT and, significantly, the power of veto over mining and development on those lands. The ALP started the process, and it was followed through by the Liberal government when Malcolm Fraser became Prime Minister.

William Cooper's dream of land rights for his people all over Australia had finally become a reality in the NT which was under Commonwealth control, but it was going to be a long time coming in the states.

At least Aboriginal trustees of the Lake Tyers and Framlingham reserves in Victoria were granted individual land title in 1970. However, most of the people wanted communal title as this would prevent sections being sold off, as they later were.

Also, William had long campaigned for a federal Department of Aboriginal Affairs. This dream was realised in 1972 with the incoming Whitlam government. His vision to have Aboriginal affairs a federal responsibility did not come until the 1967 referendum for which Ps Doug Nicholls and many others worked so hard.

New Prime Minister, Mr Gough Whitlam, at his first press conference on 5 December 1972 stated that there would be no further call-up. To this date, conscientious objectors to conscription had to go to gaol for two years for refusing to fight a war in which they didn't believe. So, this was a huge decision for the new government. Mr Whitlam said that those who had received notices would not be obliged to act on them under the National Service Act. The Prime Minister went even further. He instructed the new Attorney-General, Senator Murphy, QC, "that all pending prosecutions are to be withdrawn. The Commonwealth Police have been asked to withhold the execution of outstanding warrants and papers have been prepared for the Governor-General to remit the sentences, the remaining portion of all prison sentences, of those who are now in prison and also the remission of all outstanding fines."[123]

Gough Whitlam brought Australia's troops home from Vietnam and ended our involvement in that war. Maybe my stint in gaol helped a little, and the Aboriginal Tent Embassy was a turning point in our nation re Indigenous advancement.

Chapter 9

White Australia Policy and Social Darwinism as Foundation of Our Nation

... We continue to eject the monstrous Jap and the wily Chow with persistence...."

— Atlee Hunt, Secretary of the Department of External Affairs to Prime Minister Edmund Barton, May 1902

... no motive operated more powerfully in dissolving the .... divisions which previously separated us than the desire that we should.... remain one people without the admixture of other races...

— Attorney-General Alfred Deakin

Federation to Keep Australia White

One of the things that has shocked me most about researching this book is finding out that one of the reasons the states of Australia came together to federate in 1901 was to keep out non-British immigration. And it was reasonably successful at doing that until after World War 2. As soon as we became one nation, we passed the Australian Immigration Restriction Act of 1901, mainly to keep out Asians and Pacific Islanders. Because of the requirement of passing a dictation test in a European language, it was called the White Australia policy.

However, it was not just about keeping Australia white. It was also about keeping Australia as a nation of British stock. I have been reasonably aware of the history of Aborigines in this nation, but seeing the DVD "Immigration Nation" on TV shocked me also. It suggested that Australia is racist to the core. My research about Jewish refugees and the Australian response has also brought these issues to the fore.

Aborigines Rendered Stateless on Federation

So, Australia, as a nation of settlers, was founded on racism. There was no place for Aborigines, the original inhabitants, in the constitution. All inhabitants of Australia, settlers and Aborigines, were British citizens until 1901. However, on federation, Aborigines were not given citizenship. They were rendered stateless in their own land. This was flawed nation-building.

Our first Prime Minister, Edmund Barton, asserted that Australians were "guardians in the last part of this world in which the higher races can live and increase freely for the higher civilisation."

Attorney-General Alfred Deakin claimed that ".... no motive operated more powerfully in dissolving the .... divisions which previously separated us than the desire that we should.... remain one people without the admixture of other races..."[124]

Even in 1920, Senator Drake-Brockman said, "The whole existence of this democracy depends upon our maintenance of the great principle of a White Australia."[125] Our nation-building was flawed.

On 28 May 1902, the Secretary of the Department of External Affairs, Atlee Hunt, wrote the following to Prime Minister Edmund Barton:

> ... We continue to eject the monstrous Jap and the wily Chow with persistence. The IR Act has not exhausted its

> possibilities yet. I have four matters now with the A_G for opinion. The April returns show that no coloured aliens passed the test, over 40 were rejected, mostly chows who tried to enter Queensland on false papers.[126]

When it came down to it, the British settlers turned white Australians just wanted to get rid of the Chinese who'd come with the gold rushes and the South Sea Islanders or "Kanakas" who had been indentured, sometimes against their will, to work on Queensland's cane farms. Some Australians saw these hardworking peoples as a threat to jobs as they might work for lower wages and accept a lower standard of living. There was a concern amongst some Queenslanders that the colony would be left out of federation if it did not stop employing Pacific Islanders. The new immigration act now meant the government could prevent them from entering Australia and could send them home. Many "Kanakas" were repatriated, being forcibly and callously separated from wives and children they had in Australia.

Apology for Anti-Kanaka and Anti-Chinese Attitudes

When we hosted the Bethany Gate All Pacific Prayer Assembly in Cairns in May 2006 with over 2,000 people attending from the Pacific and Asia, my husband Norman apologised to delegates affected by this policy towards Kanakas. I also said sorry for this when we spoke at the Vanuatu Prayer Assembly in May 2012. The representatives accepted the apologies in the heartfelt manner they were given. At a conference we hosted in Cairns in July 2009, I apologised to Chinese delegates for racism to Chinese on the gold rushes of north Queensland but also in Australia generally. It needed to be said. So, I was aware of course of the White Australia Policy, just not aware that it was the basis of federation, of why we became a nation.

Origin of White Australia Policy

The origins of the White Australia Policy can be traced back to the 1850s when the resentment of the white miners towards Chinese diggers resulted in violence in Victoria at Buckland River and in NSW at Lambing Flat (now Young). These two colonies then introduced restrictions on Chinese immigration.

There were other categories of prohibited immigrant, e.g. the insane, those with infectious diseases, prostitutes, criminals, anyone likely to become a charge on the public and those of dangerous character.

During the Second World War, Prime Minister John Curtin reiterated the White Australia Policy saying, "This country shall remain forever the home of the descendants of those people who came here in peace in order to establish in the South Seas an outpost of the British race."[127]

Steps to Ending White Australia Policy

During the war, many non-white refugees entered Australia, with most leaving voluntarily at the end of the war, but some had married Australians and wanted to stay. When Australia's first Immigration Minister, Arthur Calwell, tried to deport them, there were many protests. The first step towards a non-discriminatory immigration policy was taken in 1949 by Liberal Prime Minister Harold Holt who allowed 800 non-European refugees to stay and Japanese war brides to be allowed entry.

The revised Migration Act 1958 removed the dictation test and references to race, but March 1966 was a watershed moment in abolishing the White Australia Policy with further restrictions on non-Europeans eased.

In 1973, the Whitlam government took three further steps in what had been a gradual process of removing race as a factor in our immigration policy. These were:

- Legislate that all migrants, of whatever origin, be eligible to obtain citizenship after three years of permanent residence
- Issue policy instructions to overseas posts to totally disregard race as a factor in the selection of migrants
- Ratify all international agreements relating to immigration and race[128]

Australia's Changing Identity

Immigration Department records show that by 2009 "Australians identify with some 250 ancestries and practise a range of religions. In addition to Indigenous languages, around 200 other languages are spoken in Australia. After English, the most common languages spoken are Italian, Greek, Cantonese, Arabic and Mandarin."[129]

This is changing. In 2012, Mandarin was the second most spoken language in Australia and Cantonese was fourth. According to the Australian Bureau of Statistics,

> At 30 June 2016, 28.5% of the estimated resident population (ERP) was born overseas (6.9 million persons). This was an increase from 30 June 2015, when 28.2% of the population was born overseas (6.7 million persons). In 2006, ten years earlier, 24.6% of the population was born overseas (5.0 million persons) …
>
> Persons born in the United Kingdom continued to be the largest group of overseas-born residents, accounting for 5.0% of Australia's total population at 30 June 2016. This was followed by persons born in New Zealand (2.5%), China (2.2%), India (1.9%) and the Philippines and Vietnam (both 1.0%).[130]

Australia was dragged, kicking and struggling, into changing its identity from a nation of British stock (apart from the Aborigines) into one of the most multicultural nations in the world with a reasonably harmonious record of race relations with immigrants. Regarding

Australia's attitude to refugees, especially boat people who are perceived as a border security threat and to be "jumping the queue," that is outside the scope of this book. This is a very divisive issue between those who want a more humanitarian approach and those who want safe borders.

On the centenary of federation in 2001, Prime Minister John Howard said that the celebrations are designed to remind us "of that enduring truth – that the things that unite us as Australians are always more important and more substantial than the things that might from time to time divide us." This is a laudable goal.

Social Darwinism and White Australia

Racism has been around in world events for a long time and well before Darwin, but Social Darwinism was an important factor which underpinned racism towards Australian Aborigines until the theory got discredited due to its association with the Holocaust.

Social Darwinism, a term popularised by Richard Hofstadter, is the name given to theories of society that emerged in England and the USA in the 1870s which sought to apply the biological concepts of Darwinism or evolutionary theory to society and politics. The theory was that superior groups would out-compete inferior ones, conflict leading to progress. The term was used by the opponents of such thinking rather than those who promoted it.

This theory led white Europeans to believe that they were superior to other races and therefore, destined to rule over them. As European nations built empires in the third world, they used terms about native peoples such as "white man's burden." Not only was survival of the fittest deemed natural, it was deemed morally correct.

One commentator said, "Colonialism was seen as natural and inevitable, and given justification through Social Darwinian ethics – people saw natives as being weaker and more unfit to survive, and therefore felt justified in seizing land and resources. Social Darwinism applied to military action as well; the argument that the strongest military would win, and would, therefore, is the most fit. Casualties on the losing side, of course, were written off as the natural result of their unfit status. Finally, it gave the ethical nod to brutal colonial governments who used oppressive tactics against their subjects."[131]

Those who oppose charity and government welfare sometimes use arguments rooted in Social Darwinism, i.e. that the weak and unfit should be allowed to die.

Survival of the Fittest

The term "survival of the fittest" was coined by sociologist Herbert Spencer to describe the competition between individuals for limited resources. Social Darwinism influenced eugenics, scientific racism, imperialism and fascism. However, using biological evolution to justify policies promoting inequality commits the "naturalistic fallacy, which consists of trying to derive an *ought* statement from an *is* statement. For example, the fact that you stubbed your toe this morning does not logically imply that you ought to have stubbed your toe." [132] It assumes that what is naturally occurring in the world is morally correct. It was not something that Darwin himself fell into.

The Concise Dictionary of Politics in its definition of Social Darwinism shows that it was not a uniform field of thought but meant different things to different people:

> Part of the difficulty in establishing sensible and consistent usage is that commitment to the biology of natural selection and to 'survival of the fittest' entailed nothing uniform either for sociological method or for political doctrine. A 'social Darwinist' could just as well be a defender of laissez-faire as a defender of state socialism, just as much an imperialist as a domestic eugenist.

In other words, Fascist and National Socialist ideology had a different kind of Social Darwinism than the laissez-faire variety because they did not promote individualism.

Where do the Aborigines, the original owners of the land, fit in all of this? They didn't. They were expected to die out as they were part of an evolutionary backwater. It appears that the nineteenth-century Social Darwinist theory of the survival of the fittest was the primary source of this thinking. It was alright for British settlers to come to Australia with their superior weaponry (read superior civilisation) and subdue a race of inferior weaponry and civilisation. This was not a moral issue of one race destroying another and stealing their land but part of evolution, the advance of civilisation. Might was right.

Because Aborigines were a hunter-gatherer society, they were considered far lower on the evolutionary ladder despite their complex laws, customs and social relations. Because they did not build permanent dwellings and fence off areas but moved around according to the seasons to where food was most plentiful, they were considered by the British settlers not to own the land which settlers could then take off them with abandon. However, Aboriginal tribes knew their boundaries and only moved around within them, respecting each other's territory.

Because of their supposed inferior status, marriage between races was discouraged, but Aboriginal women could be used and discarded, including the children of such liaisons. Hunting parties of white settlers could shoot Aborigines just as they would shoot kangaroos for sport. If they were a nuisance, if they had speared the introduced cattle and sheep because they were starving, Aborigines could be similarly removed. Some settlers gave Aborigines poisoned flour, poisoned their waterholes and gave them blankets infected with smallpox to hasten the process of the race dying off.

So, we have a nation in the Asia Pacific region, which expects, even hopes, its Indigenous population will die out, and it puts up the barriers to Asian immigration, especially after some scuffles with Chinese on the Australian goldfields. The Kanakas who were "blackbirded" (read stolen) from New Hebrides (now Vanuatu) to work on the sugar plantations of Queensland were repatriated after federation even though some had married Australians.

Aryan Australia

A book by David Bird called "Nazi Dreamtime, Australian Enthusiasm for Hitler's Germany" details how strong the regard for Hitler and National Socialism was among several Australia's intellectuals and literary fraternity. However, they espoused a home-grown version where they tried to build a white dreamtime based on the Aboriginal dreamtime. They wanted to get in touch with the "spirit of the land" and used Australian animals such as the mythical bunyip, the kangaroo etc. in their writing. Blood and soil featured in their dreams of a future national socialist Australia and they believed that because Aborigines were Caucasian or Aryan, then they could co-opt them rather than reject them as inferior.

P. R. "Inky" Stephensen or the "Bunyip Critic" as he liked to be called seemed to be the main inspiration for the "Aryan Australia" but there were many others like Miles Franklin, Xavier Herbert, Alexander Mills, W. J Miles, William Hardy Wilson, Reginald (Rex) Ingamells, Ian Mudie, Adela Pankhurst Walsh (the suffragette's daughter) and Manning Clark. [133] Some of these well-known names will surprise readers.

Stephensen and others set up the Australia First Party, and Stephensen and Miles produced and wrote for the *Publicist* to promote their views. Mills published the *National Socialist.* The symbol of an Aboriginal seated around a campfire was adopted by Ingamell's *Jindyworobak* literary club to promote their vision of a nativist literature drawing on white and Aboriginal influences.

When I saw the reference to Stephensen, who was later interned during the war for his Nazi sympathies, I wondered if it was the same Stepensen Jack Horner had mentioned was helpful to Jack Patten and Will

Ferguson in printing their Day of Mourning pamphlet for Australia Day 1938. What gave me a clue was that Patten met Xavier Herbert at the printers. Sure, enough it was the same Stephensen[134] who printed the pamphlet and Herbert's book *Capricornia*. It is not likely Patten and Ferguson would have known of Stephensen's Nazi sympathies but would have appreciated his help to get their policy printed. The *Publicist* gave more coverage to their meeting and the New Deal they subsequently asked for than the mainstream media. However, coverage of William Cooper and the AAL's protest at the German Consulate in Melbourne re the persecution of the Jews, was notably missing because of Stephensen's anti-Semitic beliefs.

Genocide, the Holocaust and Immigration

Blakeney in a detailed study of Jewish refugees in Australia makes a startling comparison:

> That a modern government could implement a policy of genocide was unthinkable before reliable evidence of the Holocaust began to trickle out of wartime Europe. In attempts to explain and possibly excuse the insanity of the Germans, historians have pointed out that the intellectual roots of Nazi racial policies can be traced back to the nineteenth century Social Darwinist theories which animated the American immigration laws of 1921 and 1924 and, before that time, the Australian Immigration Restriction Act of 1901. Intellectually there was not too much distance between preventing eugenic pollution, by the erection of immigration barriers against genetically undesirable races, and the purification of the population by the elimination of existing pools of genetic weakness.[135]

This is a very serious assertion, and Blakeney is quick to point out that there is a considerable difference between believing in Social Darwinism and implementing its race theories in a systemic policy of genocide. I am not aware of anyone in Australia being killed on account of being Jewish. Australian authorities did attempt unsuccessfully to wipe out every Aboriginal person in the state of Tasmania. However, there is contention about the accuracy of this assertion by Keith Windschuttle[136] and others who deny it and those who support this view of history like Henry Reynolds.[137]

How do we explain the impassivity of the Allies when eyewitness accounts and photographs showed them what was happening to trainload after trainload of Jews headed for concentration camps and extermination? Martin Gilbert in *Auschwitz and the Allies* documents this failure to act in the light of much concrete evidence and puts it down to their finding it hard to believe and understand and even their sympathy with the German predicament.[138] This same inaction is seen in revelations before the war of the Nazi treatment of Jews.

Blakeney makes the startling conclusion that just as the Holocaust can be considered as a logical result of intellectual developments in Germany, Allied inaction could be seen as stemming from immigration policies which shared the same roots as the Nazi policies that resulted in Jewish refugees. This is ironic. Furthermore, Blakeney asks - is Australia an accessory before the fact when only about 7,500 Jewish refugees came to Australia in the nine years from Hitler's rise to power to the closure of shipping lanes in 1941 while hundreds of thousands came after 1945? How culpable are we in the deaths of Jewish refugees who applied for refuge in Australia but never made it because they died in concentration camps?

Eugenics and Genocide

An extreme form of Social Darwinism has been used to justify eugenics programs. These programs aimed at "weeding 'undesirable' genes from the population. Sterilisation laws directed against 'unfit' individuals sometimes accompanied these programs. For example, "The American eugenics movement was relatively popular between about 1910-1930, during which twenty-four states passed sterilisation laws and Congress passed a law restricting immigration from certain areas deemed to be unfit.

Social Darwinist ideas, though in a different form, were also applied by the Nazi Party in Germany to justify their eugenics programs."[139] The Nazis claimed that they were cleaning out inferior genetics when they committed wholesale murder of six million Jews during the Holocaust.

The frightening thing is that Hitler got inspiration, research and funding from American eugenicists who were approving of what Hitler was doing though he took it to more extreme levels.

Hitler told his colleagues, "I have studied with great interest the laws of several American states concerning prevention of reproduction by people whose progeny would, in all probability, be of no value or be injurious to the racial stock."[140]

In 1934, ten years after Virginia passed its sterilisation act, superintendent of Virginia's Western State Hospital, Joseph DeJarnette, told the *Richmond Times-Dispatch* "The Germans are beating us at our own game."[141]

World War 11 Liberation of KZ Buchenwald 16.04.1945 (Yad Vashem Photo Archives)

Black writes, "The most commonly suggested method of eugenicide in America was a 'lethal chamber' or public locally operated gas chambers. In 1918, Popenoe, the Army venereal disease specialist during World War 1, co-wrote the widely used textbook *Applied Eugenics* which argued "From an historical point of view, the first method which presents itself is execution.... Its value in keeping up the standard of the race should not be underestimated." *Applied Eugenics* also devoted a chapter to 'Lethal Selection' which operated through the destruction of the individual by some adverse feature of the environment, such as excessive cold, or bacteria, or by bodily deficiency'. Eugenic breeders believed American society was not ready to implement an organised lethal solution. But many mental institutions and doctors practiced improvised medical lethality and passive euthanasia on their own."[142]

After the Second World War, eugenics was declared a crime against humanity, an act of genocide, but the Americans were never held to account the way the Germans were. Governors of five states, including California, did, however, offer public apologies to their citizens. In its first twenty-five years of eugenic legislation, California had sterilised by coercion nearly 10,000 people, mostly women classified as oversexed or sexually wayward.

Chapter 10

Eugenics, Stolen Children and Black Armbands

... the younger people coming through, who really shouldn't have to deal with that continual stuff to have to justify their identity."

— Dr Atkinson, a descendant of William Cooper, 2011

Eugenics

US historian Kevles writes, "The word eugenics was coined in 1883 by the English scientist Francis Galton, a cousin of Charles Darwin, to promote the ideal of perfecting the human race by, as he put it, getting rid of its 'undesirables' while multiplying its 'desirables' – that is, by encouraging the procreation of the Social Darwinian fit and discouraging that of the unfit."[143] He says that eugenics was popular in the first half of the twentieth century and that social prejudice diffused human genetics.

Robbing of Aboriginal Graves

The eugenicists considered IQ tests the main measure of human worth, ignoring other abilities this did not measure as well. It also ignored the cultural bias of the IQ tests. In early settlement history of Australia, Aboriginal gravesites were robbed of heads and skeletons to send to English and other museums for 'scientific' testing. Aboriginal skulls were measured as it was thought that larger skulls meant higher intelligence, and it was assumed that Aborigines would have smaller skulls than Europeans. In the last couple of decades, there has been a campaign by Aboriginal groups to have these human remains repatriated to Australia to be buried by their relevant tribal group or descendants on the land of their origin. There has been a great deal of resistance to this, certain museums considering these remains their property, and only some museums have returned remains for family burial services. It is Aboriginal belief that their spirits would be roaming and not properly put to rest until they were returned and buried by their people.

Australia Was Non-White from Within

Commentators usually think of the White Australia Policy in terms of immigration, but it also affected policy towards Aborigines. Why go to all that trouble to keep "coloured" races out of Australia and then have a growing group of mixed-race within your borders? Australia was non-white from within. These were mostly children born to Aboriginal mothers and fathers of European or occasionally, Chinese or Pacific Islander fathers. Sometimes these relationships were fleeting, even exploitative and sometimes they were more permanent, leading to marriage. However, such children were considered a social problem and inferior because of Social Darwinist theories. Humankind was seen in a civilisational hierarchy with northern Europeans at the top and Aborigines at the bottom. So, these children were looked at with contempt, distaste and alarm. What would Australia do with this third race if it grew to hundreds of thousands in 50-100 years?

Segregation

One solution was segregation with full blood Aborigines separated from whites geographically on reserves and to knowingly not do anything when they are starving. This would weaken them in fighting off disease. This was one of the things that William Cooper was fighting against even for places like Cummeragunga, which was not a remote full blood community. Withholding of government rations was used to control Aborigines, including during the Cummera strike.

Breeding out the Colour

Eugenics came to the rescue with the solution of "breeding out the colour" as it was called, really breeding out the Aboriginality. This involved child removal. Take the children from their parents, either forcibly, or with permission for educational purposes and break the connection with their family and culture, encouraging the girls to marry white, thus "breeding out the colour" over time.

All states and the NT appointed Protectors of Aborigines were appointed and given guardianship rights over Aborigines to the age of 16 or 21. It was heartbreaking enough for Aborigines to lose their land and autonomy but to lose their children and for the children to lose their parents and families was even more tragic. Police would raid Aboriginal communities without warning and rip part Aboriginal children from the arms of wailing mothers. Often, their families never saw them again. Mothers would run after their children as they were dragged away screaming, till they could run after the vehicle no more and they dropped, exhausted, on the ground.

The children were taken to government or missionary institutions to receive some schooling and be taught domestic work, becoming a cheap labour force for white society. Authorities thought they were doing them a favour, rescuing them from the black's camp for a better life. But the grief was immense, and many girls and boys were physically and sexually abused on a repeated basis over many years.

Some were fortunate to go to caring white homes and receive a good education and were in fact taken, just as other Australian children were, out of situations of neglect, but this the exception. Some parents gave permission for their children to be taken away for education, and the authorities told them they would see them again but then prevented the parents from doing so. Other children did receive visits. Educators returned only some children after their education.

Many children didn't know who they were as their identity was hidden from them. Eventually, as adults, when they tracked down their parents, it was often too late as they had died. Being stranded between the white and black worlds was so difficult. Identity was a struggle. Some were taught to despise their Aboriginal inheritance or brought up without knowledge of it. These children, denied the arms and advice and examples of loving parents, found it hard to parent the next generation when their turn came. But this was the price authorities were prepared to pay for a white Australia. Who really paid the price?

Where did the idea of "breeding out the colour" originate? In the 1920s and 1930s, eugenics was influential in the western world, and it maintained that a nation should improve its racial stock by breeding programs. Eugenics suggested that people with genetically transmitted diseases, sub-normal intelligence or mental illness be sterilised and this was implemented not only in Nazi Germany but also in some Scandinavian countries and some states of the USA. Some circles in Australia saw this as a solution to the "half-caste problem" and called it "the policy of biological assimilation or absorption".

Richardson describes this train of thought in Australia in 1933, interestingly during the rise of Nazism in Germany, "...' The application of Mendelianism is the only solution, and that urges the mating of the half-caste with the quadroon and the octoroon so that the confirmed infiltration of white blood will finally stamp out the black colour which, when all is said and done, is what we really object to'. The eugenics program of constructive miscegenation, of breeding out the colour of the half-castes, might have represented a mere footnote in the history of Australian ideas were it not for the fact that in the late 1920s and early 1930s two of the three most important administrators of Aboriginal affairs, the Protectors in the NT and WA, Dr Cecil Cook and A. O. Neville were enthusiastic converts to this cause"[144] and worked out blueprints to implement it.

Neville got the West Australian government's approval to restrict the marriage of part Aborigines to full bloods for example. Neville was able to persuade the first national meeting of key administrators of Aboriginal affairs in 1937 to agree to the total absorption of all non-full blood natives into the white community.

Dr Cecil Cook, the Chief Protector of Aborigines in the NT, reported in 1937, "We have to keep in mind the need for the maintenance in its inviolability of the national policy of a White Australia. This is something which the Australian people regard as sacrosanct ...All sections of the people are united in an ardent desire to maintain racial purity."[145]

It may seem strange that mating between part Aboriginal and white Australians was encouraged rather than discouraged as part of a racist policy, but Aborigines were considered to be Caucasian or Aryan rather than Negroid and so in the process of outbreeding, there would be no tendency towards "throwbacks". [146]

I was well aware of the stolen generation from firsthand accounts of Aboriginal friends and my husband's family as well as from the media and well informed for a long time of the government's policy of assimilation. But I was shocked to find out the purpose was to "breed out the colour" or breed out a race of people. The deliberate expunging of Aboriginality, the deliberate theft of children to take away their ethnic and family inheritance, the obnoxious social experiment to dislocate generations of Aborigines to wipe out part Aborigines as a group, is appalling. And at the same time, a cheap labour force was provided.

Needless to say, their experiment with eugenics failed. We still have large numbers of part Aboriginal people with us. However, it introduced such a measure of social dislocation from which it is hard to recover. The government sometimes complains when these people speak up but, in a sense, they created them. Government policies have brought, in some instances, a disconnect between part and full blood Aborigines and then Aboriginal people get blamed for it. I will probably get criticised for speaking of part and full blood Aborigines because these terms are not in favour, but I can't describe our history without doing so.

It is hard to understand how people could administer these policies, e.g. the removal of part Aboriginal babies from their mothers, but they considered that the mothers would soon forget their offspring. They did not grasp the intensity of the suffering they caused, perhaps because they did not see Aborigines as fully human.

However, others were affected by the work. A letter appeared in the *age* in 1997 from Lang Dean talking about how, as a young boy in Echuca in 1937-8, he used to often see his policeman father crying and sobbing after coming home from work. This was because he had accompanied welfare officers to Cummeragunga where they entered nice clean, simple homes and removed children 9-12 years old from loving mothers and fathers. They were taken to Echuca railway station and sent to the far reaches of NSW or Queensland to work for wealthy businessmen and graziers. The need for a job and deference to authority may be reasons for such compliance, but this man left the police force after some time.

National Inquiry into the Stolen Generations

A National Inquiry into the Separation of Aboriginal and Torres Strait Islander Children from Their Families was established in May 1995 and took evidence from 535 Indigenous people, and in 1997 the Human Rights Commission released its 689-page report accusing the government of genocide. It was called "Bringing Them Home", and it called the children "the Stolen Generation" though sometimes two or three generations had been removed. About 30,000 children are estimated to have been affected. International law defines genocide as including the forcible removal of children to a different cultural group "with the intent to destroy, in whole or part, the group."

The report called for an official apology and financial compensation because thousands of Aborigines were involved in family breakdowns, mental health issues, drug and alcohol abuse and violence linked to the assimilation policy. Successive federal governments have not supported such compensation.

The report triggered an unprecedented debate on black-white relations in Australia and a campaign to discredit the claim that generations of Aboriginal children were stolen. Some sections of Australia could not face the shame of our history. Historian Robert Manne is a key defender of the claim while historian Keith Windshuttle is a key denier. Manne does claim that the Bringing Them Home report's numbers of three in ten Aboriginal children removed between 1910 and 1970 is wrong and it is closer to one in ten.

The ABC 7.30 Report arranged a debate on the Stolen Generation report with Manne, Associate Professor, La Trobe University and Ron Brunton on 29 March 2001. Brunton, an anthropologist, was working with the conservative think-tank, the Institute of Public Affairs and wrote a scathing critique of the Bringing Them Home report. There was a debate on the numbers involved and reasons for removal:

To interviewer Kerry O'Brien's questioning, Brunton said:

> "I don't deny that there was the forced removal of children with no justification whatsoever."
>
> Manne asked, "I was going to say, Ron, do you accept that the Commonwealth had a policy of breeding out the colour?"
>
> Brunton replied, "I accept there were a number of officials in the 1930's who spoke in these terms."
>
> At another point in the interview, O'Brien asked:
>
> "Ron Brunton, what judgment do you make in the end about, for instance, the chief protector in the NT between '27 and '39, Mr Cook, who could approve or veto marriages.... between half-castes and full bloods?"
>
> Brunton replied, "I think it's appalling. I have made this point time and time again. I have said that we have to recognise

that there was a degree of interference and surveillance of Aboriginal people that is absolutely unconscionable and Australians have to come to terms with that." (He agreed it was officially sanctioned).

Later in the interview, O'Brien asked Manne:

"Robert Manne, you acknowledged yourself that there were many well-meaning people involved in the process. Do you accept that an unknown number of children, significant or otherwise, who did benefit in terms of education or other opportunity, from leaving their families, whether they were removed, whether there was some consent, whether that consent was as a result of pressure or otherwise, whose lives might have been saved by their removal?"

Manne: "Well, can I say about the well-meaning – the point I make about this is that there were very many well-meaning people and very many brutes involved. The well-meaning people could not emancipate themselves from the racism of the time, up till the mid-50s. So, you find even the finest people thinking it was right to segregate half-castes and full bloods.

I suppose there were some people who benefited; there must have been. But by-and-large, the overwhelming majority of the Stolen Generations suffered terribly because it's not fine to be brought up in an institution when the colour of your skin is a matter for shame, and it's not fine to not know from where you come or who your parents are. It's a terrible thing."

It has been asserted that the White Australia Policy, the basis of Australian federation, was based on eugenics. The first Prime Minister of Australia, Edmund Barton declared, "I don't think the equality of man was ever intended to include racial equality".[147]

However, while race appears to be a significant issue, separate races do not really exist. There is more genetic variation within what we call races than between them. This was borne out by a worldwide study commissioned by United Nations Educational, Scientific and Cultural Organization (UNESCO) in the 1950s.

Culture Wars and History Wars

While Australia predates white settlement, it has experienced some cultural cringe concerning its European foundation as a convict settlement. More recently, it has been haunted by its foundation on the dispossession and deaths of many Aborigines.

There has been a debate in recent years over the history of the British colonisation of Australia and the development of Australian society called the history wars. No historians contend that there wasn't a degree of violence or dispossession, but there is a debate about whether the conflict was minor and treatment of Aborigines humane or if it was an invasion with violent conflict involving massacres and genocide.

The Boyer Lecture by Professor Bill Stanner "After the Dreaming" in 1968 seemed to be a watershed moment when he coined the term the 'Great Australian Silence' to assert that Indigenous people had been written out of Australian history. He saw this as a deliberate process to omit "several hundred thousand Aborigines who lived and died between 1788 and 1938... (who were but) ...negative facts of history and ...were in no way consequential for the modern period."[148]

Manning Clark and Henry Reynolds were among a group of historians in the 1970s and 1980s who then proceeded to correct this historiography. There was a reaction from Geoffrey Blainey, another historian in the journal *Quadrant* in 1993 saying Australian history had moved from an overly positive view – the "Three Cheers View" to an overly negative view – "the black armband" view. [149]

Liberal Prime Minister John Howard promoted the new term, a black armband view of history, and interpretations of Aboriginal history became part of the broader political debate with previous Prime Minister

Paul Keating opposing it and arguing for a symbolic apology to Aborigines. This became known as the "culture wars" and was extended to high school history curricula and controversy over the National Museum of Australia with its Aboriginal Director, Dawn Casey, not having her contract renewed. Regular debate in the Australian media ensued.

After the 1999 release of the Bringing Them Home report, Howard passed a Parliamentary Motion of Reconciliation describing the treatment of Aborigines as the most blemished chapter in Australian history, but he would not make a parliamentary apology as it would imply intergenerational guilt and he believed that practical measures were needed instead.

Australian Reconciliation Convention

My husband Norman and I were at the landmark Australian Reconciliation Convention May 26-28 1997 (Reconciliation Week) in Melbourne where almost 1800 attended – Aborigines, government officials, religious leaders, lawyers, teachers, health workers, students etc. This was the culmination of a year of consultation and education events around the nation of which we were a part. We met Jeremy Jones, Executive Director of the Executive Council of Australian Jewry who we invited to be a speaker at an international conference on reconciliation we hosted in Cairns, our home town, in 1998. While it was successful in many ways, the Melbourne conference was overshadowed by the opening address made by then Prime Minister John Howard:

> In facing the realities of the past, …. We must not join those who would portray Australia's history since 1788 as little more than a disgraceful record of imperialism…such an approach will be repudiated by the overwhelming majority of the Australians who are proud of what this country has achieved although inevitably acknowledging the blemishes of its past history.[150]

Describing what happened to Indigenous people as a mere blemish, the Prime Minister dismissed centuries of dispossession and violence as insignificant and did it at a conference aimed to bring reconciliation and on the anniversary of the release of the Bringing Them Home report. Many Indigenous delegates in the audience turned their backs on John Howard in protest.

Nevertheless, much healing of relationships between Indigenous and non-Indigenous people occurred, and delegates reached fresh understandings. One commentator wrote, "But most telling I think is the sheer integrity of the Indigenous leaders.... and people who can find it in their hearts to forgive. To witness the peace and tranquillity emanating from those leaders, rather than the anger and rage emanating from our political masters, made me truly humbled in their presence." [151]

Three Cheers, Black Armband or White Blindfold?

The Three Cheers or self-congratulatory view of Australian history that nearly everything that happened after the convict era was pretty good was now facing a pendulum swing as a more critical history was being written, and such historians were accused of wearing a black armband of mourning, grieving and shame.

As a counter-response to the black armband view of history, the 'white blindfold view' came into use by Anna Clark, [152] Carole Ferrier[153] and others.

In the 1996 Sir Robert Menzies Lecture, John Howard argued that the "balance sheet of Australian history" had been misrepresented:

> The black armband view of our history reflects a belief that most Australian history since 1788 has been little more than a disgraceful story of imperialism, exploitation, racism, sexism and other forms of discrimination...I believe that the balance sheet of our history is one of heroic achievement and that we have achieved much more as a nation of which we can be proud than of which we

> should be ashamed. In saying that I do not exclude or ignore specific aspects of our past where we are rightly held to account. Injustices were done in Australia, and no one should obscure or minimise them. .... but ...our priority should...(be) to commit to a practical program of action that will remove the enduring legacies of disadvantage.[154]

Keith Windshuttle escalated the history wars with the publication of his book in 2002 *The Fabrication of Aboriginal History, Volume 1: Van Diemen's Land 1803-1847*. In the book, he questioned the evidence used by other historians to calculate the number of Aborigines killed during European colonisation. He focused on the Black War in Tasmania and argued there is evidence of only 118 Tasmanian Aborigines killed directly by the British, the rest dying out through introduced diseases and infertility caused by these diseases. He challenged the view by Henry Reynolds and Lyndall Ryan that Aborigines fought guerrilla warfare for their land, maintaining they only attacked settlers for food and blankets.[155]

The publication of *Whitewash, On Keith Windschuttle's Fabrication of Aboriginal History*[156] was used to refute Windschuttle's claims. Edited and introduced by Robert Manne, it also had articles by Henry Reynolds and Lyndall Ryan. In the "culture wars", Keith Windschuttle and Robert Manne were often described as "culture warriors" for their respective viewpoints.

Did European colonisation of Australia result in genocide? This depends on whether people see genocide as deliberate mass killings of Aborigines by settlers or the unintended consequences or omissions of the settler. International law takes a much broader approach than deliberate mass killings of a group. Tony Barta[157] and other historians argue that for the victim group, the result is the same. If a group is decimated by the deliberate or accidental transmission of smallpox or by introduced farming methods that cause a group of Aborigines to starve to death, he says it is still genocide. Both occurred in Australia as well as a frontier war.

The interaction of Aboriginal Australians with settlers was neither one of unrelenting violence nor one where Aborigines opened their arms to settlers and were placidly displaced.

On national commemorations like Australian and New Zealand Army Corps (ANZAC), we think about the past, and most are proud, but usually, the past doesn't intrude too much on our daily activities. Shaun Carney wrote in *The Age* that the history wars debate had affected us in the present by Australians asking the question, "Are we nice people?"

Debra Jopson, writing for the *Sydney Morning Herald* in 2003 remarked on the effect of Windschuttle's book on lessening public confidence in Aborigines:

> Tim Rowse, a political scientist and historian at the Australian National University, said that in the mid-1990s, in critical parts of the electorate, 'moral capital' was 'the primary resource of the Indigenous constituency in Australia' and governments had to get around that.
>
> Since Windschuttle's book appeared, key Indigenous institutions have faltered. Aboriginal and Torres Strait Islander Commission's (ATSIC)[158] head was suspended. Reconciliation Australia pleaded for adequate funding. The NSW Aboriginal Land Council board was sacked. The book has helped to break down the 'moral capital' Aborigines built up in the lost era of reconciliation.[159]

In the thick of the debate, another book was written – *The History Wars* by Stuart Macintyre and Anna Clarke (2003). In launching this book, former Prime Minister, Paul Keating urged us as a nation to think about ourselves in geo-political terms, as a nation in Asia and in a post-colonial world and to rethink who we are. He said this book:

> … sheds light on the political battle which is carried on in the pubs and on the footpaths about who we are and what has become of us……

We should reflect on this: alone, amongst the peoples of the world, we have possession of a continent, a continent we laid claim to as part of an empire, one we expropriated from another race, but a continent that is no longer an island in a sea of subjugated and colonial places. The Dutch no longer run Indonesia, the French no longer control Indo-China. And the Chinese now run China for themselves.

We occupy a continent surrounded by ancient societies; nations which have reclaimed their identity and their independence.

The Australian story, for it to be a record of continuing success has to come to terms with our expropriation of the land, our ambivalence about who we are and our place in the new geo-political make-up of the region. That is, being part of it, rather than simply being tolerated in it.

… Their (the Howards and the Blaineys) is not simply one of crabbiness or rancour; it's a failure of imagination, a failure to read our historical coordinates correctly but usefully to move to as bigger construct, a bigger picture as to who we are and what we can be. That's the real job of political leadership.

… A national leader, I think, should always be searching for the threads of gold in a community. Nurturing and bringing them out. Focusing on the best instincts – running with the human spirit and not punishing it…[160]

The Apology

As the debate continued, an election dramatically removed John Howard and his team from running the country, and he even lost his own seat. However, there were many reasons for this, and it's not in the scope of this book to go there. The first item on the agenda for the incoming ALP government under Prime Minister Kevin Rudd was to apologise to the stolen generation of Aboriginal people. This was a bipartisan event in parliament with the new Leader of the Opposition, Brendon Nelson. The tide had turned.

Norman's Grandfather

Aborigines came from all over Australia to sit in Parliament House to hear the apology, wiping the tears from their eyes, as I do as I write this. My husband Norman's grandfather, Thomas Miller, was taken from his mother in Nyleta, north Queensland in 1905 when he was about five years old. His mother was a full blood Aboriginal woman, and his father was Scottish. He was taken not only from his mother but his brothers and sisters. They were taken too, but the children were split up. He never saw his mother again, and in adult life, he was always searching for his brothers and sisters, finally finding some of them. It was too hard for him to talk much about it.

Norman's father, Barclay Miller, was a much-loved character around Cairns and Far North Queensland. His wife, Shirley Miller, is also much loved and respected, not only by her family but by all who know her. She is a woman of strong faith, fervent prayer and much wisdom. It seemed like Dad would know everyone in town. He was always stopping to say hello to someone and often introduced himself to people he didn't know and strike up a friendship with them. It would take a long time for Mum to get from one end of the street to the other to do her shopping when she was with Dad. He knew all his neighbours, and he liked to regularly go to an egg farm and buy many cartons of eggs and then give them away to neighbours (all white) as a friendly gesture and to help with their food bills. He would do the same with bread.

Barclay and Shirley Miller with Barbara (Miller collection)

Though only educated to Grade Four like Aborigines of his generation, Dad taught himself to read and write. Queensland government policies prohibited further education at the time he was growing up. Dad worked tirelessly for government housing and employment agencies to help Aboriginal people get homes and jobs. In his spare time, he would help homeless Aboriginal people who had come to Cairns from remote Aboriginal communities for hospital treatment or to serve prison sentences. They were often stranded, unable to afford to return home, and they camped out in the open in small groups. They would even ring him during the night asking for food, and he would get what he could from his fridge and cupboards and take it down. When the local Mayor had difficulties with business owners because of homeless people camping on their doorstep, he would ring Dad to come down and sort the problem out.

He served on ATSIC which was an elected Indigenous body to advise the government on Indigenous affairs as well as being on the boards of some Aboriginal organisations.

I remember Dad once telling me the government refused him permission to go to Weipa South Aboriginal community because they thought it was me seeking a permit to go there as we have the same initials – B. Miller.

Later in life, Dad worked for the Queensland government, helping Aborigines stolen from their families to locate them or at least research their family history with government records.

Also, he helped eligible Aboriginal people and were lucky enough to be able to prove their entitlement, get compensation for stolen wages. Over many years, the wages of many Queensland Aborigines were paid to the government instead of the workers and put into the Aborigines Welfare Fund. Aborigines had to go to the police station and ask for some money for food etc. and they received only small amounts, the government keeping most of the money. Eventually the Queensland government agreed to pay a compensation to a limit of $7,000 per person but people found it hard to prove their claims because they were often not given pay slips. Many died before they could receive compensation. This was another policy that contributed to the poverty of Aborigines. In 2019, the Queensland government finally made an out of court settlement with Hans Pearson and others to compensate workers $190 million. This was a watershed moment.

Unfortunately, we lost Dad in late 2007, so this great man was not there to hear the apology for the dislocation of his family that caused his father so much pain. But Dad himself was a very forgiving person, and I believe his Christian faith helped him in that. He was an example of practical reconciliation in action.

Removal of My Son's Grandparents

So, Norman stood in for his family in Canberra during the apology, and I was with him. When we arrived, we lined up at the doors to Parliament House and met Lydia and Marilyn Miller, my stepdaughters from my marriage to Mick Miller. The Queensland government removed Mick's father to the penal settlement of Palm Island. Mick Miller Snr as a young man was sent to Palm Island as punishment for speaking up for himself, and Mick's mother, Cissie Sibley, was sent there with her parents. Her father, George Sibley had been "cheeky," in other words, was assertive and so had to be punished. It was a common thing in those days.

While Mick's parents, my son Michael's grandparents, were not stolen from their families as children, they were removed from family members, their land and their community to live in a penal settlement, an authoritarian, harsh, government-controlled environment. They had to establish a new identity as Bwgcolman or Palm Islanders, while not forgetting their roots. This was where Mick Miller was born on 16 January 1937.

Palm Island was part of a group of islands, one of them Fantome Island, which was set aside as a leper colony. Many an Aborigine lost their life trying to swim to freedom from their island prison.

It is not possible to do justice to the life of Mick Miller in this book. When he passed away in April 1998, it was on the 30th anniversary of the death of one of his heroes – Martin Luther King Jnr. The students loved him he taught at Cairns North State School for many years before he went full time into political activism. He was not only vice president of FCAATSI, but he held many positions on national Aboriginal organisations – the National Aboriginal Education Committee (NAEC), the Aboriginal Arts Board, the national Aboriginal Sports Foundation, the National Aboriginal Consultative Committee (NACC) established in 1973 to advise the Federal Government, the Aboriginal Development Commission (ADC) set up in 1980 promoting economic opportunities for Indigenous people and many others. In 1985, we spent a year based in

Melbourne, where he travelled the country and headed up the Committee of Review of Aboriginal Employment Training Programs that resulted in the Miller Report, a widely acclaimed document. In response, the Federal Government set up the Aboriginal Employment Development Policy (AEDP).

At the local level in Cairns, he was instrumental in setting up many Aboriginal organisations – Woompera-Muralug Housing Society, Wu Chopperen Health Service, Niku Jowan Legal Service etc., organisations which provided vital support services to Indigenous people who often had difficulty accessing mainstream services.

At a regional level, Mick set up, with my help, the North Queensland Land Council. This was his great passion to work for land rights and self-management for Aboriginal people. It was never a funded or government recognised organisation like the land councils in the NT, but it was an effective lobby group. It was a thorn in the side for the Queensland Government of Premier Joh Bjelke-Petersen. This Premier was responsible for discriminatory legislation which controlled the lives of Queensland Aborigines and Torres Strait Islanders up until 1984 when local government legislation replaced it. I edited and wrote for the newspaper of the North Queensland Land Council – the North Queensland *(NQ) Messagestick*.

Mick gave a great of support to the 1978 campaign of the Aborigines at Aurukun and Mornington Island to have self-government and to the campaigns of Aurukun and Weipa Aborigines against mining on their land. He also supported the outstation movement at Aurukun and Yarrabah and the move back to Mapoon in 1975.

Mick travelled a lot to get support for his work from church groups, aid agencies, students and trade unions and to support others in their work for Aboriginal rights. I travelled with him to meetings of the Northern Land Council in Darwin, e.g. and to Noonkanbah station in WA in 1979 when the Kimberley Land Council was supporting local Aboriginal people who were concerned to protect their sacred sites against mining.

There were two important cases before the courts in 1982 with which Mick was very involved in lobbying support. One was the Koowarta v Bjelke-Petersen where the High Court upheld the constitutional validity of the Racial Discrimination Act 1975 and that the Queensland government's blocking of a land purchase of a station on his land at Archer River, Aurukun, was discriminatory.[161]

The other was the case of Mabo v Queensland (No 2) where Eddie Mabo, Dave Passi and James Rice brought an action against the State of Queensland and the Commonwealth government claiming native title to Mer (Murray Islands) in the Torres Straits. The latter case is better known and its eventual success on 3 June 1992 had far-reaching effects on Indigenous people in Australia. However, Koowarta's case was successful as well and influential, and he has recently been hailed as "the Mabo of the mainland". Neither Koowarta nor Mabo lived to see their success after very long battles.

At a state level, Mick set up the Aboriginal and Islander Health Worker Education Program (AIHWEP) at the Tropical North Queensland Institute of Technical and Further Education (TAFE) to train Indigenous health workers statewide to deal with appalling health statistics. He became the founding president of the State Tripartite Forum, where Indigenous people and State and Federal Government worked together to improve Indigenous health.

At an international level, Mick travelled to Stockholm for a World Conference of Indigenous People (WCIP) in 1977, raising support for and awareness of Indigenous issues in Australia. As Chairman of the North Queensland Land Council, Mick led a delegation to Europe in 1978 where they talked to officials of the International Commission of Jurists, the UN Commission on Human Rights and the ILO particularly taking up the issue, among others, of mining on Aboriginal land. Joyce Hall from Weipa and Jacob Wolmby from Aurukun accompanied Mick.

Joyce Hall, Jacob Wolmby and Mick Miller in London 1978 (Miller collection)

Thirty years later, it was time for the apology. It was 13 February 2008.

The Nation Stands Still

Our local Member of Parliament, Jim Turnour, organised for Norman and me to be sitting in the parliamentary gallery for the apology and to go to the reception afterwards. The gallery was full, the Great Hall which can seat about 1,000 was overflowing, the lawns in front of Parliament House were crowded, and schools and offices around the nation stopped to watch and listen on TV. The only other thing that stops the nation is the Melbourne Cup horse race every year as we are a nation of horse race enthusiasts and gamblers. The only other thing that generates such excitement as the apology did is football matches which regularly fill stadiums. But this was the Parliament House of our nation – not dry old politics that day – and not a dry eye either.

It was such a momentous moment in the history of our nation when Kevin Rudd said sorry, Brendon Nelson said sorry, the country said sorry. A wave of tears was shed across the nation, washing away much pain, much hurt, much sorrow. Many non-Indigenous Australians stood with our government and shared in saying sorry. It is not the end of the story, but a journey of healing started, which is ongoing and real. Some Aboriginal people held up signs saying, "We forgive you." Others said they were finally able to move on.

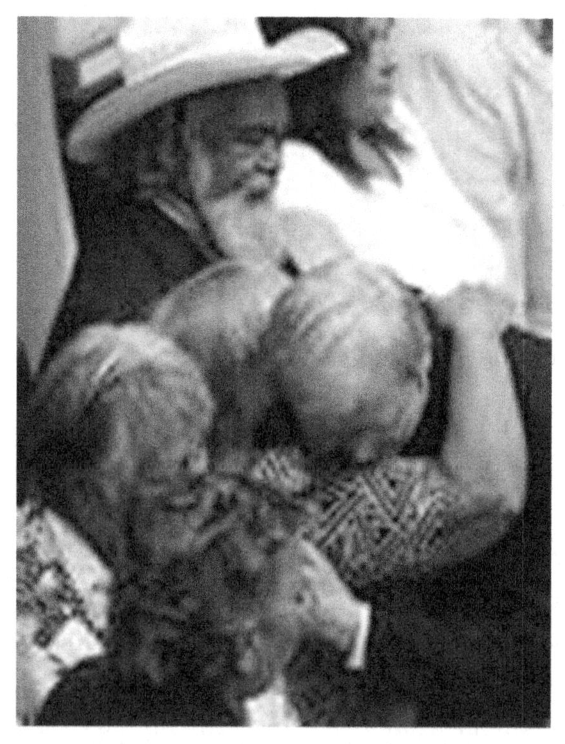

Kevin Rudd hugging Indigenous people after the apology, Bob Randall with hat on, singer of signature song "My Brown Skin Baby They Take Him Away"

Excerpt of Kevin Rudd's Speech to Parliament 13 February 2008

... To the stolen generations, I say the following: as Prime Minister of Australia, I am sorry.

On behalf of the government of Australia, I am sorry.

On behalf of the parliament of Australia, I am sorry.

I offer you this apology without qualification.

... I know that, in offering this apology on behalf of the government and the parliament, there is nothing I can say today that can take away the pain you have suffered personally.

Whatever words I speak today, I cannot undo that.

Words alone are not that powerful; grief is a very personal thing.

... My proposal is this: if the apology we extend today is accepted in the spirit of reconciliation, in which it is offered, we can today resolve together that there be a new beginning for Australia.

And it is to such a new beginning that I believe the nation is now calling us.

... Surely this is the unfulfilled spirit of the 1967 referendum. Surely, at least from this day forward, we should give it a go.

... So, let us seize the day. Let it not become a moment of mere sentimental reflection.

Let us take it with both hands and allow this day, this day of national reconciliation, to become one of those rare moments in which we might just be able to transform the way in which the nation thinks about itself, whereby the injustice administered to the

> stolen generations in the name of these, our parliaments, causes all of us to reappraise, at the deepest level of our beliefs, the real possibility of reconciliation writ large …

It was truly a historic moment, and it held out a vision of what Australia could be. It was a new beginning. A page in history had been turned and a life-changing moment experienced by many as tears flowed around the nation.

Some Aborigines wore T-shirts thanking the Prime Minister

Norman is also an artist, and he painted a large canvas to record the apology. His wish was for it to sit in Parliament House to commemorate the event. We had some difficulty organising this, however. Then we attended the Parliamentary Prayer Breakfast in February 2011 and met and became friends with Kevin Rudd's sister, Loree, a devout Catholic. Loree organised for Norman to present the painting to Kevin Rudd who by then was Foreign Minister, after a leadership challenge. Norman presented the painting to him on the anniversary of the Bringing Them Home report's release, 26 May 2011. It was an important moment for Norman who wanted to recognise and honour Kevin Rudd for what he had done.

26 May is celebrated each year as part of Reconciliation Week. Initially known as Sorry Day after the Bringing Them Home report came out, it was changed to Journey of Healing Day so that people could work through their healing and move on.

Kevin Rudd at Parliament House Canberra with Norman and Barbara and the painting presented to him (photo Darren Coyne Koori Mail)

Kevin Rudd tried to move the nation on from the history wars and was largely able to do so. His apology became the nation's apology. He inspired other governments to apologise to their Indigenous people.

There are arguments saying we should have practical not symbolic gestures towards reconciliation. We need both. Kevin Rudd followed the apology with the Closing the Gap program to reduce the considerable disparity in socio-economic indicators between Indigenous and other Australians. While it has had limited success, it is being updated in 2019 to try to generate better outcomes.

A Positive Portrayal of Australia

Australia, a vast continent, is a land of contrasts. Where I live, in Cairns, we have two beautiful World Heritage Areas on our doorstep – the Great Barrier Reef and the Wet Tropics rainforest. In the centre of Australia, we have the stark beauty of the desert and in the south, the snow-capped Snowy Mountains, to name just a few. We see the beautiful beaches and the tourist advertisements – "put another shrimp on the barbe (que)" ring in our ears.

Australia is recognised as having one of the best economies in the world, though there are still people living in poverty. Australia came out relatively well from the global financial crisis.

It sees itself as the land of the fair go and egalitarianism has always been strong. There is a strong sense of what is just and unjust and support for the 'underdog'. However, there is also the 'tall poppy' syndrome where, if someone is successful, we feel we need to bring them down a peg or two to our level, so they don't look down on us.

Australia has a relatively stable parliamentary democracy, and this probably is not as appreciated as it could be because we haven't had to struggle for it. We have freedom of speech and assembly and freedom to criticise the government.

We are somewhat laid back as a nation, and while we will come out and demonstrate at times about unpopular decisions or policies, we are relatively peaceful about it and don't do it often. We are relatively apathetic compared to some other nations, and it will take a lot to stir most people to action, except of course for the lobbyists who take regular action.

Australia was a leader in good working conditions and the right of women to vote in the early part of this century. We have a high rate of home ownership, good wages and a welfare system for the unemployed, elderly, sick and disabled.

Australia has always been proud of its sporting prowess, but it is also a nation of scientific discovery. Until recently, the state I live in, Queensland, has called itself the "Smart State".

We are one of the most multicultural nations in the world and live in relative harmony between the ethnic groups. However, there is considerable concern about boats of refugees, at times turning up on our doorstep.

While Australia is an isolated Island continent in the Asia Pacific region, it is 'punching above its weight' in the international political arena, particularly since the formation of and its involvement in the G20.

Australia is not only proud of its achievements in many areas but also its ANZAC (Australia and New Zealand) fighting tradition and its spirit of courage and mateship. Australians see themselves as independent, resourceful and a bit irreverent. Australians are probably not as patriotic as Americans, but they still love Australia.

One of the most encouraging moments in our history was the reconciliation marches in the year 2000 when one million Australians marched across bridges in the capital cities of Australia in support of reconciliation between Indigenous and non-Indigenous people.

Bridge Walk for Reconciliation Brisbane 2000

If William Cooper had lived to see this day, I think tears would have come to his eyes to see the hundreds of thousands of ordinary Australians walk across bridges in Australia to say their hearts were open to Indigenous people and they wanted to reconcile or make peace with them. With every fibre of his being, he would have walked with them. He laid the foundation that many others would build on.

Chapter 11

Honouring of William Cooper in Australia

For Castan, the answer to the Holocaust deniers and those who use terms like 'black armband' is 'to write more books, give more talks, fight more native title cases in the courts, tell more stories of the Stolen Generation...so that the cult of disremembering may never take hold again.

Editorial, *The Australian Jewish News* 20 December 2002 on the late Ron Castan, QC, lead counsel in the historic Mabo Case

Protest re Kristallnacht

William Cooper and the Australian Aborigines League protested against *Kristallnacht*, the Night of the Broken Glass, the start of the Holocaust in Germany and Austria 9-10 November 1938. The broken glass of 7,000 Jewish businesses and synagogues littered the streets and rioters ransacked Jewish homes, schools and hospitals. The Germans forced thirty thousand Jews into concentration camps and killed over 91 Jews. It shattered William to think that such tragedy and savagery could occur. He led the walk to the German Consulate in Melbourne on 6 December, concerned at the inaction and ineffectiveness of governments around the world.

William attempted to hand them a letter of protest but was not able to. This protest was remarkable because Aborigines were not even citizens in their own land. The Jewish community in Australia has regularly honoured William Cooper because he led this protest. Yad Vashem World Holocaust Remembrance Center in Israel honoured Cooper in 2010 with an Academic Chair of Resistance to the Holocaust named after him. My husband Norman and I were privileged to be there with William's descendants and a bipartisan group of 17 Australian federal parliamentarians to witness the event.

However, this book is concentrating on William's activism for Indigenous Australians, and his stand for Jewish people is covered in another book by the author – *William Cooper, Gentle Warrior, Standing Up for Australian Aborigines and Persecuted Jews.*[162]

Western Suburbs Indigenous Gathering Place

The Western Suburbs Indigenous Gathering Place under the leadership of Colleen Marion decided to become a champion of the legacy of William Cooper and have now been running several events in his honour since 2004. Avraham (Abe) Schwarz, a Jewish friend of the Cooper family, has been an enthusiastic proponent of William Cooper's legacy and worked for a time for the Gathering Place setting up events in his honour.

Colleen first became interested in telling William's story after she had attended an event in 2002 where Maribyrnong Council recognised him. Abe became interested when he was working in Echuca where many of William's relatives live, and he heard the story.

Footscray, where William lived is a suburb west of Melbourne, and its local government area is the City of Maribyrnong. It is home to the Aboriginal Woimurrung and Boonwurrung tribes of the Kulin nation. In 2019, it has a population of over 19,000 with more than half its residents born overseas. Footscray is very multicultural, and where it was once a centre for Italian, Greek and Yugoslavian migrants, it is now home for migrants from South East Asia and East Africa.

NAIDOC and Annual William Cooper Cup

On 3 July 2004, Colleen organised a NAIDOC football match between the Victorian police and Aborigines. This is a successful reconciliation initiative in building good relationships and recognising William as the founder of NAIDOC. This has become a yearly event Uncle Boydie, William Cooper's grandson comes from Shepparton to Melbourne to be honoured and to hand out the trophy each year.

The free event is a family day and includes a barbeque (BBQ), face painting, Police and Emergency Service displays, Indigenous cultural events and children's activities.

William Cooper Memorial Walk

Forty years after the 1967 referendum, the Western Suburbs Indigenous Gathering Place organised the William Cooper Memorial Walk to honour both William Cooper and the 1967 referendum which changed the constitution to give Aboriginal people the right to be counted in the census. It also gave the Federal Government the right to make laws for Aborigines as a group across the nation; this previously has been a state government responsibility. The Federal Government was then able to enact the Racial Discrimination Act 1975 and other laws.

When William was unsuccessful with having his petition of about 2,000 signatures sent to the King of England because Aborigines were not citizens of Australia, the fight to change the Australian constitution began. William started it but was not around to see the victory. However, he mentored some of those, like Pastor Sir Doug Nicholls, who carried on the baton and saw the success of this struggle.

William Cooper Footbridge

Footscray footbridge at Footscray train station was named in honour of William Cooper. Two residents of the area, Anthony Balla and the owner of William Cooper's former house, Christine Newman, independently nominated William in a competition and their nomination was successful.

William Cooper Bridge (www.treatyrepublic.net)

"He played an important part in Australia's Aboriginal history, and it is fitting to pay tribute to his legacy in this way," Planning Minister Justin Madden said at the christening of the footbridge on 20 May 2010.[163]

Petitions Exhibition at Museum of Australian Democracy

William Cooper was an active participant in Australia's democratic process initiating several petitions to influence politics and policy making. His petition to the King of England was the most ambitious. The Museum of Australian Democracy at Old Parliament House Canberra held a Petitions Exhibition which included William's petitions. It was part of a collaboration between the National Centre of Biography and the Museum of Australian Democracy in the production of a Timeline of Australian Democracy. The new museum opened on 9 May

2009, and the interactive Timeline was a significant element in the exhibition - Australian Democracy: More than 2000 years in the making. I was pleased to be able to visit this Petitions Exhibition.

They set the display up so visitors would walk along a bank of interactive screens and select from a menu of nine subjects: Colonisation; Rule of law; Politics; Parliament; the right to vote; Defence; International affairs; Freedoms; and Equal rights. The museum honoured key people associated with each milestone and provided a sketch on the person's role and influence on the evolution of Australian democracy. The display added the valuable human dimension to historical events.

Bennet condensed the biographies of major figures in the history of Australian democracy from the Australian Dictionary of Biography (ADB). He said, "The individuals on whom sketches have been prepared from *ADB* articles include statesmen, such as Sir Henry Parkes and Sir Samuel Griffith; pioneer women in politics such as Edith Cowan and Dame Edith Lyons; Aboriginal leaders such as William Cooper and William Ferguson; and a wide range of other persons, among them Jessie Street, Vida Goldstein, William Charles Wentworth and Henry Bournes Higgins, whose vision and endeavours helped to shape Australian democracy."[164]

The setting in Old Parliament House provides an apt place for the museum and this exhibition honours men and women of considerable note in Australian history, and William Cooper and William Ferguson should be among them. The House of Representatives and the Senate have been left exactly as they were when they were in use from 1927-1988.

Only one petition was presented to the house in 1927 when Federal Parliament moved from Melbourne to Canberra. In opening the exhibition, Wilson referred to this, "On 20 October, a petition was presented by the member of Angas, Walter Parsons [National Party, SA] which stated:

> The Aboriginal races are dying out and praying that a model Aboriginal State be established.

The petition was signed by 7113 residents of Australia and supported with the reference of two full-blooded Aboriginals who would assist in the founding of the proposed state, listed as Reverend John Noble and David Unaipon. The member for Bass, Tasmania, Mr Jackson, had made a plea to the house in the previous weeks for the need to protect the Aboriginal tribes of Australia against disease and other effects of their contact with modern conditions. Debate was also held in the house on the issue of the apparent exploitation of northern Aboriginal labour force with low wages. The question of an Aboriginal state was defeated with seventeen for and thirty-two against."[165]

Besides William Cooper's petitions, there were petitions to Federal Parliament starting in 1957 that led to the 1967 referendum to change the constitution so Aborigines could be counted in the census.

William Cooper Justice Centre

The Victorian Government opened The William Cooper Justice Centre (WCJC) at 223 William Street Melbourne on the 6 October 2010. It was previously the vacant Old County Court which required upgrading to meet environmental standards. It completed the court precinct at the William and Lonsdale Street corner.

William Cooper Justice Centre (www.v-arc.com.au)

Deputy Premier and Attorney-General Rob Hulls announced on 17 August 2010 that they would dedicate this new court building would to the memory of William Cooper.

VCAT recognised that William was someone "whose tireless pursuit of justice for his people and for other disadvantaged communities in the early 20th century laid the groundwork for contemporary advocates of Indigenous rights. He has been described as 'a man who...knew that we must keep testing the limits of the law if we're to deliver on the promise of justice.' Notably, the first sitting at the WCJC coincides with Reconciliation Week."[166]

However, as it was completed mid-year, the Victorian Civil and Administrative Tribunal (VCAT) made history on Tuesday, 29 May as the first ever jurisdiction to sit at the refurbished William Cooper Justice Centre (WCJC) with Senior Member Nihill presiding over an anti-discrimination case. The WCJC has good facilities, including multi-jurisdictional courtrooms, mediation and conference facilities. It will improve community access to justice services in the CBD. Bush-themed colour schemes were used, and crafted wood beautifies the furnishings in the courtrooms. Uncle Boydie has asked that there be an exhibit on the life and work of William Cooper on the ground floor.

At the official October opening, Kevin Russell gave the main address. As part of the dedication, he said:

> And of course, we only need to look at Uncle Boydie for further reflection of his grandfather. Everything you see in Uncle Boydie, the dignity, and the way he has lived his life for the community (Current Board Member Rumbalara) reflects his grandfather William. Williams' legacy is being honoured today with the opening of the William Cooper Justice Centre, a court precinct where justice shall be delivered. What an appropriate way to honour a man who fought all of his life seeking justice, not only for his people, but for all marginalised and oppressed peoples.
>
> We, the Aboriginal community and family of William Cooper, are proud of our great ancestor, and are delighted that this Justice Centre is being named in his honour. Many of us here today continue to strive for justice, just as William did 100 years ago. Let us not give up in our endeavours to make sure justice prevails, and in the face of adversity, fight as William did, and his message will not be in vain.
>
> I would like to thank The Koorie Justice Unit and Andrew Jackomos, for the wonderful recognition you have bestowed upon a Truly Great Man, William Cooper my great grandfather (GGF). In line with this years' NAIDOC Theme: 'A True Unsung Hero'.
>
> In closing I would like to quote former Chief Executive Officer of Melbourne Jewish Holocaust Centre Mr Bernard Korbman: "William should be remembered for not only what he tried to do for his people, but as a Global Warrior for Humanity.[167]

Uncle Boydie and Kevin Russell (photo J-Wire, 28 November 2010)

Chapter 12

Connecting with William's Family and Country

NAIDOC Cairns

As an Aboriginal pastor, Norman would get an opportunity each year to open the official NAIDOC celebrations in prayer, and he would also talk about William's legacy. This is what he said on 8 July 2011 at the Cairns NAIDOC celebrations:

I would like to honour God, who gave us this land and created us and I would like to honour the traditional owners of this country. I acknowledge all the elders who have come before us and paved the path for us to follow. I also want to bless this present generation and the generations to come who are our future.

I ask our Father in Heaven to rain down his blessings on this gathering today and each one here …

Pastor Norman Miller shared some reflections with the Cairns community.

Norman Miller (photo Koori Mail)

This year, the national theme is "Change, the next step is ours". Our future is in our hands. Change is inevitable, but we want to shape that change to the benefit of our community. We need to have a positive vision of the future and strategies of how to get there. We need to boldly step into the future and take our community to the place where we have pride in what we have achieved and hope for the future. Let's take the next step together as we climb the ladder of opportunity...

Before closing, I particularly want to honour William Cooper of Victoria, who was the originator of NAIDOC. He persuaded the churches to institute Aboriginal Sunday which later became Aborigines Day, a secular observance and later NAIDOC Week ...

We hand the baton on today to the youth who will link arms together to walk into the future – black and white Australians together. We have hope. We have a dream. It can be achieved. It will be achieved.

40th Anniversary of 1967 Referendum

The Centre for International Reconciliation and Peace which was founded by Norman and me in 1998 held a Christian conference in July 2007 in Melbourne. As it was the 40th anniversary of the 1967 referendum, we honoured both Pastor Sir Doug Nicholls and William Cooper for their ground-breaking work, and it was good to have Ps Doug's daughter Lillian and grandson Jason with us to honour them as well.

2007 Melbourne conference L-R Norman Miller, Rev Neville Lilley, Doug Nicholls' daughter Lillian Tamiru and grandson Jason (Miller collection)

Shepparton Youth Inspired by William Cooper

La Trobe University Equality and Diversity Centre researcher, Beth Rankin, wanted to help local young people through its Shepparton campus to tell a story about themselves, and Shepparton's diversity, through musical theatre. It was also a way of reaching out to disadvantaged young people, including Congolese and Iraqi refugees and Indigenous and other youth to provide a life-changing learning experience.

She engaged two professionals from London's West End to help with the musical and artistic direction of the performance – Warren Wills and Yamin Choudury who had been involved with a multicultural youth program at London's Haringey Shed. Thus, Shepp Shed was born.

Warren and Yamin used the story of local hero William Cooper to inspire the disparate group and Uncle Boydie came along to tell his grandfather's story igniting further interest. The youth worked on their own script called "Ghost Gum High" based on the theme of what might they do if they were a present-day William Cooper It was a big success with its world premiere on January 2011.

It was also an interesting story for Warren, whom Norman and I met when he performed at a concert in Melbourne the same day Uncle Boydie, Abe and I were fine tuning the book. Warren commented:

The striking coincidence for me is that my grandparents were refugees from the ovens of Poland and came here and were located in Shepparton. Thus, my Australian roots are born from displacement of the Jewish peoples as a result of the Jewish persecution and genocide. And here am I, some 70 years later on the home soil of Uncle Boydie whose grandpa took a stand, a crusade to shout about the injustice inflicted on these very same people.[168]

Visit to Cummeragunja and the Murry River

I decided to write William's story about May 2011, and I felt a need to visit the place where he was born, where he lived and where he was buried. I wanted to see the beautiful Murray River where the paddle steamers plied their way up river with bales of wool in William's time and see the beautiful forests. In particular, I wanted to get to know the people of the land more.

Indigenous Gathering Place Cooper Gala Dinner

So, Norman and I timed our visit to Cummera to follow on from the William Cooper Gala Dinner organised by Colleen Marion, Abe

Schwarz and the team from the Western Suburbs Indigenous Gathering Place. For us, Melbourne and country Victoria is a long way away from north Queensland, and we don't travel there often. We stayed with our friends David and Carol Jack and, after introducing David to Abe, David's help was enlisted to make a DVD of the proceedings.

Flemington Racecourse is well known in Australia as we are a nation of horse race enthusiasts. The Melbourne Cup is said to be the one thing that can stop the nation. Workplaces around Australia run sweepstakes on the race so that people who don't usually bet have a "flutter" as they call it on the Melbourne Cup. The women (and men) go to considerable trouble to wear fashionable outfits and prizes are awarded for the best dressed.

But on this night, we weren't gathered around the racetrack cheering on the horses. We weren't going to leave rich or broke, depending on the outcome of a horserace and our propensity or not to bet and take risks. We were indoors at the Atrium to witness another important event. People arrived dressed very formally and spent time chatting, having pre-dinner drinks and looking at the paintings and sporting memorabilia on display for the silent auction. There was an air of anticipation and a chance to catch up with old friends and maybe make new ones. The Jewish community had turned up in force, and so had the Aboriginal community, many coming from Shepparton and Mooroopna - Cooper country.

Colleen Marion, Uncle Boydie Turner, Kevin Russell and Joy Wandin-Murphy at Gala Dinner (Photo David Jack)

Aunty Joy Wandin-Murphy welcomed us to country. During the night, we enjoyed the One Fire Dancers and a performance by Aleesha and Sarina Dean.

The Reagan Milstein Foundation co-hosted the dinner celebrating William's life. It is a charity named in honour of the Bialik College student who died the year before tragically in a scuba diving accident. Funds were raised to help get Indigenous youths involved in soccer, a passion of the late Reagan. The dinner was held on 16 June with Warren Mundine, chief executive of native title advisory group Native Title Service Provider (NTS) Corp as Master of Ceremonies. The Israel Ambassador, the Hon Yuval Rotem attended and Mr Simon McKeon, Australian of the Year, was the event patron and one of the speakers. Jacqui and Colleen Marion and the Hon Nigel Scullion, Shadow Minister for Indigenous Affairs, spoke briefly.

Gala Dinner, Warren Mundine standing behind Hon Yuval Rotem and Boydie Turner seated, Abe Schwarz on right and Hon Kevin Rudd talking to his sister, Loree, nephew Rad and author in the background (Photo David Jack)

Kevin Milstein, Reagan's father, said William's story was inspirational and educating people about it was very important "… It comes back to that *tikkun olam* (healing the world) feeling; we're all on this planet together, we all need to live together, we all need to honour each other, we all need to respect each other."

Milstein's foundation helped raised money to send a delegation, including members of Cooper's family, to Israel, for the ceremony at Yad Vashem. Colleen, CEO of the Gathering Place, was one of them. She said she was committed to telling Uncle William's story.

Colleen said in her message to those attending the Gala Dinner:

> Uncle William continuously fought for our people's rights more than 70 years ago – as well as standing up against the persecution of Jewish people and other instances – whenever and

wherever he saw injustice. In the spirit – and legacy – of William Cooper, I commit to likewise tirelessly continue his stance, to rid this world of oppression, ensuring people are treated with the dignity, and access to services, that we all deserve irrespective of race, religion or colour.

Simon McKeon, Australian of the Year 2011, Tamara Newing, Kevin Milstein, Colleen Marion, the Hon Nigel Scullion and Warren Mundine (Photo David Jack)

Foreign Minister Kevin Rudd gave a stirring and heartfelt key address on "Walking together: Celebrating the Legacy of William Cooper." He said:

And yet, we know that humanity is also capable of listening to better angels. Capable of overcoming a natural tendency to stand with the herd, impotently on the sidelines. Capable of taking action.

Capable of confronting hatred.

Never to sit safe on the sidelines when great wrong is being done.

Always seeking to stand up for the weak.

Always seeking to give voice to the voiceless.

And to inspire others to do the same.

Those who stand up to racism, to xenophobia, have the power to prick our consciences, to whisper in our hearts, to inspire action, even long after their lifetime.

We often look abroad for such heroes….

We can also look here at home for those who also swam against the tide in defence of a people oppressed.

Tonight, we gather together to honour such a man.

A man named William Cooper …

In pushing for these fundamental democratic rights, William Cooper used the weapons of peace – words, principles, faith, letters, petitions, protests, an appeal to basic principles.

And like the democrat he was, he argued with a generous spirit.

He believed firmly that when fair people heard what was really going on, what the plight of his people really was, they would make the changes that would give everyone a fair deal…

It was an inspiring speech. We had some friends join us on our table - Kevin Rudd's sister Lorree, her nephew Rad and Sally Humphrey and her husband. David sat down only briefly to eat as he was busy with the camera. It was at the dinner that I was able to ask Uncle Boydie if I could write a book on William and he was happy for me to do so.

Visit to Cummera 18 June 2011

Norman and I attended the dinner Thursday night and organised with Melbourne Aboriginal people to visit Cummera on Saturday. However, the ride didn't work out. Also, Uncle Boydie would be returning to Shepparton on Friday but would be tied up at a Yorta Yorta meeting in Echuca from 10 am Saturday, and we'd not be able to catch up with him. Still, we had an interesting visit with Esme Bamblett of the Aborigines Advancement League on Friday.

I'd phoned some Aboriginal contacts in Shepparton and Moama and found that they'd all be at a football match a couple of hours away from Cummera, so no one was able to meet us or show us around. A local Aboriginal pastor, Joe Day who lives at Moama, was going to be coaching a football team and driving them to the venue on a bus. He ministers at Cummera and, when we asked him, he said it would be fine to visit. We were staying with friends, David and Carol Jack and David offered to drive us there.

We made an early start from Montmorency after saying prayers together and putting our luggage in the car as David would be taking us to the airport at the end of our trip for an evening flight home, ready for our local church service the next day. It was a chilly morning and overcast.

Beautiful forests opened up before us. It was Victorian country scenery. The land was grassy and hilly, and a heavy fog hung over it. We were near the Great Dividing Range.

We started to see dead trees, stripped of their leaves as a result of the deadly fires that occurred about two years previously. The area was still recovering. David said that the fire raged along the road we were travelling on and went into some houses, destroying them and taking lives and then might skip the next house and go into the one after it. He knew some people felt guilty that they had cheated death while so many perished. He told of people trying to escape in their cars, only to find trees fallen over the road making their escape by road impossible. Cars piled up, and others bumped into the back of them in the dense fog and smoke.

After about 20 minutes, we came across a small old church with much character on the right and David said it was his mother's church. He and Carol and their three adult sons, Tim, Andrew and Ali would be moving to this area in October to be near David's aging mother. They are a close-knit and talented family of artists and IT specialists.

About 2 hours into our trip, we came to Tatura where David and Andrew had worked on a large mural in three pieces that showcased the town's history and natural features. The three murals represented water, land and sun and one side featured the birdlife and the other side the people, Aborigines, famous settlers and industry. We had a coffee break there. The area is very flat. David said there had been a sizable Italian population here growing tomatoes etc. who had been imprisoned during World War 2 as aliens and repatriated after the war. Many returned to this area in the years to follow.

As we drove on to Echuca, we passed through Nagambi, known as the rowing capital of Victoria where many schools would bring their children to compete in rowing contests on Lake Nagambi near the Goulbourn River. I was surprised how quiet these country towns were small with a lot of character.

We finally reached Echuca port and the Murray River. Norman spotted a statue of Ned Kelly in the town. We didn't have much time to have a look around, but we went to the river bank and saw the place where William was born – somewhere along this beautiful river. The bridge over the Murray River into NSW was above us on the right. The ground beside the river was cracked and mossy. The river had risen and overtaken a plastic rubbish bin that was now mostly submerged. There were large stately gum trees near the river bank. A few paddle steamers were moored at the jetty. The paddle steamer had several large bales on it to make it look like the cargo of days gone by. Echuca was the largest port outside the capital of Melbourne in the early days, buzzing as it was with paddle steamers carrying wool to market.

Millers at Echuca on banks of Murray River 2011 (Photo David Jack)

A little further down, there was a bend in the river, and we could see a fair way downstream. There was a huge wharf area on the left and many paddle steamers anchored. They were very picturesque, ready to be hired out to take passengers for a ride or even accommodate them for an overnight stay on board.

Paddle steamers in background at Echuca on banks of Murray River 2011 (Photo David Jack)

We then made our way over the bridge and into NSW, driving into the beautiful little town of Moama just inside the border. We followed the road through forest land on the way to Barmah forest where William lived for a time. We were keeping an eye out for the Aboriginal community of Cummeragunja. We drove past a turn off to the right and noticed some houses in the distance. Thinking it might be Cummera, we turned around and looked closer at the open, wooden gates. On each side was a tiny Aboriginal flag. There was one notice with the name Cummeragunja on it. We found it and drove in.

Cummeragunja 2011 (Photo David Jack)

Here was a small community of well- kept brick houses. It was quiet as most people were at football. We stopped at the house where there was some activity, and the eldest Koori[169] came out to greet us. He was from Swan Hill but married to a Yorta Yorta woman. We told him who we were, where we were from, and why we were there. We asked him if it was okay to visit William's grave, and he said yes and gave us directions.

We drove around the corner and to the graveyard which had a high arched entrance to it. As we entered on foot, there were clumps of cow dung and patches of an unusual green leafy plant. William's grave was further away near the fence with towering pine trees providing shelter on the other side of the fence. On the way to it, I saw the graves of other famous Yorta Yorta people like Selwyn and Geraldine Briggs and Hyllus Maris. However, there were not a large number of graves there.

Millers at entrance Cummera cemetery 2011 (Photo David Jack)

William's grave had a branch with fresh eucalyptus leaves on it. It seemed a new headstone might have been built in 1995. Around the grave was grey granite edge with a black basalt headstone. The top of the grave was covered with white quartz gravel and moss. A small angel adorned it and a teddy bear with a football.

It was a blessing to pay tribute to this man of God, this pioneer for the uplift of his Aboriginal people who also had a heart for the Jews. As I prayed a blessing over him, his family and the Yorta Yorta people, I felt to compare him to another William - William Wilberforce and his long struggle to rid the British Empire of slavery.

William Cooper's headstone (Photo David Jack)

We then drove into the small village of Barmah, which was very close and which had a caravan park. It was time then to make the journey back as we had to catch a plane and it would be about a two-and-a-half-hour trip. We ate the roll and fruit Carol had prepared for us as we drove. We passed through Shepparton on the way back. Uncle Boydie would probably still have been at Echuca at his meeting with the Yorta Yorta people, so we blessed him as we drove through the town. He lives in nearby Mooroopna, about 4km from Shepparton. It was at Mooroopna hospital that William passed away, after which he was taken to his beloved Cummera to rest.

Honouring Uncle Boydie and William in Parliament House Canberra

At our yearly Centre for International Reconciliation and Peace conference in July, we decided 2011 was a time to honour Uncle Boydie who has been such a role model to his people with the same dignity and grace as his grandfather William. Uncle Boydie is the longest-serving board member of the Rumbalara Cooperative in Shepparton, Victoria.

On the first night of our conference (21 July) in Parliament House Canberra, we presented a plaque to Uncle Boydie in recognition of William's work. We were blessed that Abe Schwarz accompanied Uncle Boydie and was able to address our conference as well. Colleen Marion and the Gathering Place supported them to come, and they were able to visit the Petitions Exhibition at the Museum of Australian Democracy and see William's petitions while in Canberra.

Uncle Boydie centre, receives plaque from Barbara & Norman Miller Canberra 2011 (photo David Jack)

Uncle Boydie's Story

We were able to have some time out with Uncle Boydie who told us he was born in Carlton, Melbourne on 25 October 1928. His Dad was Alf Turner, and his mother was Amy Cooper, William's daughter. Uncle

Boydie married Amy Briggs in 1951, and they were happily married till she passed away, so he lives on his own in Mooroopna. He had two older sisters – Edna and Valda. Valda, 84 years old, is still alive and lives in Melbourne. Uncle has a cousin John living in the Gold Coast. He said:

> My family split up when I was a baby, and I went to live with William and Sarah. It was the Great Depression, and Mum couldn't keep the girls, so she sent them to Dad who put them in a convent. Men cut trees and worked on the roads, and they got sustenance (the dole). Things were not good until the 2nd World War. Then there was work because most men had gone to war.
>
> In his middle 70's, grandfather took me on as a baby. That was in Barmah on the banks of the river opposite Cummera. I was probably four or five when they moved to Melbourne in 1933. Sarah came back to Echuca and picked me up from Mum. They were used to having me. We lived somewhere else in Footscray before Southampton St.
>
> I was the youngest of four grandchildren because William's other daughter died and left three children. She died during childbirth because they took Bruce as a young baby and reared him. Grandfather had Cyril and Esme till they were able to look after themselves.
>
> I left there in 1941 at 12 years old and went back to Mum. Grandfather got sick in 1940. He moved to Mooroopna, and they put him in hospital the following year, and he died.

When I asked Uncle Boydie about living in Footscray with William, he said:

> Grandfather had meetings at the house we lived in, so I knew these people. Uncle Lynch Cooper, William's youngest son, won the Stawell Cup in 1928 and in 1929 he won the world sprint championships. He was the first Aboriginal to win a world title.

To leave the mission with kids and come out was a big thing. Grandfather started a fish shop at Mulwala near Albury with fish he caught himself in 1906 or 1907. He ran that for a few years. He worked shearing, fencing and labouring because he did not have much education.

Remembering the story of Maloga, Uncle said, "grandfather was 14 years old when the Mathews set up Maloga. The Mathews went out with their buggy and brought the family in. William came behind on a horse. There was not much food. Shadrach was a brother-in-law and helped him with writing." William used electric light in Melbourne and lamps at Barmah to write his famous letters.

Uncle Boydie has a son in Perth called Lance and Lance has four children. Uncle also has a daughter Leonie living in Shepparton with her husband Ben Drummond and three children. Leonie works at a secondary school in Shepparton and is studying Aboriginal culture at a Brisbane university by distance education. Uncle says, "I visit her every day. If I get lonely, I jump in the car and go over. It only takes me seven minutes."

Now retired from the board, Uncle had been a board member of Rumbalara for 14 years at the time of our talk and is the longest-serving director. He says it is the only Aboriginal cooperative in Shepparton and Mooroopna. It is a big responsibility. "We've got a medical centre and run forty different programs, including alcohol rehabilitation. It's a big place. We employ about 150 people. We're building a new medical centre and renovating Rumbalara, so probably we'll need more. We're building an aged care centre. It is $70-$80 million worth."

He sees himself carrying on William's legacy at Rumbalara. In the 1950's they moved people off Rumbalara, and that's when Uncle got involved. He was eighty-three when we talked in Canberra, so he got involved in Aboriginal affairs at 69 years of age and is active in his old age like William. The board mainly consists of elders.

Uncle Boydie and 54 Elders Visit Cairns

When Norman and I heard from Uncle Boydie that he was coming to Cairns with a group of elders from all over Victoria on a boat cruise, we were excited at the prospect of having him in our own city and being able to honour him and his grandfather William. It was an excursion organised by Rumbalara Aged Care, and the elders had to make a significant contribution to the cost. It was a once in a lifetime opportunity for a group of elders from Victoria and Cairns to spend time together! We couldn't miss it!

We decided that it would be good to organise a reception for them and to organise for Aboriginal and Torres Strait Islanders from the Cairns area to welcome them. It was hard to get the arrival date in Cairns from Uncle as he hadn't been told. In the end, we had about three days' notice of their arrival, and we thought somehow, we have to get this happening in time. It was all going to happen on 17 November 2011 when this huge cruise ship came into our beautiful Cairns harbour.

I approached the Cairns and District Aboriginal and Torres Strait Islander (ATSI) Corporation for Elders (Gumba Gumba) with an invitation to a BBQ, and they were keen to come and meet the Victorian elders even at short notice. Without us asking, they donated $250 towards the food as they knew we were a small church and using our own funds.

We were going to use our church venue initially but decided we needed more room and more hands to help. We approached Wu Chopperen Health Service as we knew that they had a program where they visited the homes of elders to check on their health care needs, and we wanted to invite them to the BBQ. They agreed to be involved and offered their venue, which is large and spacious. I explained that some of the elders were on the board of Rumbalara, and it would be good if Wu Chopperen could organise a tour of their facilities for them after the BBQ. They were happy to do and provided some of their young staff to help cook the BBQ. I did the shopping and helped prepare food.

I approached two other Indigenous organisations personally and sent an email out inviting others. Dija Meta Aged and Disabled Home brought their people to the BBQ with their carers though the outing proved too long for some of them.

I put out a press release and invited local councillors, two of whom attended, Cr Rob Pyne and Cr Dianne Forsayth, and I organised the recording of the event on DVD.

Norman has a van given him by his father, and, along with a few members of our church with their private cars, we were waiting to pick the elders up from the cruise ship. Dija Meta ended up helping pick them up in a small bus. I stayed back at the BBQ to oversee everything and was keeping in touch with Lena Morris on the boat by mobile phone. She was responsible for looking after the elders.

The boat was going to be an hour or so late in docking because of the tide!! It was going to be more like 1 pm than 11.30am when we would welcome the elders and be able to eat. Fortunately, we had morning tea with cakes, cheese and biscuits to keep the elders going but little entertainment due to the three day lead time. However, local elders were able to use the time to catch up with each other and have a relaxed outing. The excitement was building towards the arrival of the Victorian elders. One young worker from Wu Chopperen played the didjeridoo for us.

Seith Fourmile was on hand to do the welcome to country but had to leave for a while because of the delay, and when the big moment came, Sandra Levers did the welcome to country with Seith doing it again when he returned later. Sandra paid homage to me for my long contribution to Aboriginal affairs.

Elders coming together ... Victorian and far north Queensland Elders meeting together at Wuchopperen Health Services.

Victorian and Cairns Elders at Wu Chopperen Health Service Cairns (Photo Christine Howes, Koori Mail 30.11.11)

It was a wonderful event. Norman opened in prayer and honoured both William and Uncle Boydie and all the elders from Victoria and Cairns. We showed a 10-minute DVD on the life of William Cooper and had speeches from Len Watson, President of Wu Chopperen and Betty Gibson, President of Gumba Gumba, Uncle Boydie and Lena Morris from Rumbalara and Cr Rob Pyne from Cairns Regional Council. He then called for a 1-minute silence to remember our elders, who are no longer with us.

Len Watson, Uncle Boydie, Lena Morris and Norman Miller (photo Christine Howes, Koori Mail 30.11.11)

I was the MC and remembered the work of the Victorian and Cairns Aboriginal Advancement Leagues as they worked together as part of FCAATSI to successfully push for the 1967 referendum. I also honoured my son Michael's father, Mick Miller, who was involved with this and much more in working for justice for Indigenous people in Australia.

We were grateful for the help of Gumba Gumba and Wu Chopperen to help us get our Victorian visitors to town for the bank and shopping and back to their boat as they were to leave the next day again to continue their journey, stopping at different ports on their way back to Victoria.

Visit to Uncle Boydie in Mooroopna February 2012

I needed to talk to Uncle Boydie some more and see Shepparton and Mooroopna where many of William's descendants live. Also, I wanted to make another visit to Barmah, Cummera and the Murray River. This time, Uncle Boydie was able to be our guide for the 3-day visit.

Norman came with me, and we timed our visit so that we would be in Shepparton for the 4th anniversary of the Apology to the Stolen Children generation on Monday 13 February. Also, we particularly timed it to be in Melbourne for Friday night's dinner on 17 February where Victorian Government would honour Aborigines, William Cooper among them.

We left Betty Jack's place at Doreen, Melbourne, where we were staying at 6, am and arrived at Queens Gardens Shepparton at 8.15am for the Apology breakfast. It was in the open with finger food, and it was hard to hear the speeches, but we were able to meet a few people. Uncle Boydie met us there and hosted us for the rest of our trip.

We met Leon Saunders at the breakfast, and he said he was a descendant of Thomas James. He said Thomas had a vision before he left Mauritius to come to Australia and work with Aborigines. He said Thomas had planned to be a doctor but went to a meeting Daniel Mathews had and offered his services to teach Aborigines.

At the Friary Coffee Shop, we spoke to Uncle Boydie, and Paul Briggs was there. Paul said Ps Doug Nicholls, a friend of his father, took him to Melbourne as an 18-year-old and found him a job. Ps Doug went to stay with Uncle Boydie when Uncle was first married.

Uncle said William was a big man, heavily built. He said:

> Mum told me he was a hard man on them, but the grandchildren could get away with a lot more. I was the youngest who lived with him in Melbourne. He was in his seventies, but he walked 12 km to the CBD. It took us 2 hours to do the (commemoration) walk in 2011.
>
> We walked over the bridge they named after him. The woman who bought the house we lived in named it after

grandfather. We walked to Federation Square and Friday night's event is at Federation Square.

He died when I was 13 years old at Mooroopna hospital. He got sick in Melbourne, and they brought him up here because Mum was here and he got worse and went into the hospital. When I asked what he died from, the doctor said he was just worn out. He was 80 years old and real bright and just after we left, he passed away. It was a big funeral. Many knew him.

When I look back now, he was a father figure to me. I was only a baby when I went to live with him. My family broke up. We lived on the Murray River before moving to Melbourne. I'm probably the only person alive who knew him.

I asked if Uncle could remember anything funny about those times and he said once he had an empty plate in front of him and said to his grandfather, "You ate my dinner, you mongrel!" I was only three years old, and they laughed. It was a great joke. They must have tipped my plate out and put an empty plate in front of me."

Uncle said his Mum was living on the riverbank and working in the fruit cannery and his step-Dad was picking fruit. He'd go to school at Mooroopna.

He remembered the people who came to meetings at William's place in Melbourne: "While with grandfather, I'd open the door for people attending meetings – Doug Nicholls, Lynch Cooper, Marg Tucker and Bill and Eric Onus and people who lived in Fitzroy, about 15-20 people.[170] A couple of white people came too – Arthur Burdeau who worked in the railways and Helen Baille."

Uncle talked a little about the family. He said William's second wife was Agnes Hamilton whose parents were Annie and William Hamilton. Agnes and William Cooper had Amy whose first husband was Alfred George Turner, and they had Boydie. After they broke up, she married Henry Charles.

Uncle Boydie said he remembered grandfather writing letters. Some days he could not get out of bed; he was so sick. He would put a red blanket around his shoulders, and he would still write letters. William had been writing for years before moving to Melbourne, but it went in the wastepaper basket because no one would listen. It was a lonely struggle for the rights of his people until he moved to Melbourne and founded the AAL.

Much earlier, William left the mission because of the regulations and went to a little place and ran a fish and chip shop for several years because he had to feed seven children. This was about 1906 at a place called Mulwala. He was about 45 years old.

William's first wife and he had two children, but one died. The other was a daughter called Emma, who married Tom Donolly. Emma's son and grandson are buried with William at Cummera.

Dan was the eldest child of William's second marriage, and he died in action in the First World War. Another son Gillison spent all his working life in the Victorian railways and became the station master at Mooroopna. He also was the "man in grey" in a cubicle at Spencer St station who you could go to and ask questions. William's son Lynch won the Stawell Gift run in 1928, the year Uncle Boydie was born, and in 1929, he was the world sprint champion. He married Eva Christian.

Amy, Uncle's mother, ran a hostel in Melbourne and Sally ran a safe house in Melbourne for young Aboriginal girls. She married Mick Russell, a New Zealander. She had one son, Kevin who is Kevin Russell's father.

William and Sarah looked after three other grandchildren – Cyril who played for Carlton, Esme and Bruce. Bruce's mother Jessie had died in childbirth. Cyril and Bruce both fought in Papua New Guinea (PNG) and were not the same when they came back.

Uncle remembered one of William's contemporaries who worked for Aboriginal rights- Jack Patten. He said "He was a funny man, jolly to be around. He was a nice fella, and everybody liked him."

After this time of talking about family history, we went to a BBQ lunch down by the river which was part of the Apology Day celebrations. One of Thomas James' descendants was very busy cooking, even though he is an elder. A couple of young girls helped him.

Yorta Yorta Nation Aboriginal Corporation

Uncle Boydie took us to the Yorta Yorta Nation offices in Shepparton, which are very impressive looking. One of their most important totems is the long neck turtle, more commonly called the broad shell turtle. It is on the Yorta Yorta Nation logo.

Yorta Yorta Nation Aboriginal Corporation (YYNAC) was incorporated in 1998 and represented the clans speaking the Yorta Yorta language, including the Kaitheban, Wollithiga, Moira, Ulupna, Bangerang, Kwat Kwat, Yalaba Yalaba and Ngurai-illiam-wurrung. Yorta Yorta country is within an area currently known as the central Murray Goulburn region in northern Victoria and southern NSW.

Yorta Yorta Nation has had a climate change working group since 2008 and when we visited were working with the universities who were offering them assistance to train youth to interview elders who have the cultural knowledge. They have already done a cultural mapping exercise looking at current harvesting activities on Yorta Yorta country and found a large number of sites of significance. Other research planned will cover sustainability of flora and what water needs requirements there are. They are planning an Indigenous Knowledge Survey.

Though they lost the Yorta Yorta native title claim, which was disappointing to many, their joint management arrangement with national parks enables them to maintain their cultural identity into the landscape.

They are continuing the work of William Cooper, lobbying the government for water allocations and land and for self-management. There have been many petitions since 1874.

A valuable lobby group is the Murray Darling River Indigenous Nations which consists of thirteen Indigenous nations in four states – Queensland, NSW, Victoria and SA – who work together to preserve Aboriginal cultural and environmental knowledge and land management of the Murray Darling river area.

Bangerang Cultural Centre

The plan for Tuesday (14 February) was to visit Barmah forest, the Murray River, Echuca and Cummeragunja. I rang Marlene Atkinson as Esme Bamblett had told me she was at Cummera, but she was running the Bangerang Cultural Centre in Shepparton, so Uncle Boydie stopped there as it was on the road out to Barmah forest. Marlene showed us around.

Opened in 1982, it is the first Aboriginal cultural 'keeping place or museum' to be developed and managed by the Aboriginal community in Australia. Artefacts and artworks from Aboriginal communities across Australia are housed there though it concentrates on local communities of the Murray and Goulburn Valleys. In Victoria, the largest number of Aboriginal people, about 7000, live in the Murray Goulburn region.

It was an amazing place, and it had a very large possum skin cloak in a case that had a map of tribal land on the back of it. Life-like scenes of traditional living of the Aborigines were displayed in dioramas designed by George Browning. The titles of the dioramas, beginning in a clockwise direction from the entrance, are: 'Bogong Moth Feast,' Riverina Economy," Mount William Technology' and 'Corroboree'. I especially liked the scene of the family on the Murray River.

What was very interesting was they had a section on the photos of elders and the Bangerang and Yorta Yorta enjoy the same elders, many of whom are famous. William Cooper and Doug Nicholls, for example, were there. It seems that that the Bangerang are part of the Yorta Yorta and some people call the Yorta Yorta land claim the Yorta Yorta/Bangerang land claim.

Bangerang Cultural Centre, Uncle Boydie beside photo of William Cooper and other elders 2012 (Photo Norman Miller)

The Banks of the Murray River

Uncle Boydie took us to the banks of the Murray River near Barmah, where he had lived with his grandfather William. There are no houses here now. They had their house a bit back from the water's edge because of flooding. William lived here after he left Cummera and his home was a very basic one made of hessian which he painted white. It had a corrugated iron roof and a fire for warmth. There were other houses here too at the time. It was stunning.

It was wonderful to be able to see the place alongside the Murray River, where Uncle Boydie lived with William. Uncle showed us the exact spot where they lived. We were on the Victorian side of the Murray River, and as we looked across the river, Uncle showed us where Cummera is located on the NSW side. He showed the land where the house of Thomas and Shadrach James had been. Families were living all along the river and all along a path to the river in the days of the 1939 strike. Being here was a very special moment!

He was disappointed to see, in the place he used to live, a fence with padlocks on it which cut off access to the river. He said it should be public access all along the river bank.

Based on what Uncle Boydie showed David Jack about where the families had their houses, David constructed a map which is shown here. Uncle Boydie explained this camp was a refuge when the black cars came to Cummera looking for children to remove from families. The people would scatter and cross the river. He remembers the names of the families based their children as he was young then. There were some missionaries and a church in the camp as well. William and Sarah Cooper's dwewlling was left of the vertical fence.

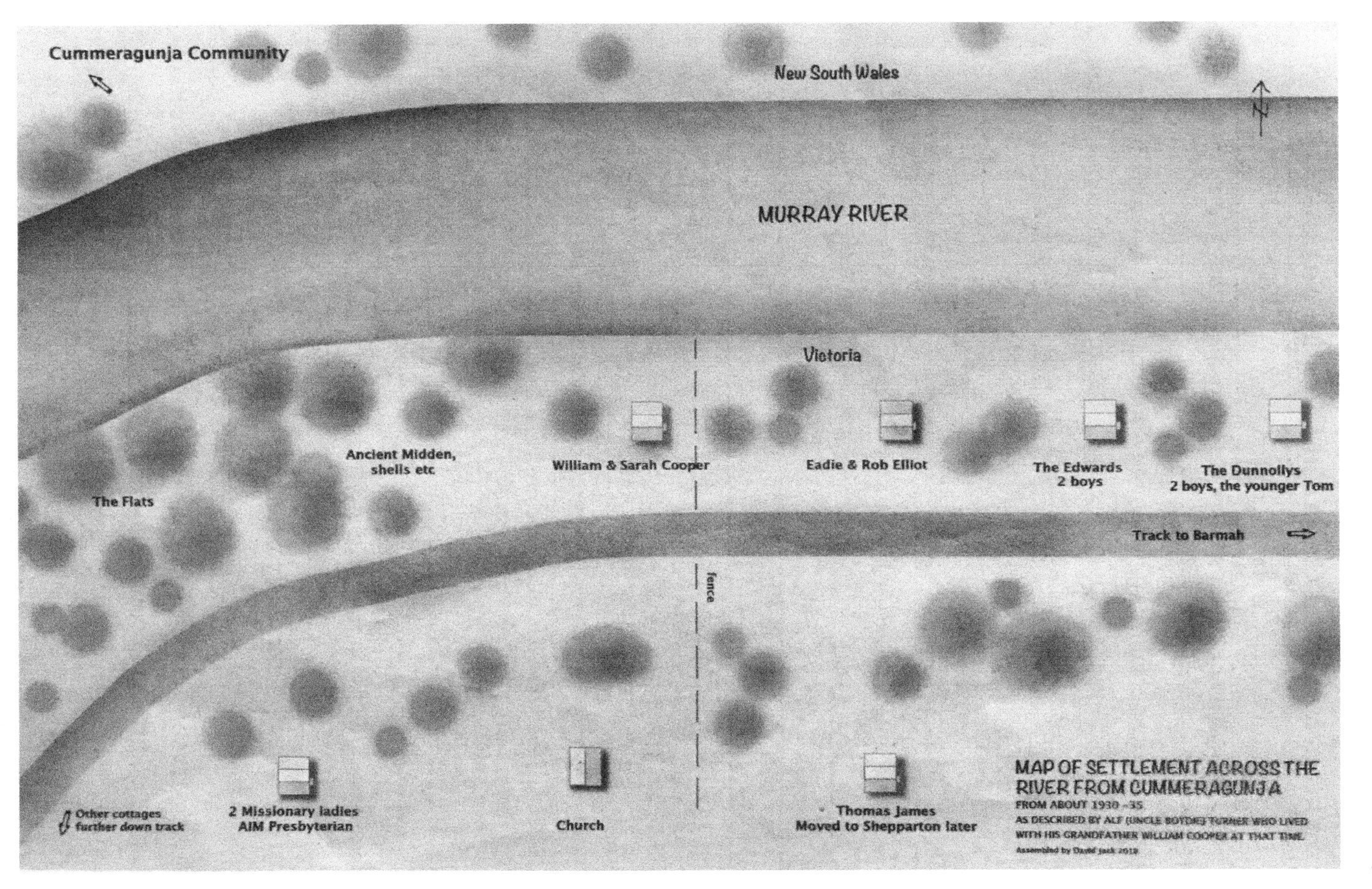

Cummeragunja Community
New South Wales
MURRAY RIVER
Victoria
Ancient Midden,
shells etc
William & Sarah Cooper
Eadie & Rob Elliot
The Edwards
2 boys
The Dunnollys
2 boys, the younger Tom
The Flats
Track to Barmah
fence
Other cottages
further down track
2 Missionary ladies
AIM Presbyterian
Church
Thomas James
Moved to Shepparton later
MAP OF SETTLEMENT ACROSS THE
RIVER FROM CUMMERAGUNJA
FROM ABOUT 1930 –35
AS DESCRIBED BY ALF (UNCLE BOYDIE) TURNER WHO LIVED
WITH HIS GRANDFATHER WILLIAM COOPER AT THAT TIME.

Yorta Yorta Nation Centre at Barmah Forest

We then went to the small town of Barmah and visited the Yorta Yorta Nation headquarters, which is linked to the Yorta Yorta Nation office in Shepparton. This is where the Yorta Yorta Nation store their the archives in a special room which they hope to make into a library. A lot of information from the native title case is stored here, and some volunteers and Yorta Yorta people have indexed it.

Colin Walker and Uncle Boydie beside Yorta Yorta Nation sign with Yorta Yorta Nation Barmah office in the background (Photo Norman Miller)

We spoke to Kellie Jones, currently Manager of Yenbena Training Centre who said they have a rangers program with Parks Victoria. They have five rangers on secondment to Parks Victoria to get skills and then they'll come back to Yorta Yorta as their own employees. Part of their work will be doing traditional burn-offs of protected areas.

Yenbena Training Centre runs Cert 1, Cert 11 and Cert 111 courses in Conservation and Land Management and delivers other accredited training and lifestyle courses to Yorta Yorta, Indigenous and mainstream students. They have a partnership arrangement with Greening Australia who will teach the students and Yenbena will own the accreditation. The students will stay in Shepparton, Echuca and Nathalia.

After a re-registration and compliance process, Yenbena is now an Indigenous-owned and operated registered training organisation (RTO). "We've got no special funding. We apply like others" said Kellie. We're just more likely to take Indigenous students and utilise elders in all cultural aspects. We plan to provide Gr 11 and Gr 12 students with a pathway to university in the future."

Uncle Boydie told Kellie about the fence with padlocks preventing access to the river where he had lived with William. She was concerned and said she'd follow up.

Kellie said that by July 2011 they hoped to open their doors officially. NSW Health would put on a 2-day course for Aboriginal and Torres Strait Islanders in Mental Health First Aid that starts in March.

She said "Yelima used to be a cattle property, but now it is Yorta Yorta Nation property (since the 1990s). We hope to establish tourism and outback accommodation there eventually. Colin Walker, Uncle Max and Aunty Rachelle camp there and look after the place."

Kellie said they planned to collect seeds in conjunction with Parks Victoria to develop a nursery to restart the native plants. The young people doing the training will develop it. She said, "I'm passionate about my work. Seeing the DVD *Lousy Little Sixpence* about the stolen children changed my life".

Colin Walker, Yorta Yorta Elder

We phoned Colin Walker hoping to catch up with him, but he was out so we left the building to get some lunch and we met him in the street. It was too late for lunch, so we went to a little shop/café instead, where I got some tourist brochures. We did manage to yarn with Colin standing up in the street for a while.

He has written a book called *Mission Voices* and his most recent book which he said he had a copy of for Uncle Boydie is *The Living History of Colin Walker*. Col and Uncle Boydie's grandmothers were sisters. Col's mother was Florence Johnston, the first Aboriginal nurse, and she worked as a nurse on the steamers on the Murray River. Florence was a sister to Agnes, William's second wife.

Uncle Boydie and Colin Walker in front of scar tree once used to make a canoe (Photo Norman Miller)

Barmah Forest and Lakes

We went down the Moira Lakes Rd. There was a Barmah Café and Park. Uncle used to milk cows for a farmer before school. During the war, he made charcoal here and would ride his bicycle the 3-hour trip from Mooroopna on Sunday afternoon for work and back Friday afternoon.

Moira Lakes (Photo Norman Miller)

As we drove along in Uncle's car, we passed cattle yards on the right where they used to do a muster and branding once a year. They don't do it now because there are only a few brumbies[171] here. We came to a place called the Dharnya Centre. The visitors centre was closed because of white ants. Before, schools would come and see Aboriginal exhibits, and there was accommodation here. The Yorta Yorta would run programs on location. The place was now deserted except for a caretaker. There are a lot of tiger snakes who now have free rein. Uncle is very fit and has a lot of energy as we were to do a lot of walking that day in the hot sun, and it didn't bother him a bit.

Uncle Boydie showing author his country where he lived with William and Sarah (Photo Norman Miller)

There's a fenced-off Aboriginal site of significance and Uncle Boydie came here during the Yorta Yorta land claim. We saw four wild emus. We went deeper and deeper in the Barmah forest. There were sand ridges and box trees and many gum trees. This is the biggest red gum forest in the world and an amazingly beautiful place. We saw some stunning lakes.

We came to Snake Is and saw two egrets. Suddenly, 30-40 birds flocked across the lake. The Barmah Lakes fill from the Murray River. When Uncle was small, they used to take horse and buggy across the lake when they could. We travelled a long way into the forest before heading back.

Birds fly over lakes in Barmah forest (photo Norman Miller)

Before leaving, we saw a national parks sign that declared that Barmah is Yorta Yorta country.

Barmah National Park sign (Photo Norman Miller)

Cummergunja Visit

We made a visit to Cummera where William lived for a time and where he is buried. The NSW Land Council runs it as it is on the NSW side of the border. A rice farm is nearby. Uncle didn't seem to know people living here or want to spend much time here apart from going to the cemetery. He said people from other places had moved in here. Uncle never lived at Cummera though he went to school there. The church sometimes holds services at the school we visited the school before we left.

We went straight to the cemetery where William is buried. Norman and I had been here before with David Jack. There are a lot of bindis. Uncle was disappointed at the lack of upkeep. There are three graves with William's, all from the Dunolly family.

It was very moving again to see William's grave. A plaque was put on it in 1995 by a great-granddaughter. Uncle Boydie's wife's parents are buried here - Sophie Amy Briggs, died 16/11/82 and William Briggs died 6/2/64. Lady Gladys Nicholls (1906-1981) and Sir Doug Nicholls (1906-1988) are buried here side by side. It says, "we pressed toward the mark for the prize of the high calling of God in Christ Jesus." Their son, Ralph Doug Nicholls is buried there too (1949-1996).

Uncle Boydie and author outside old schoolhouse at Cummera (Photo Norman Miller)

Visit to Rumbalara Aboriginal Cooperative

The following day, we visited Rumbalara Aboriginal Cooperative Ltd in Mooroopna with Uncle Boydie, who lives at Mooroopna near Shepparton. It has offices in Shepparton, but its biggest operation is in Mooroopna. Rumbalara has a Community Justice Panel, a Women's Family Violence service, Men's Offender Mentoring and Support, Men's Family Violence, Youth Justice and Women's Offender Mentoring and Support and other services.

Uncle Boydie said there were 4-5,000 Aboriginal people on Rumbalara's books and it was the biggest Aboriginal organisation outside Melbourne. It has 3-4 acres on the riverbank at Mooroopna. They couldn't build too close to the riverbank because of flooding.

We saw the new medical centre, which has three doctors. We met Bobby Parker there who recognised us from the visit to Cairns. We visited the Harmony Centre, where there are family violence classes for men and women on different days. A teacher arrived for a class while we were outside. They also have a dentist there.

We spent most of our time talking to Lance James, the Bringing Them Home worker. His grandmother was William Cooper's sister Ada who was married to Grandpa (Thomas) James. Lance lives at Barmah across the road from Yenbena and drives to Mooroopna for work. The police took Lance's mother at 14 years of age and trained her as a domestic at Cootamundra Girls Home. She had to work for two years to get her freedom. This is another incredible story of survival against the odds.

Rumbalara, Mooroopna L-R Lance James, Norman and Barbara Miller and Uncle Boydie

Rumbalara preserved some old houses to show tourists and schools what people used to live in before they moved them off the river bank into new housing because of the flooding. Lance said the Council of Elders was meeting at Yenbena on Friday which meant he couldn't go to Melbourne for the Honour Board dinner. They were expecting sixteen to come because there are sixteen family groups.

Lance spoke about the Drug and Alcohol and Mental Health and Emotional Wellbeing programs. We talked in his kitchen. He said the kindy used to be here but moved to Shepparton. We saw the aged care area which wasn't residential (that was in Shepparton) but they could have indoor meals or an outdoor BBQ here. There are thirty-five aged care beds. That is stage I and they'll expand to seventy. There are thirty-five self-contained units. He said Shepparton and Mooroopna have the highest Indigenous population in country Victoria.

Rumbalara employs about 150 people and is the biggest service provider in Victoria. There are lots of trees around and different buildings for different purposes. They have boys doing apprenticeships on building projects and getting their licences. Eighty per cent of the staff are women because of the caring role.

Lance said Rumbalara leads in Aboriginal health and aged care. Lena Morris, the manager of Home and Community Care (HACC) has taken them on holidays on house boats on the Murray River and other places. Norman and I remembered Lena from when she brought a group of fifty-four Victorian Aboriginal elders to Cairns the previous November and we hosted them with a BBQ at Wu Chopperen Health Service.

They have a Woongi Mental Health program because too many young men commit suicide. They are going to build a healing centre which will be part therapy and part counselling.

Rumbalara have community-based programs for offenders. He said, "They can clean up and do their hours here. It fits in with the Koori Court. Col Walker is on it. We need to retrain elders what to do. Not just to say I know your mother or father. We'll soon start to refer them to DV[172] programs at the Harmony Centre. There they'll learn to communicate not just with their hands."

On May 26, Lance said they'll have a march and BBQ making the point the constitution should acknowledge the first people. Lance is co-chair of the local Reconciliation Committee. He said he'd like to bring Maloga back. There are sixty odd graves there but the landowners have put a shed over it.

It was impressive to see Rumbalara and meet the people who work there, especially Lance. William, Ada and Grandpa James have left behind very capable family who are working hard for the good of their community and doing a commendable job.

Uncle drove us back to Shepparton to where our car was parked. However, he was not ready to say goodbye after three full days of spending time with us, so he invited us back to Mooroopna again, this time to his home. We happily followed him in our car.

Uncle Boydie's Home

He invited us in for a cuppa. I think he'd grown quite fond of us as family and we felt that way about him too and really didn't want to say goodbye either. He had many family photos of his beautiful wife and children. Amy had died 18 years before of cancer so Uncle had lived alone a long time. However, he lives a very full life with regular meetings of Rumbalara to attend and his daughter and her family close by.

Uncle said there is some contention as to whether a statue of his grandfather should be put outside Parliament House in Melbourne alongside the statue of Ps Doug Nicholls or by the lake in Shepparton where we had the BBQ. Shepparton Council are reluctant as William didn't actually come from there. Uncle favours beside Ps Doug's as many more people will see it. He said there had been a flurry of articles re William Cooper but it had only happened since the Jews picked it up.

On Uncle Boydie's mantelpiece lay an old certificate which amazingly predates the Jewish interest which says:

Maribyrnong City Council

Acknowledges the contribution of

William Cooper

Who has lived and worked

In the western suburbs of Melbourne

And has advanced the rights and

Community life of Indigenous and non-Indigenous Australians

Aboriginal National Reconciliation Week Ceremony 29 May 1998

What a treasure!

Victorian Indigenous Honour Roll Feb 2012

After leaving Uncle Boydie, we drove back to Melbourne. Abe had secured an invitation for us to the Victorian Indigenous Honour Roll in Melbourne on 17 February 2012. The invitations were sent out by the Hon Jeanette Powell, the Minister for Aboriginal Affairs for this inaugural Honour Roll. Federal Minister for Aboriginal Affairs, Jenny Macklin also attended. We knew it was highly likely that William Cooper would be one of those to be honoured and so he was. It was a lovely walk along the Yarra River, past stalls and displays to the venue – Zinc at Federation Square.

Aunty Joy Wandin-Murphy of the Wurudjuri did a welcome to country, waving a gumleaf branch. The One Fire dance group did three dances. This happened outside with passers by watching and the Yarra River in the background. It was so engaging that many of those passing by stopped, enthralled.

Honour Roll event (L-R) Barbara Miller, Aunty Joy Wandin-Murphy and Colleen Marion seated, (back row) Uncle Boydie and grandson Nathan Drummond (Photo Norman Miller)

We were then invited to be seated at dinner tables and Debra Cheetam was the MC. We sat with Abe, Colleen Marion, Uncle Boydie, his grandson Nathan Drummond who was on his way home from boarding school, Carol Briggs and others.

I spoke to Herb Patten who joined the band and played the gumleaf impromptu. Apparently, he is famous for it and people encouraged him to jump up and play. His wife was with him and was honoured. I asked him about Cec Patten as I knew Cec in my days with the Aboriginal movement in Sydney. He said Cec was the famous activist Jack Patten's son. I was very happy to make this connection.

Honour Roll event – Herb Patten, centre (photo Norman Miller)

Premier Ted Ballieu honoured the Kulin nation. He said in 1834, the first settlement was nearly, "where we are right now. It was Freshwater Falls. We now have here a lovely building called the Freshwater Building and it's a place of meeting."

The Premier said that the Victorian government wanted to recognise the achievements of Indigenous people, redress imbalance and promote Indigenous success. The Honour Board was a way to do that. He said Lionel Rose, the famous Aboriginal boxer, had a big impact on him which is why the government organised a state funeral for him. He hoped other states would do the same and have Honour Boards like Victoria as all the inductees were role models.

He said he personally nominated William Barak and Doug Nicholls. "Doug was the first Aboriginal to be knighted. We have a statue of him. Barak was a man of peace and diplomacy. He worked for cross-cultural understanding. William Barak's image is on a skyscraper overlooking the city."

The Premier gave a shield as a gift for the men and a coolamon[173] for the women. The list of inductees was – Geraldine Briggs, Lester Harradine, Elizabeth Pike, Lorraine 'Bunta' Patten, William Barak, Lionel Rose, Joan Vickery, Nessie Skuta, Alby Clark, Doug Nicholls, Dorothy (Dot) Peter, Joan Robinson, Alma Thorpe, Melva Johnson, Johnny Mullagh, Alf Bamblett, Merle Jackomos, William Cooper, John Stuart Murray and Archie Roach. They are all high achievers, some passed away and representatives of a number of different tribes. Their families and friends were present to celebrate this momentous occasion.

It was an opportunity for me to meet a several people including Andrew Jackomos whose mother Merle was honoured. Andrew's father Alick was a prolific photographer and Andrew said he was happy for me to use photos his father had taken for my book.

I spoke to Ron James who is the head of Rumbalara Cooperative in Shepparton. We hadn't met him while there earlier in the week. He was Advancement League chairman and is related to Thomas James. He said he knew Mick Miller, my first husband, who was a national Aboriginal leader. Esme Bamblett and her aunty were there along with many others. Colleen said it would be ten years next year since she began activities to recognise William Cooper.

Norman and I were so privileged to be part of this event. The families of those being inducted into the Honour Roll were only able to have a limited number attend, and we were able to attend as part of Uncle Boydie's family, a great honour.

Chapter 13

William's Story Lives on Through Uncle Boydie

Cooper's Unfinished Business with German Consulate and the British Crown

Norman and I met Uncle Boydie, Abe and David in Melbourne on 20 September 2012. I mentioned the idea of Uncle Boydie giving William's petition to the German Consulate in Melbourne on the same day as my first edition book launch. It made him think of presenting to the Queen of England the petition that William wanted to give to King George V, her grandfather and later King George VI, her father. William had gathered 1814 signatures on it in the 1930s. The Australian government of the time would not forward it on because even though Aborigines were British citizens, they were not Australian citizens. They had lost their citizenship at federation. This had then sparked off the Day of Mourning, Aborigines Sunday which became NAIDOC and the 1967 referendum fight to change the constitution. These were two pieces of unfinished business of William Cooper that Uncle Boydie took on as his own task to complete.

Uncle Boydie, author and Abe discussing the book in Melbourne 2012 (photo David Jack)

Norman and I had been to England in 1997 to a Reconciliation conference at Coventry Cathedral. The Anglican church had worked on reconciliation between the British and Germans from the charred remains of the Cathedral due to bombing during World War 2.

Norman gave a heartfelt apology to the British for the bitterness held by some Aboriginal people to the British for the colonisation of Australia, and I apologised for the "anti-Pommy" attitudes of Australians to the British. The conference attendees did not understand this, and no one responded. Nearly a year later, however, one of the leaders at the conference, Jacky Hopkins, whose conscience was pricked by what happened, travelled to Australia and all the way to us in Cairns and received our apology and said sorry for what the British had done.

Independently of this, the British prayer movement, led by Brian Mills and Roger Mitchell, approached the Australian Prayer Network, led by Ben Gray and Brian Pickering to do some British-Australian reconciliation over colonisation. A large team of British came to Australia in 1998, and we hosted them in Cairns at a conference while they travelled for six weeks through the land saying "sorry" to various groups, particularly Aborigines. We were part of the Australian team that travelled Britain in 1999 saying "thank you" for the apology to multiple groups.

Former Prime Minister, Kevin Rudd, made his famous apology to Aborigines in 2008, directed mainly to the stolen generation but for other events in Australia's history also. This was a watershed moment. However, Norman has always felt that it would be good for the Queen to apologise to Aborigines on behalf of the British government as the colonial power responsible for the decimation of Australia's Aboriginal population on settlement.

Abe suggested we all travel together to England next year so that Uncle Boydie could hand over the petition, Norman could further his cause for the apology from the Queen, and I could launch my first book on William Cooper. Abe would like to see us all travel together to Israel and Germany to launch the book also. We didn't have the finances to do so, but Uncle Boydie's dream of doing so was to build.

Uncle Boydie's Dream Team

Abe became Uncle Boydie's secretary as he called it but really mover and shaker and launched Uncle Boydie's Dream. It had two goals, one for Uncle Boydie to present William's letter of protest re *Kristallnacht* to the German government in Germany and secondly, for Uncle Boydie to present William's petition to the Queen in England. These goals needed, of course, high-level diplomacy and considerable finances. Norman and I, David Jack, Matthew Busby Andrews and others who joined us from time to time, formed the Uncle Boydie's Dream Team and we met regularly by phone link up to plan and progress these goals.

William's letter and the accompanying petition ended up in the National Archives, and Uncle Boydie, Abe, Norman and I were able to meet with National Archives staff in Canberra to look at the material. They brought it to the Australian Centre for Christianity and Culture ACCC) on 21 May 2013. Matt and Abe helped set this up, and Rev Prof Dr James

Haire was facilitative of the meeting. He was a Professor of Theology at Charles Sturt University and past president of the National Council of Churches. The ACCC is a national ecumenical centre encouraging dialogue with other faiths, exploring reconciliation and the interface between faith and Australian culture. We arrived at a beautiful site on a small knoll overlooking Lake Burley Griffin and just south of the Parliamentary Triangle.

It was exciting to look at these original materials. However, to our dismay, the original signatures had been lost. We needed to make a replica of William's petition and get new signatures as the original signatures had been lost.

L-R Abe Schwarz, Dr James Haire, Uncle Boydie Turner, Barbara Miller, Matt Busby Andrews and two staff of the National Archives 21.5.2013

Gathering Signatures for the Petition

We decided not to have an online petition but to get handwritten signatures as William Cooper had done. David prepared it on buff paper, and I did a cover as an explanation to people as to why they should sign it given the passage of time and its symbolic nature. David's son, Tim Jack, set up a page for me on my book website so that people could download either a petition for Indigenous people to sign or one for non-Indigenous people to sign. All petition sheets were to go to Abe who collated them. Matt set up a website called Uncle Boydie's Dream to encourage people to sign the petition. David and I helped him with photos. Abe was very active in getting signatures and Norman, and I got signatures at my book launches and at Christian conferences where Norman and I spoke.

One of the places we got signatures was at a very historic event, the launch of the Recognise campaign to promote Indigenous recognition in the constitution. I was privileged to walk alongside Michael Long, the champion Indigenous AFL player as he led off the walk of the Journey to Recognition on 27 May 2013 in Melbourne. It was Reconciliation Week. Thousands joined the walk which was taken by different teams all over Australia. I was able to get the signature of Prime Minister Tony Abbott at this event after explaining to him the purpose.

Abe Schwarz, Barbara Miller and Prime Minister Tony Abbott at Recognise Campaign launch Melbourne 27 May 2013. Barbara got PM Abbott to sign the replica of Cooper's Petition

Visit to Prince William

Once we had gathered a comparable number of signatures to the 1930s petition, negotiations got underway to deliver it. We were still meeting in phone hook-ups to progress the matter. I provided Abe with contacts I had in London, but he managed to get access to a contact in Buckingham Palace. We also had the cautious assistance of Prime Minister Tony Abbott's staff, and Abe and Matt tried to get a meeting with Prince William while he was visiting Australia.

With two days' notice, the government informed us they had arranged a five-minute stand-up meeting with Prince William for Good Friday in Sydney.

I couldn't get there from Cairns but on 18 April 2014, Uncle Boydie, Abe and Matt met the Prince in a visit that extended to about 15 minutes. Uncle Boydie said Prince William wanted to know what life was like for his grandfather and how people had made things hard for him. It was the great hope of our team that Uncle Boydie could hand the replica petition to the Prince and William Cooper's intentions would finally be achieved.

However, it was not to be. Government staff instructed Uncle Boydie before he met the Prince that he was not permitted to hand him the petition. Every part of him wanted to hand it over, but Uncle Boydie respected protocol. Prince William moved towards the petition, hoping for a look. Swiftly, a man pulled it away. He would have been a government official.

"I thought he'd be the stuffy type, but he was a genuine bloke," Uncle Boydie said, and he said that he would help me in any way that he could. Emboldened, Uncle asked, "Can you help us get this petition through to the Queen, sir?" Uncle Boydie said the Prince's reply was, 'I certainly will'."

Uncle Boydie, Matt Busby Andrews and Abe Schwarz meet Prince William in Sydney 18.4.2014

Presenting Petition to the Governor-General

Uncle Boydie was advised that the protocol was to send the petition to the Governor-General who would send it to the Queen. Rather than posting it to the Governor-General and then having him post it to the Queen, we wanted Uncle Boydie to be able to do as much in person as possible. Abe managed to get us an appointment with Sir Peter Cosgrove, the Governor-General at 3 pm 27 May 2014 at Government House, Canberra to hand over replica petition. This was a momentous occasion. Uncle Boydie, Abe and David travelled from Victoria, and I flew from Cairns.

We stayed at the Canberra House of Prayer for All Nations in Yarralumla near the Saudi Arabian embassy. Uncle Boydie doesn't share the fervent faith of his grandfather, but it was supportive of our purposes and low-cost accommodation near our meeting. The next day Uncle Boydie and I addressed the Canberra Pastors Network breakfast held at the prayer house. The son of a prominent Jewish family in Canberra drove one of the cars for us, and we met them for lunch.

David prepared a beautifully bound folder for Uncle to present that had a photo of Uncle and of King George V on the cover. He then placed the petition inside. Only three people could go inside, and David graciously allowed that to be me, and he took photos of the occasion.

It was all very formal, and the Governor-General offered us afternoon tea. Sir Peter Cosgrove warmly expressed his admiration for the achievements of both William Cooper and Uncle Boydie and promised to send the petition to the Queen. The meeting was supposed to last 20 minutes, but the Governor-General extended it to 45 minutes.

Uncle Boydie was "over the moon." He said, "I feel that my dream to complete my grandfather William Cooper's business is accomplished."

Uncle Boydie felt that he had picked up the baton of where his grandfather had left off, and he had completed the task for him. Eighteen months of work of gathering signatures and lobbying for this moment had borne fruit. He hoped it would have a practical effect for Aborigines today.

It was especially poignant that this meeting had occurred in Reconciliation Week and on the 47th anniversary to the very day of the 1967 referendum. It was also the 47th anniversary of the reunification of Jerusalem and Jewish access to the Western Wall, a sacred site.

Correspondence between the Australian Governor-Generals staff and Buckingham Palace staff would continue.

Abe Schwarz, Barbara Miller and Uncle Boydie present William Cooper's Petition to the Governor-General at Government House Canberra 27.5.2014 (photo David Jack)

Museum of Australian Democracy

The following day, 28 May, Uncle Boydie gave an address at the Museum of Australian Democracy at Old Parliament House Canberra with Abe and I accompanying him. Reconciliation Australia supported the event. It was terrific that Uncle Boydie could stand beside a statue of King George V of England, the intended recipient of William Cooper's petition.

It took until 1971 for an Indigenous Australian, Liberal member Neville Bonner of Queensland, to enter Parliament. William was not to see this day as it was 34 years after his petition was to be forwarded to the King of England.

Uncle Boydie with Statue of King George V at the Museum of Australian Democracy Canberra (photo David Jack)

The Governor-General Presents Petition to the Queen

The Governor-General was true to his word and delivered the petition to the Queen, much to the excitement of Uncle and our team. On 5 August 2014, the Australian The Governor-General, accompanied by Lady Cosgrove, was invested as a Knight in the Order of Australia by Her Majesty the Queen at Balmoral, Scotland. At a ceremony in Aberdeenshire, Scotland, Sir Peter finally relayed the document to the Queen.[174] She was able to receive it as it was not a live petition but a historical document. Prime Minister Tony Abbott was supportive of the handover.

At Balmoral, the Governor-General and Lady Cosgrove attend an audience with Her Majesty the Queen, at which the Governor-General is invested as a Knight in the Order of Australia. photo: http://www.gg.gov.au/events/audience-her-majesty-queen

Victorian Indigenous Honour Roll

Uncle Boydie had been inducted onto the Victorian Indigenous Honour Roll the week before for his own contribution to Indigenous affairs and well as being a custodian of William Cooper's legacy. They hailed him as:

> A dignified elder with a dream - Uncle Alf Turner – or Uncle Boydie to most – is a true gentleman, and believed to be the oldest living Yorta Yorta Elder in Victoria. In addition to making his own substantial contribution to his community, he is custodian of the legacy of his grandfather, the Aboriginal leader William Cooper…
>
> After suffering the loss of his wife in 1995, Uncle Boydie focused his energy on Aboriginal affairs. He was the longest-serving board member of the Rumbalara Aboriginal Co-operative, helping to develop its range of health, housing, and aged care services over 16 dedicated years. Uncle Boydie also supported the Yorta Yorta native title claim and worked closely with the Yorta Yorta Nation Aboriginal Corporation to broker land management agreements with state authorities. All the while, it was his grandfather's values that guided him…[175]

Officials honoured Jack Patten (1905-1957) and other recipients who have made an impressive contribution. Jack was recognised as, "A leader who forged a path towards equality - Jack Patten was one of the great Aboriginal leaders of the 20th century and set the agenda for the civil rights movement in Australia. The Yorta Yorta man spoke out against Aboriginal inequality with such vigour that his words resounded across the land."[176]

He settled in La Perouse, Sydney and Jack worked with Aboriginal leader William Ferguson, who launched the Aborigines Progressive Association (APA) in 1937. Jack was the organisation's first president.

Together with William Cooper, they organised the Day of Mourning in Sydney, and Jack was a key person in the Cummera walk off.

William Cooper Footbridge

The local council opened a footbridge at the Footscray railway station and named it after one of their local identities, William Cooper, in December 2014. The council put photos of William Cooper, William and his family, and of our Uncle Boydie's Dream team meeting the Governor-General on the plaque. Footscray Mayor Nam Quach officiated, and William's great-grandson Kevin Russell attended with Uncle Boydie.

Kevin Russell, Alf Turner and Footscray Mayor Nam Quach at opening 2014 (photo David Jack)

Australian Hall, Sydney

For the first time in Sydney, at Australian Hall, where the 1938 Day of Mourning event was held, supporters gathered to honour William

Cooper. It was September 2017. Speakers from the Cooper family, the Indigenous community, the Jewish community, the Christian community and the Labor movement took part. The organising committee for this event was Uncle Boydie, Abe Schwarz, Alex Kats, Vivienne Fink, Eva Sommers and Renata Schnall. It was a historic moment for them to come to the very place that William Ferguson, Jack Patten, William Cooper and other leaders had held their memorable protest.

The William Cooper Legacy Project

Abe set up the William Cooper Legacy Project to raise finances for Uncle Boydie and a team to travel to London, Belgium, Israel and Germany to further the legacy of William Cooper. A series of events ensued including concerts, film nights and educational activities. Considerable donations came in from the Jewish community. I will cover the story of this trip in more detail in the companion book to this one on William Cooper's stand for Jewish people.

Briefly, on Monday 23 October 2017, Uncle Boydie and his supporters left Melbourne on their way to London. From here they went to Ypres, Belgium to visit the grave of William Cooper's son, Dan Cooper who was killed in World War 1. They then travelled to Israel for Uncle to lay a wreath on behalf of Indigenous diggers (soldiers) at Be'er Sheva (Beersheba) on the 100th anniversary of the Battle of Be'er Sheva. And to top it all off, they went to Germany to present William Cooper's letter of protest re *Kristallnacht* to the German government. They also took part in the moving *Kristallnacht* ceremonies. Those who travelled with the 88-year-old Uncle Boydie to help make the journey a success were his son, Lance Turner, Abe Schwarz, David Jack (videographer) and Emmanuel Santos (photographer).

When they arrived in London, Uncle Boydie wanted to see the petition that Australia's Governor-General had handed to the Queen. However, Australia House was a bit embarrassed that they didn't know where it was. Uncle and team were able, however, to have afternoon tea at Australia House with the Deputy High Commissioner. They also visited Buckingham Palace, where Uncle Boydie looked longingly at the possible home of his petition. As their stay was only short, they were at London airport ready to leave for Belgium when they received a call from Australia House that they had located the petition at Windsor Castle. In a heart-rending decision, Uncle Boydie had to pass up the opportunity to see the petition at Windsor Castle as Abe had made arrangements for them to meet personnel from the French and Belgium embassies in Belgium.

L-R Dale Eaton from the Australian High Commission Uncle Boydie and Abe Schwarz at Buckingham Palace 2017 (photo David Jack)

80th Anniversary of Day of Mourning and Australia Day

Two Australia Day events were held in Sydney, one at the Block in Redfern, the centre of much Koori (Aboriginal) activity in Sydney. Following speeches, 3,000 people marched to the Yabun Festival at Victoria Park. Signs read "no pride in genocide" and "230 years, and we're still here". Speakers called for a treaty.

The Metro Aboriginal Land Council hosted the other commemoration at the historic venue of Australia Hall where descendants of the men and women who first declared the Day of Mourning had met 80 years earlier. It was also the 230th anniversary of white settlement. NSW Opposition Leader Luke Foley was one of the speakers and promised a treaty for NSW if he is elected - the first time a NSW Labor or Liberal leader has made such stand. Linda Burney, MP made an impassioned speech.

Norman and I attended the event at Australia Hall, as it was a highly significant day to honour William Cooper and the other organisers of the Day of Mourning. Uncle Boydie was not able to attend, but he spoke by phone at that event, and other descendants spoke. Barbara McDonogh, William Cooper's great-granddaughter, was there in her wheelchair and her son Michael McDonogh and daughter attended. The descendants of the key leaders of the Day of Mourning were all duly honoured.

Barbara Gravener and Barbara Miller at 80th Anniversary of the Day of Mourning at Australia Hall, Sydney (photo Norman Miller)

Norman shared that he was looking forward to having an Indigenous Prime Minister and Indigenous governors of the states. He then sang a stirring song he wrote called "Reconciliation" to the backing of didjeridoo and clapsticks. There were posters and memorabilia of the Day of Mourning on display as well as my 2012 biography of William Cooper. Joey Geia, a well-known Indigenous singer, also performed at Australia Hall.

At the end of the meeting, we all made a spirited walk to Yabun Festival with placards, slogans, Aboriginal flags and dancers in traditional regalia and paint. The busy roads of Broadway and City Road were blocked off for the long hot walk.

Cooper descendant Michael McDonogh and Norman Miller at the door of Australia Hall Day of Mourning 80th anniversary ready to join the march to Yabun Festival (photo Barbara Miller)

For a number of years, Norman and I have attended Yabun Festival on Australia Day in Sydney where Indigenous people commemorate their survival and resilience with displays of art, craft and culture, traditional dancing, a concert, activities for children, food and other stalls and a speak-out tent where speakers discuss current political issues with a number of panels. Thousands attend, including the non-Indigenous community. We did so in 2018 after the event at Australia Hall, joining the march from Australia Hall to Yabun. Marches are held from Redfern to Yabun each year.

While in Sydney, we also attended a conference on constitutional change and Norman was able to sign the Uluru Statement from the Heart. I will discuss this statement in the next chapter.

For many years now, Indigenous people call Australia Day Invasion Day or Survival Day. There is controversy around whether the date should be changed with a "Change the Date" campaign. Some local government councils clashed with the federal government over wanting to change their Australia Day celebrations to another date out of respect to the First Nations people.

The city of Yarra decided not to celebrate Australia Day on 26 January out of respect to the Aboriginal people, and the federal government reacted by removing their right to hold citizenship ceremonies at which migrants receive their Australian citizenship. Cooper's grandson, Kevin Russell always finds it hard to celebrate his birthday because it is on 26 January and he feels this date represents the dispossession of his people. Kevin read one of William Cooper's speeches at the City of Yarra's smoking ceremony.

An estimated 25,000 Aboriginal and Torres Strait Islanders and their supporters marched from Parliament House in Flinders Lane in Melbourne, calling for equal rights and a change of date for Australia Day. They closed down Melbourne's CBD, with the rallying cry "always was, always will be, Aboriginal land". About 3,000 marched in Brisbane, 2,000 in Hobart, 200 in Perth and 1,000 in Canberra, the latter marching to the

Aboriginal Tent Embassy in front of Old Parliament House. The tent embassy still stands as a reminder there is so much yet to achieve. Some see it as a symbol of resistance.

Mural and Statue of Cooper in Shepparton

A striking mural of William Cooper and Pastor Sir Doug Nicholls had already been painted in Shepparton. Now there was more recognition. There is also a mural of Dan Cooper.

Pastor Sir Doug Nicholls and William Cooper Mural Shepparton (photo David Jack)

A 1.8 metre high, bronze statue of William Cooper was unveiled in Queens Park, Shepparton. He is holding a letter of protest to the German government for the atrocities of Kristallnacht. On 4 April 2018, NITV News reported that it had been unveiled the previous week (27 March) and Executive Chairman of the Kaiela Institute, Paul Briggs, said during the ceremony:

The unveiling of this statue today is a symbolic testament to Uncle William's character, values, and enormous contribution to humanity and to the survival of the Yorta Yorta people …

Uncle William's advocacy and spirit was full of wisdom, bringing traditional values and experiences from his mother and Elders; while witnessing the war against the Yorta Yorta that was raging around him.[177]

Statue of William Cooper, Shepparton (photo David Jack)

Family and Others at Unveiling of William Cooper Statue (photo David Jack)

The William Cooper Memorial Committee was formed, led by the Director of Catholic Education Sandhurst, Paul Desmond, to build the statue. The committee raised funds from the Shepparton community, but it was a $30,000 donation from Gandel Philanthropy that was the deciding factor in enabling it to go ahead. Hundreds of people attended the unveiling ceremony last week, including descendants of Uncle William Cooper. A mural of Pearl Gibbs, the only woman speaker at the Day of Mourning in 1938, and a passionate advocate for her people, can be seen in Dubbo as well.

A bronze sculpture of Sir Douglas and his wife Lady Gladys was placed near in the Parliament House reserve in 2006, the first statue erected in Victoria to honour an Aborigine. Gladys was a charity worker and activist in her own right, as secretary of the National Aboriginal and Torres Strait Islander Women's Council and the Victorian state president in the 1970s. The statue was timed for the centenary of Doug's birth. He had come a long way from when he arrived in Melbourne in 1927. *The Age* writes:

> He had hitchhiked down to Melbourne from the bush and was living rough, sleeping in fruit boxes at the Queen Victoria Market. But he had talked his way into training with the Carlton Football Club. Doug was 20, tough, fast and skilled, but he had not lasted long. He was cut from the list when the other players said they didn't want him on the team and the trainers refused to rub him down. Because he was black, they said, he smelled.[178]

The Dubbo community erected a statue of William Ferguson (1882-1950) in the NSW town on 4 May 2019 to commemorate his pioneering efforts in Indigenous affairs. He was a strong Christian to the end and died speaking up for his people. He had just finished a speech on his soapbox in Dubbo and collapsed of heart failure, and his statue is just steps from where he made his last speech. The statue features him with a rolled-up newspaper in hand. When he drew a crowd, he would smack a rolled-up newspaper into his hand to make a point. The Council, the State government and donations from Aboriginal and other citizens, funded the statue. Uncle Boydie and Abe travelled to Dubbo to honour William Ferguson and support his family.

Treaty Legislation Passed in Victoria

Australia's first treaty bill passed the Victorian Parliament on 21 June 2018. It is called Advancing the Treaty Process with Aboriginal Victorians Bill 2018. It was a historic moment that William Cooper would have loved to live to see, especially in his own state

In an amazing coincidence, the Australian Electoral Commission, a federal body, announced the next day the renaming of the electoral seat of Batman to Cooper to honour William Cooper. Batman, the founder of Melbourne, was said to have made the only treaty with Aborigines in Australia, so it was a big thing to dump him for Cooper. However, there are queries over Batman's claims, and there are concerns also that he killed Aborigines in Tasmania. *The Guardian* newspaper reported:

... there remains a sizeable question mark over Batman's claims he traded axes, mirrors, scissors and flour for 240,000 ha of land on which present-day Melbourne presently sprawls. He also insisted he walked the boundary of his new acquisition in a day, which may have been the straw that tipped Governor Arthur to scrutinise the dates on Batman's report, which in turn led to the Batman deed being stamped null and void. That was 183 years and 15 days ago. (1836)[179]

William wanted to be a Member of Parliament but decided he was too old (and probably not well enough.) However, he campaigned for an Aboriginal parliamentarian. Many of his numerous letters to politicians and newspapers were written from his bed by candlelight because of his health and poverty. Many of the AAL meetings were in his home and sometimes at his bedside. On Sundays, however, he regularly walked the 10km from his home during the Depression to Yarra Bank. This was just down the road from Melbourne's Parliament House, and he would join Melbourne's orators expounding their views to the public. People would gather and listen.

Batman Electorate Renamed Cooper

The Australian Electoral Commission was redrawing electoral boundaries and taking submissions on boundaries and the possible renaming of electorates. The Labor Party campaigned to change the name of the federal electorate of Gellibrand to Cooper. Local MP Tim Watts backed in the party's official submission to remove the name of Joseph Gellibrand - an early British explorer of the Australian mainland and one of the negotiators of the Batman Treaty. He said the Wurundjeri probably thought they were offering safe passage, not selling their land. He believed as well as being a questionable treaty, it was outdated, and it would be a matter of practical reconciliation to name it after Cooper as the AAL had been located in this electorate. He was disappointed that the seat of Batman was renamed Cooper instead.

Batman electorate was renamed Cooper on 13 July 2018. The Wurundjeri and Yorta Yorta elders, who lobbied for this for many years, spearheaded the campaign to change the name. John Batman (1801-1839) set himself up in the northeast of the Van Diemen's Land Colony (now Tasmania) in the 1820s and was a major player in the founding of a settlement on the Yarra River, the forerunner of the city of Melbourne. A long campaign had been waged to rename the seat of Batman due to the pioneer's chequered past as a bounty hunter in Van Diemen's Land specialising in hunting Aborigines.

Cummera Walk Off 80th anniversary

Hundreds gathered excitedly at Cummera to celebrate the 80th anniversary of when the people walked off due to mistreatment and starvation rations. Visitors camped for the weekend or drove in daily from nearby towns, swelling the local community. The three-day event from Saturday to Monday included sharing stories, singing and dancing. The final day included a walk-on starting in Barmah, with participants walking across the bridge and back onto the reserve. Banners and flags marked the event, and those attending were able to get a sense of what it was like for their early generations.

Located on Yorta Yorta country along the Murray River in NSW, the station was founded in 1888. As discussed in Chapter 3, the people went on strike, and about 200 walked off the reserve on 4 February 1939, camping on the riverbank. They did this because there were too many deaths from starvation rations, inadequate sanitation and poor living conditions. The autocratic rule of the manager, bullying and mistreatment was also a significant reason.

They crossed the Murray River, leaving NSW and some never returned settling in the nearby towns of Mooroopna, Shepparton. Echuca, Barmah and Kyabram.

Yorta Yorta Nation Aboriginal Corporation CEO Monica Morgan, who lives at Cummera, and chairman Uncle Lance James organised the anniversary. Mr James' grandparents, Thomas Shadrach James and Ada Cooper (William's sister), and other family members settled in Shepparton after the walk-off. He said his Yorta Yorta people were 15,000 strong:

> We've retained our culture, our knowledge, our language, who we are, our identity — and those things are really important to us ...The thing that has made us who we are today is our family connection. We all have a story to tell, rich in family values. We have our history - which we are really proud of - as well as our achievements.[180]

Lynch Cooper Remembered

Ninety years ago, on 24 February 1929, Lynch Cooper, William's son became the first Aboriginal World's Sprinting Champion. A gifted runner from an early age, he did not run as a professional until he was 21 years old. Lynch was passionate about Indigenous rights and was the secretary for the AAL, working alongside his father. Lynch later in life became president of the Aborigines' Progressive Association.

He won the Stawell Gift in 1928. Lynch's self-confidence is shown in a report by NITV that, "he won a prize of 250 pounds for his win, but is reported to have won around 3000 pounds in bets he placed on himself. After his retirement, he remained active in sports training several runners and football players. He was an original inductee in the Aboriginal Sports Hall of Fame and is believed to be the first Aboriginal person to win a world title in any sport."[181] Born in 1905 at Moira Lake in Yorta Yorta country, Lynch Cooper passed away in 1971.

NAIDOC Events

As William Cooper is the father of NAIDOC, events are held in his honour during NAIDOC Week in Victoria in July each year. Colleen Marrion of the Gathering Place initiated the William Cooper Cup Football Match between Victorian Aborigines and the police and they held the 16th annual event in 2019 on 14 July. The Westgate Police hosted a 2019

NAIDOC event with a walk from Footscray Police Station to Maribyrnong River to honour William Cooper. Aunty Faye Muir, a Boon Wurrung elder, spoke on Indigenous languages. At the river, where William Cooper used to speak, there was a smoking ceremony and cultural dances and Abe, Uncle Boydie and Colleen shared about the Cooper legacy.

Norman and I always honour William Cooper each year in the Cairns NAIDOC celebrations as the Father of NAIDOC and share his story. Norman, as a pastor, opens the official NAIDOC event in prayer.

The interfaith community commemorated United Nations Mandela Day in Melbourne with a musical event which also honoured William Cooper on 7 July 2019 during NAIDOC Week. International Composer and Director, Warren Wills launched the 'Young World Choir' Project, and Abe Schwarz made comparisons between the legacies of Cooper and Mandela.

The Catholic Secondary Student Social Justice Day was held at the Australian Catholic University by the Justice Education in Catholic Schools (JECS) initiative on the first day of Reconciliation Week, 27 May 2019 with a focus on William Cooper. Abe and Uncle Boydie's daughter, Leonie Drummond shared as well.

Many Events with Jewish Community

I will cover the honouring of William Cooper by the Jewish community in Australia and Israel in a companion book. The Jewish community have praised him for leading the AAL in a protest to the German Consulate in Melbourne on 6 December 1938 to protest Kristallnacht, the start of the Holocaust. There are a number of events each year, but the main one is a walk on the anniversary of this event.

Chapter 14

Conclusion

40th anniversary of the Aboriginal Tent Embassy

On 26 January 2012, Australia Day, it was the 40th anniversary of the Aboriginal Tent Embassy outside Old Parliament House Canberra. Some people see the tent embassy as an eyesore and not needed any more. Others see it as a symbol of the continuing work for Aboriginal rights. The effective work of Indigenous organisations goes on without much involvement from it.

Constitutional Change

In January 2012, 45 years on from the 1967 referendum, the Expert Panel on the Constitutional Recognition of Indigenous Australians released its report recommending the removal of sections 25 and 51 of the constitution and recommending the inclusion of a new section 51A that recognises that the continent and its islands now known as Australia were first occupied by Aboriginal and Torres Strait Islander peoples. There is still a need to eliminate racism from the constitution. For this reason, a proposed section 116A would say that the Commonwealth, a State or a Territory shall not discriminate on the grounds of race, colour or ethnic or national origin.

Miller Boomerang Petition

Norman Miller framed a petition around the recommendations of the Expert Panel and called it the Miller Boomerang Petition, reminiscent of the Yirrkala Bark Petition. He travelled Australia, with me accompanying him, and gathered, at his own expense, over 5,100 signatures from Indigenous and non-Indigenous people. Norman also made a giant boomerang with the words "No Discrimination in the Constitution" and gained 360 signatures on the back of it. He presented it to then-Speaker Bronwyn Bishop on 27 November 2013. On 12 December 2013, the Hon Mr Entsch MP presented Miller's on-paper petition with 2115 signatures to Parliament.

L-R Hon Warren Entsch, the Hon Bronwyn Bishop, Norman Miller, Hon Ken Wyatt and Barbara Miller, Parliament House Canberra as Norman presents the boomerang to the Speaker 27.11.13 (photo Geoff Bagnall)

Norman continued to gather signatures until over 5,100 had been collected and presented them to the Speaker Hon Tony Smith MP in the presence of the Clerk of the House and the Hon Warren Entsch on 8 February 2016. Mr Entsch then presented the petition to the Parliament - https://www.youtube.com/watch?v=4LSEErGV1rI&feature=youtu.be

L-R Warren Entsch MHR, Norman and Barbara Miller presenting the final signatures of the Miller Boomerang Petition to the Speaker and Clerk of the House at Parliament House 8.2.16

Recognise Campaign

Recognise was set up under Reconciliation Australia by then Prime Minister Julia Gillard in 2012 in response to recommendations from an expert panel with the charter to raise awareness of Australians of the need for constitutional recognition of Indigenous people. This was successful in raising awareness, but as there was no model for it to promote, the government closed Recognise in August 2017.

Referendum Council

The Referendum Council was jointly appointed by Prime Minister Malcolm Turnbull and Leader of the Opposition Bill Shorten on 7 December 2015. Its job was to advise on the next steps towards a successful referendum to recognise Aboriginal and Torres Strait Islander peoples in the constitution. Building on the work of the Expert Panel, and by a Parliamentary Joint Select Committee that completed its work in 2015, it handed down its report on 30 June 2017.

The Referendum Council held twelve Dialogues or meetings of Indigenous Australians around Australia between December 2016 and May 2017. They were by invitation only and capped at 100 persons to try to reach consensus. Feedback from these dialogues was given to a First Nations National Constitutional Convention at Uluru in May 2017.

Uluru Statement from the Heart

Uluru, the large red rock in the centre of Australia is an iconic image that often symbolises Indigenous Australia and is a favourite spot for tourists. To the traditional owners, the Anangu, it is a sacred site. Many say it is the sacred heart of Australia. It was to Uluru, in the shadow of the rock, that the Referendum Council took the First Nations Convention.

Uluru at Sunset (photo Wikimedia Commons)

While there were sometimes heated discussions over whether sovereignty should be part of the outcome, they reached a consensus, and Megan Davis read out what became the Uluru Statement from the Heart on 26 May at the end of the Convention. The 250 Aboriginal and Torres Strait Islander delegates adopted it. Here is an excerpt:

> … We call for the establishment of a First Nations Voice enshrined in the constitution.
>
> Makarrata[182] is the culmination of our agenda: the coming together after a struggle. It captures our aspirations for a fair and truthful relationship with the people of Australia and a better future for our children based on justice and self-determination.
>
> We seek a Makarrata Commission to supervise a process of agreement-making between governments and First Nations and truth-telling about our history.
>
> In 1967 we were counted, in 2017 we seek to be heard…

So, the Indigenous cry from the heart of Australia is VOICE TREATY TRUTH. The reception from Prime Minister Malcolm Turnbull was not positive, and he called it a "third chamber" of Parliament. Opposition leader Bill Shorten was supportive and committed to implementing it if he won government. It had languished until the 18 May 2019 federal election when Prime Minister Scott Morrison and his Minister for Indigenous Australians, Ken Wyatt said they would support the voice but it would be achieved through legislation rather than constitutionally. Mr Wyatt hopes to put it to a referendum in this 3-year term of Parliament. Indigenous proponents of the voice want it enshrined in the constitution, so the government can't abolish it as they did the former national body - the Aboriginal and Torres Strait Islander Commission.

The debate is continuing. Eminent former High Court Chief Justice, Murray Gleeson, who was on the Referendum Council that supported the Uluru Statement, gave an address at a symposium and *The Australian* reported his views on 19.7.19. He declared the voice was advisory and not a third chamber to Parliament and could be created through legislation. Its structure, function and composition could be determined through legislation with the possibility of change. At the same time, there could be minimal change to the constitution to ensure its continued existence and essential features.

Indigenous Parliamentarians

William had wanted to be a Member of the Federal Parliament himself. He lobbied for Aborigines to take their place in the Parliament of Australia. This was to come to pass after a long time waiting with the first Aboriginal Senator, Neville Bonner (Liberal, Queensland) in 1971 followed by Senator Aden Ridgeway (Australian Democrats, NSW) in 1998. Ken Wyatt (Liberal, Hasluck) WA became the first Aboriginal Member of the House of Representatives in 2010. There have been a number of Aboriginal members in State and Territory Parliaments.

The Morrison Federal Parliament elected in May 2019, made history by appointing the first Indigenous Minister for Indigenous Australians. It is also the first time an Aboriginal person has been in the cabinet. The minister is the Hon Ken Wyatt, who was also a member of the Expert Panel on constitutional change. The shadow minister for the ALP is also Indigenous for the first time and is the Hon Linda Burney, the Member for Barton, NSW. There are two Indigenous ALP Senators in the 2019 parliament, the Hon Sen Pat Dodson, WA and the Hon Malarndirri McCarthy, NT.

William Cooper may not have been in Parliament, but he was the voice of Indigenous people for much of his life, and particularly in the 1930s. He did not see constitutional recognition and removal of racism from the constitution in his time, but he started the journey to the counting of Aboriginal people in the census, which required the constitutional change of 1967. William did not see a treaty or treaties in his lifetime, but he knew how to engage with governments state and federal for his people. He was one of the first Indigenous people to get truth-telling about Australia's history regarding its First Nations people into public discourse. In his time, he did what he could re the 2019 theme of NAIDOC, which is the theme of the Uluru Statement from the Heart – Voice, Treaty, Truth.

Speaking Out

William Cooper spoke up. William Cooper stood up and was counted. So, should we all in whatever way we can. The price of freedom and justice is high, but the cost of losing it is higher.

Sometimes we don't stand up for fear of criticism, fear of disagreement, fear of conflict, fear of standing out and having our "head chopped off," fear of not being able to "stand the heat". Fear of retribution can hold us back – loss of job or reputation; attacks on our family. In totalitarian societies, some have paid the price through torture or even death. But down through the centuries, change for the good has been made by those who were prepared to make a stand. They have, by their sacrifice, made a better world for those who followed. And we remember them.

In William Cooper's case, we have a man who could have rested in his final years of failing health. But we find a man who would not give up; who persevered in the face of incredibly slow progress: who showed much resilience and commitment as he continued to work for the human rights and betterment of his people. Till his last breath, he was a national figure whose heart was for his beloved people and all peoples in need. His Christian faith in God gave him a vision of what could be and sustained him through the hard times.

However, William was not alone in what he did. Margaret Tucker, Ps Doug Nicholls, Lynch Cooper, Bill and Eric Onus, Grandpa James, Shadrach James, Caleb and Anne Morgan, Nora Clark and white supporters Arthur Burdeau and Helen Baillie were some of the key people who worked with him.

What a legacy William and the AAL have left, not just for their family, but for Aboriginal Australia, and not just for Aboriginal Australia but for all Australians and not just for Australia, but for the world. We are better for William's life lived among us. He is an inspiration.

So, what is his legacy? What is the inheritance that he has left for his family and for those who become part of his and the AAL's ongoing story?

Above all, it was his fight for human dignity. He did not use guns or swords or spears. He used the pen, his oratory and the moral force of a righteous personality. As it is said, "the pen is mightier than the sword." He was a prolific letter writer to politicians and newspapers. He would regularly be seen at the Domain in Melbourne on his soapbox, speaking to whoever would listen. He travelled the country, seeing what needed to be done and talking to Aboriginal people about their concerns. His good character shone through and made him a force to be reckoned with. He was a gentle warrior.

In Aboriginal affairs, he set the agenda or platform for succeeding generations who built on this platform or base. Issues he fought for were issues for which the next generation and beyond fought. Sometimes victory came slowly, but it did come. William mentored the next generation of leaders, including Ps Doug Nicholls, and his struggle for the rights of his people lived on through them.

Great Leaders

I think of the great Jewish leader Moses as he stood on Mt Nebo in present-day Jordan and looked at the Promised Land which he was prevented from entering. Norman and I have stood there to get an idea of what it must have been like for Moses and felt sad for him to be on the brink but not enter in, especially after such an arduous journey. But he knew his people would enter in and he had led them there. He had fulfilled his purpose and led his people out of slavery in Egypt.

In Martin Luther King Jnr's famous speech "I have a dream," made in 1963 in Washington, we see how he paved a path for Black Americans to freedom, equality and human dignity. But he was cruelly gunned down before he saw it achieved. It seems from his last speech that he knew he wasn't going to make it himself. Yet he had a vision of a freer, more tolerant future that he held with passion and which sustained him. He famously said at Memphis, 3 April 1968, the night before he was shot and killed:

> Like anyone, I'd like to live a long life. Longevity has its place. But I'm not concerned about that now. I just want to do God's will. And he's allowed me to go up the mountain, and I've looked over, and I've seen the Promised Land. I might not get there with you. But I want you to know that we as a people will get to the Promised Land. So, I'm happy tonight. I'm not worried about anything. I'm not fearing any man. My eyes have seen the glory of the coming of the Lord![183]

He was only 39 years old, but he turned the tide of American history.

William Cooper was a national Australian Aboriginal leader. He too had a vision of the future to which he was leading his people. He too had led his people on a difficult journey of disappointment and setbacks. He too was not there to see his dreams come true, though most of what he worked for has been achieved in succeeding generations. He said:

> Are you prepared to admit that since the Creator said in his Word all men are of "one blood," we are humans with feelings like yourselves in the eyes of Almighty God, that we have our joys and our sorrows, our likes and our dislikes, that we can feel pain, degradation and humiliation just as you do. If you admit that, will you like true men do your bit to see a great injustice at least mollified by agitating for us to get a fair deal before it is too late?[184]

Different times and different places but all three men – Moses, Martin Luther King Jnr and William Cooper – had a faith in the God of Abraham, Isaac and Jacob that sustained them and gave them hope. God told Moses He had heard the Israelites crying out because of their slavery in Egypt and He was concerned about their suffering and had come down to rescue them by calling Moses to lead them out. [185]

No doubt God spoke to Martin Luther King Jnr and William Cooper and many others, men and women, throughout history. They heard the call and took up the challenge. They stood up and were counted.

Unexpectedly, in telling William Cooper's story, we became part of the story. Maybe you will feel inspired to tell William's story and become part of the story too.

Epilogue

by ***James Wilson-Miller***

The writers and proponents of the (Day of Mourning) Manifesto (Patten, Ferguson and Cooper) have been rightfully or wrongfully attacked by (others) ...

Just what led these people to take on a monumental challenge to change a nation? Many of these people were only two generations removed from tribal days. Many had slipped through the education system unnoticed because most 'whites' then only thought of them as being under-educated, unintelligent and therefore not in their class. What motivated these people when most would have hardly been to school and if they did, they would have only received a third-grade standard no matter how old they were? Their achievements in the teeth of entrenched racism and against all odds demonstrates they were the parents of Indigenous political activism who forged the way the Indigenous struggle would be fought and won.

Since the 1930s contemporary Indigenous visionaries have really not deviated too far from the ideals of the 1938 Aboriginal Day of Mourning Manifesto. Such visionaries have included: Mum Shirl Smith, Bert Groves, Kumanjayi Perkins, Mick Miller, Oodgeroo Noonuccal, Pat O'Shane, Faith Bandler, Lowitja O'Donoghue, Charles Dixon, and a host of others I haven't mentioned, because the list of our Indigenous visionaries is just so long. Regardless of what organisations they belonged to or what they did, when they did it, how they did it and why they did it, post-1930s visionaries at some stage in their struggles highlighted and progressed issues raised in the Manifesto. [186]

It is also important for me to mention that both historically and in contemporary times there have been decent non-Indigenous Australians who have risen above entrenched ignorance and racism at great personal cost to lead initiatives and proactively contribute to driving the vision. Often these people have been ridiculed from both non-Indigenous and Indigenous Australians so much so that their efforts have been devalued by both groups..........

It is also important for me to note the everyday non-Indigenous people who have proactively supported the struggle and I would particularly like to commend the everyday Aussies and people from other cultural backgrounds who walked the Harbour Bridge and other bridges around this country, wrote sorry in sorry books or apologised at meetings, the individual local, state and federal politicians, the states whose Premiers have apologised on behalf of their people, in the face of the deafening silence from the Australian Prime Minister (John Howard) to say the 'S' word on behalf of all non-Indigenous Australians. In doing what you did does not entirely let you off the hook, for it is what you do in the future, to further the ongoing legacies still faced by the majority of Indigenous Australians. Your actions have been recorded and have also spoken to the future, because future non-Indigenous visionaries will take what you have done and move positively further forward in making this country a just country. [187]

Appendices

Appendix 1 Maloga Petition to Governor of the Colony of NSW 1881

Appendix 2 Maloga Petition signatures 1881

Appendix 3 AAL and William Cooper's petition to King George V of England

Report of APA meeting concerning land, 1881

PETITION FOR LAND

The following petition, signed by forty-two of the aboriginal inhabitants of the colony (most of them only with their marks) has recently been presented to his Excellency the Governor.

The matter has not as yet, we understand come under the consideration of the Cabinet, but will probably be taken into consideration in the course of a few days –

"To his Excellency Lord Augustus Loftus, G.C.B., Governor of the colony of New South Wales – The humble petition of the undersigned aboriginal natives, residents on the Murray River in the colony of New South Wales, members of the Moira and Ulupna tribes, respectfully showeth:-

1. That all the land within our tribal boundaries has been taken possession of by the Government and white settlers; our hunting grounds are used for sheep pasturage and the game reduced and in many places exterminated, rendering our means of subsistence extremely precarious, and often reducing us and our wives and children to beggary.
2. We, the men of our several tribes, are desirous of honestly maintaining our young and infirm, who are in many cases the subjects of extreme want and semi-starvation, and we believe we could, in a few years support ourselves by our own industry, *were a sufficient area of land granted* to us to cultivate and raise stock.
3. We have been under training for some years and feel that our old mode of life is not in keeping with the instructions we have received and we are earnestly desirous of settling down to more orderly habits of industry, that we may form homes for our families.

   We more confidently ask this favour of a grant of land as our fellow natives in other colonies have proved capable of supporting themselves, where suitable land has been reserved for them.

We hopefully appeal to your Excellency, as we recognise in you, The Protector specially appointed by Her Gracious Majesty the Queen "to promote religion and education among the aboriginal natives of the colony", and to protect us in our persons and in the free enjoyment of our possessions, and to take such measures as may be necessary for our advancement in civilization.

and your petitioners, as in duty bound will ever pray."

(signed by 42 aboriginals)
Maloga Mission – Murray River, New South Wales, 1881

Cato, Nancy (1976) "Mister Maloga, Daniel Matthews and his Mission, Murray River, 1864-1902" St Lucia, Qld: University of Queensland Press, Appendix 10

NAMES OF 42 MALOGA ABORIGINAL MEN

(A Petition for Land Reserve)

Bobby Wilberforce (Cooper)
Richard (X, his mark)
Thomas Williams
Aáron Atkinson
George Charles
Freddy Walker
Daylight
David Berrick
Peter Stuckey
Jacky Wilberforce (Cooper)
Jimmy Turner
Sydney
George Keefe
James Coghill
Sampson Barber
Bagot Morgan
John Atkinson
Peter
Robert Taylor
David Taylor
Jasper Angus

George Aben
Bradshaw
Harry Fenton
Thomas Fenton
Alowidgee
Johnny Galway
Charlie Stewart
Ted Robertson
Rochford Robertson
Gibson Platt
Jackie John
Tommy Hawke
Robertson
Boney Cockie
Barralta
Harry
Jimmy Martin
Blucher
Dick Richards
James Edgar
Whyman McLean

[Sydney Daily Telegraph 5 July 1881]

Cato, Nancy (1976) "Mister Maloga, Daniel Matthews and his Mission, Murray River, 1864-1902" St Lucia, Qld: University of Queensland Press, Appendix 10

COPY. 29

P E T I T I O N.

of the Aboriginal Inhabitants of Australia to His Majesty George V by the Grace of God of Great Britain Ireland and the British ---- Dominions beyond the seas King Defender of the Faith Emperor of - India.

TO THE KING'S MOST EXCELLENT MAJESTY IN COUNCIL.

THE HUMBLE PETITION of the undersigned Aboriginal Inhabitants of the Continent of Australia respectfully showeth:

THAT WHEREAS it was not only a moral duty, but also a strict - - - injunction included in the commission issued to those who came to - people Australia that the original occupants and we their heirs and successors should be adequately cared for.

AND WHEREAS the terms of the commission have not been adhered to in that :

(a) our lands have been expropriated by Your Majesty's Government in the Commonwealth.

(b) legal status is denied to us by Your Majesty's - - Government in the Commonwealth.

AND WHEREAS all petitions made on our behalf to Your Majesty's Government in the Commonwealth have failed.

YOUR PETITIONERS therefore humbly pray that Your Majesty will intervene on our behalf and through the instrument of Your Majesty's Government in the Commonwealth of Australia:

To prevent the extinction of the Aboriginal Race and better - conditions for all and grant us power to propose a member of --- parliament in the person of our own Blood, or White man known to have studied our needs and to be in Sympathy with our Race to represent us in the Federal Parliament.

AND YOUR PETITIONERS will ever pray:

SIGNATURES OF PETITIONERS ADDRESSES.

Endnotes

1 One of the 500 plus Aboriginal tribes or language groups in Australia before white settlement

2 Clark, Mavis Thorpe (1972) "Pastor Doug: The Story of Sir Douglas Nicholls, Aboriginal Leader," Melbourne: Lansdowne Press, P14

3 ibid P15

4 Harris, John (1994) "One Blood, 200 Years of Aboriginal Encounter With Christianity: A Story of Hope" Sutherland, NSW: Albatross Books, P223

5 Cato, Nancy (1976) "Mister Maloga, Daniel Matthews and his Mission, Murray River, 1864-1902" St Lucia, Qld: University of Queensland Press P9

6 ibid

7 Daniel Mathews diary entry cited in ibid P69

8 Daniel in ibid P79

9 (Cato cites 1833 as the year Kitty was born, based on Maloga Mission records

10 Clark, Mavis Thorpe (1972) "Pastor Doug: The Story of Sir Douglas Nicholls, Aboriginal Leader," Melbourne: Lansdowne Press P12-13

11 Cato, Nancy (1976) "Mister Maloga, Daniel Matthews and his Mission, Murray River, 1864-1902" St Lucia, Qld: University of Queensland Press P117

12 ibid P167

13 ibid

14 Clark, Mavis Thorpe (1972) "Pastor Doug: The Story of Sir Douglas Nicholls, Aboriginal Leader," Melbourne: Lansdowne Press, P19

15 Cato, Nancy (1976) "Mister Maloga, Daniel Matthews and his Mission, Murray River, 1864-1902" St Lucia, Qld: University of Queensland Press P180

16 Ibid P192-3

17 Harris, John (1994) "One Blood, 200 Years of Aboriginal Encounter With Christianity: A Story of Hope" Sutherland, NSW: Albatross Books P227

18 Clark, Mavis Thorpe (1972) "Pastor Doug: The Story of Sir Douglas Nicholls, Aboriginal Leader," Melbourne: Lansdowne Press, P22-23

19 Cato, Nancy (1976) "Mister Maloga, Daniel Matthews and his Mission, Murray River, 1864-1902" St Lucia, Qld: University of Queensland Press, P220

20 ibid P243

[21] Attwood, Bain and Markus, Andrew (2004) "Thinking Black, William Cooper and the Australian Aborigines" League" Canberra: Aboriginal Studies Press P27

[22] Goodall, Heather (1982) "The history of Aboriginal communities in NSW 1909–1939", Unpublished PhD thesis, Department of History, The Australian National University, Canberra P36 in Harris, John (1994) "One Blood, 200 Years of Aboriginal Encounter With Christianity: A Story of Hope" Sutherland, NSW: Albatross Books P618

[23] Markus, Andrew (1988) "Blood From a Stone: William Cooper and the Australian Aborigines' League" Sydney: Allen and Unwin P7

[24] Harris, John (1994) "One Blood, 200 Years of Aboriginal Encounter With Christianity: A Story of Hope" Sutherland, NSW: Albatross Books P225

[25] ibid P236

[26] ibid P226

[27] Clark, Mavis Thorpe (1972) "*Pastor Doug: The Story of Sir Douglas Nicholls, Aboriginal Leader*", Melbourne: Lansdowne Press P31

[28] ibid P40

[29] Horner, Jack (1974) "Vote Ferguson For Aboriginal Freedom, A Biography by Jack Horner" Sydney: Australia and New Zealand Book Company, P47

[30] Clark, Mavis Thorpe (1972) "*Pastor Doug: The Story of Sir Douglas Nicholls, Aboriginal Leader"*, Melbourne: Lansdowne Press P160

[31] ibid P161

[32] Aborigines would settle their differences by tribal law, sometimes resulting in a killing. Police would use neck-chains to march outback Aborigines beside the trooper's horse to the nearest white settlement to face justice.

[33] Clark, Mavis Thorpe (1972) "*Pastor Doug: The Story of Sir Douglas Nicholls, Aboriginal Leader"*, Melbourne: Lansdowne Press P89-90

[34] Markus, Andrew (1988) "Blood From a Stone: William Cooper and the Australian Aborigines' League" Sydney: Allen and Unwin P1983

[35] Ibid.P9

[36] Clark, Mavis Thorpe (1972) "*Pastor Doug: The Story of Sir Douglas Nicholls, Aboriginal Leader"*, Melbourne: Lansdowne Press P97

[37] Markus, Andrew (1988) "Blood From a Stone: William Cooper and the Australian Aborigines' League" Sydney: Allen and Unwin P16

[38] Ibid. P18

[39] Gribble Papers, ABM Archives 20/9/1937 in Harris, John (1994) "One Blood, 200 Years of Aboriginal Encounter With Christianity: A Story of Hope" Sutherland, NSW: Albatross Books P629

[40] Clark, Mavis Thorpe (1972) "*Pastor Doug: The Story of Sir Douglas Nicholls, Aboriginal Leader"*, Melbourne: Lansdowne Press P98

[41] ibid

[42] ibid.

[43] Horner, Jack (1994) "Bill Ferguson: Fighter for Aboriginal Freedom" Canberra: self-published P57

[44] ibid P59

[45] ibid P58

[46] Australian Inland Mission

[47] Harris, John (1994) "One Blood, 200 Years of Aboriginal Encounter With Christianity: A Story of Hope" Sutherland, NSW: Albatross Books P629. AIM stands for Australian Inland Mission.

[48] Horner, Jack (1994) "Bill Ferguson: Fighter for Aboriginal Freedom" Canberra: self-published P64

[49] Ibid P65

[50] ibid

[51] *Australian Abo Call,* 1 (1) April 1938, a magazine put out by Jack Patten

[52] Ibid P70

[53] Markus, Andrew (1988) "Blood From a Stone: William Cooper and the Australian Aborigines' League" Sydney: Allen and Unwin P9, 17

[54] Ibid P76

[55] Clark, Mavis Thorpe (1972) "*Pastor Doug: The Story of Sir Douglas Nicholls, Aboriginal Leader*", Melbourne: Lansdowne Press P112-113

[56] Horner, Jack (1994) "Bill Ferguson: Fighter for Aboriginal Freedom" Canberra: self-published P76

[57] Ibid P79

[58] Mathews, Daniel Diary 1884 cited in Cato, Nancy (1976) "Mister Maloga, Daniel Matthews and his Mission, Murray River, 1864-1902" St Lucia, Qld: University of Queensland Press P 167

[59] Attwood, Bain and Markus, Andrew (2004) "Thinking Black, William Cooper and the Australian Aborigines' League" Canberra: Aboriginal Studies Press

[60] Ibid P34

[61] Attwood, Bain and Markus, Andrew (2004) "Thinking Black, William Cooper and the Australian Aborigines' League" Canberra: Aboriginal Studies Press P127

[62] Cooper to Prime Minister Lyons 26/10/1937 in Attwood, Bain and Markus, Andrew (2004) "Thinking Black, William Cooper and the Australian Aborigines' League" Canberra: Aboriginal Studies Press P18

[63] Cooper letters cited in Markus, Andrew (1988) "Blood From a Stone: William Cooper and the Australian Aborigines' League" Sydney: Allen and Unwin P18

[64] Herald 7 August 1937

[65] Gribble, Ernest (1932) "The Problem of the Australian Aboriginal" Sydney: Angus and Robertson P112 in Harris, John (1994) "One Blood, 200 Years of Aboriginal Encounter With Christianity: A Story of Hope" Sutherland, NSW: Albatross Books P517

[66] Attwood, Bain and Markus, Andrew (2004) "Thinking Black, William Cooper and the Australian Aborigines' League" Canberra: Aboriginal Studies Press P95

[67] ibid P96

[68] ibid P97-98

[69] ibid P127

[70]ibid P94

[71] ibid P109

[72] ibid P112-113.

[73] Ibid P125

[74] Ibid P125

[75] Victorian Aborigines Advancement League (1985) "Victims or Victors: The Story of the Victorian Aborigines Advancement League" Melbourne: Hyland House Publishing Pty Ltd P42

[76] www.indigenousrights.com.au

[77] Clark, Mavis Thorpe (1972) "*Pastor Doug: The Story of Sir Douglas Nicholls, Aboriginal Leader*", Melbourne: Lansdowne Press P173

[78] Aborigines living on the edge of towns, generally in makeshift camps

[79] Bryant later became Minister for Aboriginal Affairs, and Beazley became Minister for Education in the Whitlam government

[80] Ibid P53

[81] Ibid P27

[82] Taffe, Sue "The Cairns Aboriginal and Torres Strait Islander Advancement League and the Community of the Left" "Labour History" Vol 97, Nov 2009

[83] Ibid P6

[84] FCAA became FCAATSI to include Torres Strait Islanders.

[85] Miller, Barbara (1986) "The Aspirations of Aborigines Living at Yarrabah in Relation to Local Management"

[86] Roberts, Jan, Parsons, Michael, McLean, David and Russell, Barbara (1975) "The Mapoon Story" Vol 1-3. Melbourne: International Development Action.

[87] See Miller, Barbara (2018) *White Woman Black Heart: Journey Home to Old Mapoon, A Memoir,* Createspace.

[88] Op. Cit. P58

[89] Attwood, Bain and Markus, Andrew (2004) "Thinking Black, William Cooper and the Australian Aborigines' League" Canberra: Aboriginal Studies Press P122

[90] the person Douglas Lockwood wrote about in the book "I, the Aboriginal."

[91] Clark, Mavis Thorpe (1972) *"Pastor Doug: The Story of Sir Douglas Nicholls, Aboriginal Leader",* Melbourne: Lansdowne Press P230-231

[92] "Aborigines need less than the cost of a jet", The Sydney Morning Herald, 1 December 1965 http://www.creativespirits.info/aboriginalculture/history/referendum-1967.html#ixzz259yzoib7

[93] 'I want to be a human being', The Sydney Morning Herald, 21 May 1967, p.47, http://www.creativespirits.info/aboriginalculture/history/referendum-1967.html#ixzz25A1sdWlC

[94] http://indigenousrights.net.au, National petition campaign, 1962-63, P2

[95] http://indigenousrights.net.au, Parliamentary and Cabinet debates, 1964-66, P2

[96] Miller, Barbara (2018) "The Dying Days of Segregation in Australia: Case Study Yarrabah" Cairns: Barbara Miller Books.

[97] Miller, Barbara (1994) "Options for the Future: Local Government and Native Title on Queensland Aboriginal Communities" Cairns: Aboriginal Co-ordinating Council

[98] Victorian Aborigines Advancement League (1985) "Victims or Victors: The Story of the Victorian Aborigines Advancement League" Melbourne: Hyland House Publishing Pty Ltd P86

[99] ibid P93

[100] Miller, B (1986) "The Aspirations of Aborigines Living at Yarrabah in Relation to Local Management and Human Rights" Canberra: Human Rights Commission; Miller; Barbara (1990) "ACC Submission to the Royal Commission into Aboriginal Deaths in Custody" Cairns: Aboriginal Co-ordinating Council; Adams, J., Venables, P. & Miller, B. (1991) "Wayan Min Uwanp Aak Ngulakana, Finding the Right Road Ahead" Cairns: Queensland Department of Aboriginal and Islander Affairs; Miller, B. (1992) "A Social-Historical and Psychological Perspective on Aboriginal Intra-Cultural Aggression" in Thomas, D.R. & Veno, A. (Eds) (1992) Psychology and Social Change, Creating an International Agenda Palmerston North, NZ: Dunmore Press; Miller, B (1993)" Queensland Aboriginal Trust Community Initiatives in taking Responsibility for Social Control", Cairns: Aboriginal Co-ordinating Council; Miller, B (1994) "Options for the Future: Local Government and Native Title on Queensland Aboriginal Communities" Cairns: Aboriginal Co-ordinating Council; Miller, B (2005) "Community Transformation – Building Spiritual Capital at Aurukun Project Report" Cairns: Queensland Department of Communities.

[101] National Aboriginal and Islander Day Observance Committee

[102] Clark, Mavis Thorpe (1972) "Pastor *Doug: The Story of Sir Douglas Nicholls, Aboriginal Leader"*, Melbourne: Lansdowne Press P111

[103] National Aboriginal Day Observance Committee

[104] Australian National University

[105] See Appendix 4 for a copy of the article

[106] http://vietnam-war.commemoration.gov.au/conscription/save-our-sons.php

[107] 'Commonwealth policy in relation to land and related matters', 7 July 1971, file 29, Barry Dexter papers, Menzies Library, ANU, Canberra, accessed on www.indigenousrights.net.au

[108] Taylor, Chris "Australia's Heritage National Treasures" video.

[109] www.indigenousrights.net.au, National Museum of Australia, Collaborating for Indigenous Rights

[110] "The Age", 8 February 1972; John Newfong. 'The Aboriginal Embassy: its purpose and aims,' Identity, 1 (5):4-6, July 1972.

[111] "The Australian", 9 February 1972; "Sydney Morning Herald", 9 February 1972; "The Age", 10 February 1972.

[112] "The Age", 24 July 1972; Stewart Harris (Canberra correspondent to the "London Times"), quoted in *The Age*, 29 July 1972; Scott Robinson. 'The Aboriginal Embassy: an account of the Protests of 1972.' "Aboriginal History" Vol.18 (1) 1994, pp. 49-63.

[113] "The Age", 31 July 1972.

[114] Hansard" 13 September 1972 P1315-1330

[115] That included me

[116] Hansard 13/9/72 P1318

[117] "Hansard" 13/9/72 P1319

[118] "Hansard" 13/9/72 P1319

[119] "Hansard" 13/9/72 P1320-1321

[120] On September 5-6, there was a massacre where eleven Israeli athletes at the 1972 Summer Olympics in Munich were murdered after eight members of the Arab Terrorist group Black September invaded the Olympic Village. Also, five terrorists and one policeman were killed in a failed hostage rescue. There is no real comparison here as there were no deaths in Canberra but the Munich event, which shocked the world, was still fresh in people's minds.

[121]"Hansard" 13/9/72 P1326

[122] Taylor, Chris "Australia's Heritage National Treasures" video. Mate is an Australian term for friend

[123] http://vietnam-war.commemoration.gov.au/conscription/moratoriums-and-opposition.php

[124] Small, Jerome "100 years or racism: federation and the white Australia policy" Social Alternative Ed 48, Feb 2001.

[125] Commonwealth Parliamentary Debates, 1920 P4863

[126] Barton Papers, National Library of Australia, MS 51/1/976 in ABC "Australia's Centenary of Federation", http//www.abc.net.au/federation/fedstory/ep2/ep2_institutions.htm

[127] Australian Government Department of Immigration and Citizenship (2009) "Fact Sheet 8 – Abolition of the White Australia Policy" P1

[128] Australian Government Department of Immigration and Citizenship (2009) "Fact Sheet 8 – Abolition of the White Australia Policy" P3

[129] ibid.

[130] Australian Bureau of Statistics (2017) *Migration, Australia (cat. no. 3412.0)* https://www.abs.gov.au/ausstats/abs@.nsf/previousproducts/3412.0main%20features32015-16

[131] http//.library.thinkquest.org/C004367/eh4.shtml, P2

[132]Ibid P3

[133] Bird, David S. (2012) "Nazi Dreamtime, Australian Enthusiasts for Nazi Germany" Melbourne: Australian Scholarly Publishing Pty Ltd, P223-224

[134] Ibid P71 and Horner, Jack (1994) "Bill Ferguson: Fighter for Aboriginal Freedom" Canberra: self-pub P57

[135] Blakeney, Michael (1985) Australia and the Jewish Refugees 1933-1948" Sydney: Croom Helm Australia

[136] Windschuttle, Keith (2002) "The Fabrication of Aboriginal History, Volume One: Van Diemen's Land 1803-1847". Sydney: Macleay Press.

[137] Reynolds, Henry (1981) "The Other Side of the Frontier: Aboriginal Resistance to the European Invasion of Australia." Sydney: UNSW Press

[138] Gilbert, Martin (1981) "Auschwitz and the Allies" New York: Holt, Reinhart and Winston in Blakeney, Michael (1985) "Australia and the Jewish Refugees 1933-1948" Sydney: Croom Helm Australia, preface

[139] http//.library.thinkquest.org/C004367/eh4.shtml, P2

[140] Black, Edwin (2003) "The Horrifying American Roots of Nazi Eugenics" George Mason's University History News Network, http://hnn.us/articles/1796.html, P3

[141] ibid.

[142] ibid P2

[143] Kevles, Daniel J. "In the Name of Darwin" adapted from his 1995 book "In the Name of Eugenics", Harvard University Press, http://www.pbs.org/wgbh/evolution/darwin/nameof/index.html

[144] Richardson, Tim "The Stolen Generations: Robert Manne" http://www.tim-richardson.net/joomla15article-list-personalmenu-7, P3

[145] "The High Cost of Whitewash" 27/9/2003 Sydney Morning Herald, http://www.smh.com.au/articles/2003/09/26/1064083186575.html

[146] Richardson, Tim "The Stolen Generations: Robert Manne" http://www.tim-richardson.net/joomla15article-list-personalmenu-7, P4

[147] Woorama (2007) "Eugenics and Aborigines, Genetic Science – Its Role in Indigenous Policy, Identity, Genocide" http//suite101.com/article/eugenics-and-aborigines-a22972, P2

[148] Stanner, W.E.H. (1979) "After the Dreaming" in Stanner, W.E.H. *White Man Got No Dreaming: Essays 1938-1973* pp198-248

[149] http://en.wikipedia.org/wiki/History_wars

[150] http://ergo.slv.vic.gov.au/explore-history/fight-rights/indigenous-rights/reconciliation-convention-1997, 2011 State Library of Victoria, P1

[151] ibid

[152] Clark, Anna "History in Black and White: a critical analysis of the Black Armband debate, originally published in Richard Nile (ed) *Country: Journal of Australian Studies* no 75, St Lucia, UQP, 2002. http:/www.api-network.com/main/pdf/scholars/jas75_clark.pdf

[153] Ferrier, Carole "White Blindfolds and Black Armbands: the uses of whiteness theory for reading Australian cultural production", *Queensland Review*, vol 6, no1, p42-49.

[154] Howard, John "The Liberal Tradition: The Beliefs and Values That Guide the Federal Government, 1996 Sir Robert Menzies Lecture. Sir Robert Menzies Lecture Trust http://www.menzieslecture.org/1996.html

[155] Windschuttle, Keith (2002) "The Fabrication of Aboriginal History, Volume One: Van Diemen's Land 1803-1847" Sydney: Macleay Press.

[156] Manne, Robert (ed) (2003) "Whitewash: On Keith Windschuttle's Fabrication of Aboriginal History", Melbourne.

[157] Barta, Tony, "Relations of Genocide: Land and Lives in the Colonization of Australia, in Wallimann, Isidor & Dobkowski, Michael N. (eds) (1987) Genocide and the Modern Age: Etiology and Case Studies of Mass Death, New York: Greenwood Press pp 237-251, http://hyperhistory.org/index.php?option=displaypage&Itemid=364&op=page#arti. Australian Government Department of Education, Science and Training.

[158] The Aboriginal and Torres Strait Islander Commission (ATSIC), the only national elected Aboriginal body, was later axed, though it was having some difficulties.

[159] Irving, Helen, Bolton, Geoffrey, Ricketson, Matthew and Jopson, Debra "Footnotes to a war" 13/12/2003, Sydney Morning Herald, http://www.smh.com.au/articles/2003/12/15/1071336875054.html

[160] Keating, Paul "Keating's 'History Wars'", 5/9/2003 *Sydney Morning Herald*, http://www.smh.com.au/articles/2003/09/05/1062549021882.html

[161] Dow, Coral and Gardiner-Garden, John "Overview of Indigenous Affairs: 1901 to 1991" Parliament of Australia 2011

[162] Miller, Barbara (2012) "William Cooper, Gentle Warrior: Standing Up for Australian Aborigines and Persecuted Jews" Xlibris, see barbara-miller-books.com

[163] *Cannon, Anthea* "Footscray bridge named in honour of Aboriginal leader" *20 May 10* http://maribyrnong-leader.whereilive.com.au

[164] Bennet, Darryl "NCB Collaborates with Museum of Australian Democracy" http://ncb.anu.edu.au/book/export/html/103

[165] Jennifer Wilson, National Museum of Australia, 12 May 2010 "Parliament for the people" http://www.nma.gov.au/audio/transcripts/landmarks/NMA_Parliament_for_people_20100512.html

[166] "VCAT cuts the ribbon at William Cooper Justice Centre, 6 June 2012", http://www.vcat.vic.gov.au/news/vcat-cuts-ribbon-william-cooper-justice-centre

[167] "William Cooper's Great Grandson Walks the Walk" J-Wire 28 November 2010 Agencies

[168] www.splitter.com.au/warrenmillsmusic/shep-shed-2011.php

[169] Aboriginal

[170] Caleb Morgan and Shadrach James were also key members of AAL

[171] A free-roaming wild horse

[172] Domestic violence

[173] Coolamons were traditionally used by Aboriginal women to carry water, fruits, nuts, as well as to cradle babies.

[174] Jacks, Timna (2014)" Queen accepts petition for Aboriginal rights, 80 years on". *Sydney Morning Herald* 4.10.14 https://www.smh.com.au/politics/federal/queen-accepts-petition-for-aboriginal-rights-80-years-on-20141003-10ksh6.html#ixzz3lcYds1kZ

[175] 2014 Victorian Aboriginal Honour Roll. https://w.www.vic.gov.au/aboriginalvictoria/community-engagement/leadership-programs/aboriginal-honour-roll/2014-victorian-aboriginal-honour-roll.html

[176] Ibid.

[177] Hayman-Reber, Madeline (2018) "A statue celebrating the life of Yorta Yorta man Uncle William Cooper has been unveiled in the town of Shepparton, Victoria." *NITV News* 4.4.2018

[178] The Age (2006) A lasting tribute to an Australian Gandhi 18.2.2006 https://www.theage.com.au/national/a-lasting-tribute-to-an-australian-gandhi-20060218-ge1s7y.html

[179] Latimore, Jack (2018) "Treaty Legislation Passed and William Cooper Honoured. This week there was hope". *The Guardian* 22 June 2018

[180] Witoslawski, Ashlea (2019) "Cummeragunja walk-off anniversary celebrated." 4.2.19 Shepparton News

[181] Pearson, Luke (2017) "Lynch Cooper: the first Aboriginal World's Sprinting Champion" 24.2.17 *NITV*

[182] Yolgnu Aboriginal word for treaty or peace after conflict

[183] http://blogs.riverfronttimes.com/dailyrft/2012/01/martin_luther_king_jrs_prophetic_last_speech.php

[184] Attwood, Bain and Markus, Andrew (2004) "Thinking Black, William Cooper and the Australian Aborigines' League" Canberra: Aboriginal Studies Press P95

[185] Exodus 3:7-8

[186] Wilson-Miller, James "Visionaries of Change", Self-Concept Enhancement and Learning Facilitation Research Centre, University of Western Sydney, Australia http://www.aare.edu.au/05pap/wil05320.pdf P5

[187] Ibid P7

References

Books and Reports

Adams, J., Venables, P. & Miller, B. (1991) *Wayan Min Uwanp Aak Ngulakana, Finding the Right Road Ahead* Cairns: Queensland Department of Aboriginal and Islander Affairs

Attwood, Bain and Markus, Andrew (2004) *Thinking Black, William Cooper and the Australian Aborigines' League* Canberra: Aboriginal Studies Press

Bird, David S. (2012) *Nazi Dreamtime, Australian Enthusiasts for Nazi Germany* Melbourne: Australian Scholarly Publishing Pty Ltd

Blakeney, Michael (1985) *Australia and the Jewish Refugees 1933-1948* Sydney: Croom Helm Australia

Cato, Nancy (1976) *Mister Maloga, Daniel Matthews and his Mission, Murray River, 1864*-1902 St Lucia, Qld: University of Queensland Press

Clark, Mavis Thorpe (1972) *Pastor Doug: The Story of Sir Douglas Nicholls, Aboriginal* Leader Melbourne: Lansdowne Press

Commonwealth of Australia (1920) *Hansard* Commonwealth Parliamentary Debates

Commonwealth of Australia (1972) *Hansard* Commonwealth Parliamentary Debates, 13/9/72

Dow, Coral and Gardiner-Garden, John (2011) *Overview of Indigenous Affairs: 1901 to 1991* Canberra: Parliament of Australia

Gilbert, Martin (1981) "Auschwitz and the Allies" New York: Holt, Reinhart and Winston in Blakeney, Michael (1985) *Australia and the Jewish Refugees 1933-1948* Sydney: Croom Helm Australia, preface

Goodall, Heather (1982) "The history of Aboriginal communities in NSW 1909–1939," Unpublished PhD thesis, Department of History, The Australian National University, Canberra in Harris, John (1994*) One Blood, 200 Years of Aboriginal Encounter With Christianity: A Story of Hope* Sutherland, NSW: Albatross Books

Gribble Papers, ABM Archives 20/9/1937 in Harris, John (1994) *One Blood, 200 Years of Aboriginal Encounter With Christianity: A Story of Hope* Sutherland, NSW: Albatross Books

Gribble, Ernest (1932) "The Problem of the Australian Aboriginal" Sydney: Angus and Robertson in Harris, John (1994) *One Blood, 200 Years of Aboriginal Encounter With Christianity: A Story of Hope* Sutherland, NSW: Albatross Books

Harris, John (1994) *One Blood, 200 Years of Aboriginal Encounter With Christianity: A Story of Hope* Sutherland, NSW: Albatross Books

Horner, Jack (1974) *Vote Ferguson For Aboriginal Freedom, A Biography by Jack Horner* Sydney: Australia and New Zealand Book Company, P47

Horner, Jack (1994) *Bill Ferguson: Fighter for Aboriginal Freedom* Canberra: self-published

Manne, Robert (ed) (2003) *Whitewash: On Keith Windschuttle's Fabrication of Aboriginal* History Melbourne: Black Inc.

Markus, Andrew (1988) *Blood From a Stone: William Cooper and the Australian Aborigines' League* Sydney: Allen and Unwin

Miller, B (1986) *The Aspirations of Aborigines Living at Yarrabah in Relation to Local Management and Human Rights* Canberra: Human Rights Commission

Miller, Barbara (1990) *ACC Submission to the Royal Commission into Aboriginal Deaths in Custody* Cairns: Aboriginal Co-ordinating Council

Miller, B. (1992) "A Social-Historical and Psychological Perspective on Aboriginal Intra-Cultural Aggression" in Thomas, D.R. & Veno, A. (Eds) (1992) *Psychology and Social Change, Creating an International Agenda* Palmerston North, NZ: Dunmore Press

Miller, B (1993) *Queensland Aboriginal Trust Community Initiatives in taking Responsibility for Social Control* Cairns: Aboriginal Co-ordinating Council

Miller, B (1994) *Options for the Future: Local Government and Native Title on Queensland Aboriginal Communities* Cairns: Aboriginal Co-ordinating Council

Miller, B (2005) *Community Transformation – Building Spiritual Capital at Aurukun Project* Report Cairns: Queensland Department of Communities.

Miller, Barbara (2012) *William Cooper, Gentle Warrior: Standing Up for Australian Aborigines and Persecuted Jews* Xlibris

Miller, Barbara (2018) *The Dying Days of Segregation in Australia: Case Study* Yarrabah Cairns: Barbara Miller Books.

Miller, Barbara (2018) *White Woman Black Heart: Journey Home to Old Mapoon, A Memoir,* Createspace

Reynolds, Henry (1981) *The Other Side of the Frontier: Aboriginal Resistance to the European Invasion of Australia* Sydney: UNSW Press

Roberts, Jan, Parsons, Michael, McLean, David and Russell, Barbara (1975) *The Mapoon Story* Vol 1-3. Melbourne: International Development Action.

Stanner, W.E.H. (1979) "After the Dreaming" in Stanner, W.E.H. *White Man Got No Dreaming: Essays 1938-1973*

Victorian Aborigines Advancement League (1985) *Victims or Victors: The Story of the Victorian Aborigines Advancement League* Melbourne: Hyland House Publishing Pty Ltd

Windschuttle, Keith (2002) *The Fabrication of Aboriginal History, Volume One: Van Diemen's Land 1803-1847* Sydney: Macleay Press.

Newspapers, Journals and Articles

Australian Bureau of Statistics (2017) *Migration Australia* *Migration, Australia (cat. no. 3412.0)* https://www.abs.gov.au/ausstats/abs@.nsf/previousproducts/3412.0main%20features32015-16

Australian Government Department of Immigration and Citizenship (2009) *Fact Sheet 8 – Abolition of the White Australia Policy*

Barta, Tony, "Relations of Genocide: Land and Lives in the Colonization of Australia", in Wallimann, Isidor & Dobkowski, Michael N. (eds) (1987) *Genocide and the Modern*

Age: Etiology and Case Studies of Mass Death New York: Greenwood Press http://hyperhistory.org/index.php?option=displaypage&Itemid=364&op=page#arti.

Bennet, Darryl *NCB Collaborates with Museum of Australian Democracy* http://ncb.anu.edu.au/book/export/html/103

Black, Edwin (2003) "The Horrifying American Roots of Nazi Eugenics" in George Mason's University *History News Network* http://hnn.us/articles/1796.html

Cannon, Anthea (2010) "Footscray bridge named in honour of Aboriginal leader" 20 May 10 http://maribyrnong-leader.whereilive.com.au

Clark, Anna (2002 "History in Black and White: a critical analysis of the Black Armband debate, originally published in Richard Nile (ed) *Country: Journal of Australian Studies* no 75, St Lucia, UQP, 2002. http:/www.api-network.com/main/pdf/scholars/jas75_clark.pdf

Commonwealth of Australia http://vietnam-war.commemoration.gov.au/conscription/moratoriums-and-opposition.php

Commonwealth of Australia http://vietnam-war.commemoration.gov.au/conscription/save-our-sons.php

Dixon, Chicka (1967) quoted in "I want to be a human being", *The Sydney Morning Herald*, 21 May 1967 http://www.creativespirits.info/aboriginalculture/history/referendum-1967.html#ixzz25A1sdWlC

Ferrier, Carole "White Blindfolds and Black Armbands: the uses of whiteness theory for reading Australian cultural production,"*Queensland Review*, vol 6, no1, p42-49.

Hayman-Reber, Madeline (2018) "A statue celebrating the life of Yorta Yorta man Uncle William Cooper has been unveiled in the town of Shepparton, Victoria." *NITV News* 4.4.2018

Herald 7 August 1937

Howard, John (1996) "The Liberal Tradition: The Beliefs and Values That Guide the Federal Government", Sir Robert Menzies Lecture. Sir Robert Menzies Lecture Trust http://www.menzieslecture.org/1996.html

Irving, Helen, Bolton, Geoffrey, Ricketson, Matthew and Jopson, Debra(2003) "Footnotes to a war" 13/12/2003, *Sydney Morning Herald* http://www.smh.com.au/articles/2003/12/15/1071336875054.html

Jack Patten (1938) *Australian Abo Call,* 1 (1) April 1938

Jacks, Timna (2014) "Queen accepts petition for Aboriginal rights, 80 years on" *Sydney Morning Herald* 4.10.14 https://www.smh.com.au/politics/federal/queen-accepts-petition-for-aboriginal-rights-80-years-on-20141003-10ksh6.html#ixzz3IcYds1kZ

Jennifer Wilson, National Museum of Australia (2010) *Parliament for the people* 12 May 2010 http://www.nma.gov.au/audio/transcripts/landmarks/NMA_Parliament_for_people_20100512.html

John Newfong (1972) "The Aboriginal Embassy: its purpose and aims,: Identity, 1 (5):4-6, July 1972

J-Wire (2010) "William Cooper's Great Grandson Walks the Walk" *J-Wire* November 28, 2010 Agencies

Keating, Paul (2003) "Keating's 'History Wars,'"5/9/2003 *Sydney Morning Herald* http://www.smh.com.au/articles/2003/09/05/1062549021882.html

Kevles, Daniel J. "In the Name of Darwin" adapted from his 1995 book *In the Name of Eugenics,* Harvard University Press, http://www.pbs.org/wgbh/evolution/darwin/nameof/index.html

Latimore, Jack (2018) "Treaty Legislation Passed and William Cooper Honoured. This week there was hope." *The Guardian* 22 June 2018

Menzies Library, ANU, Canberra (1971) *Commonwealth policy in relation to land and related matters*, 7 July 1971, file 29, Barry Dexter papers, accessed on www.indigenousrights.net.au

National Library of Australia, MS 51/1/976 "Barton Papers," in ABC *Australia's Centenary of Federation* http//www.abc.net.au/federation/fedstory/ep2/ep2_institutions.htm

National Museum of Australia, Collaborating for Indigenous Rights *National petition campaign, 1962-63* http://indigenousrights.net.au

National Museum of Australia, Collaborating for Indigenous Rights *Parliamentary and Cabinet debates, 1964-66* http://indigenousrights.net.au

News Blog "Martin Luther King's Prophetic Last Speech" http://blogs.riverfronttimes.com/dailyrft/2012/01/martin_luther_king_jrs_prophetic_last_speech.php

Pearson, Luke (2017) "Lynch Cooper: the first Aboriginal World's Sprinting Champion" 24.2.17 *NITV*

Richardson, Tim "The Stolen Generations: Robert Manne" http://www.tim-richardson.net/joomla15article-list-personalmenu-7

Robinson, Scott (1994) "The Aboriginal Embassy: an account of the Protests of 1972" *Aboriginal History* Vol.18 (1) 1994

Small, Jerome (2001) "100 years or racism: federation and the white Australia policy" Social Alternative Ed 48, Feb 2001.

SMH (1965)"Aborigines need less than the cost of a jet," *The Sydney Morning Herald*, 1 December 1965 http://www.creativespirits.info/aboriginalculture/history/referendum-1967.html#ixzz259yzoib7

SMH (2003) "The High Cost of Whitewash" 27/9/2003 *Sydney Morning Herald* http://www.smh.com.au/articles/2003/09/26/1064083186575.html

State Library of Victoria (2011) Reconciliation Convention 1997 http://ergo.slv.vic.gov.au/explore-history/fight-rights/indigenous-rights/reconciliation-convention-1997

Sydney Morning Herald 9 February 1972

Taffe, Sue (2009) "The Cairns Aboriginal and Torres Strait Islander Advancement League and the Community of the Left" *Labour History* Vol 97, Nov 2009

Taylor, Chris *Australia's Heritage National Treasures* video.

The Age (2006) *A lasting tribute to an Australian Gandhi* 18.2.2006 https://www.theage.com.au/national/a-lasting-tribute-to-an-australian-gandhi-20060218-ge1s7y.html

The Age 8 February 1972, 10 February 1972, 24 July 1972 and 31 July 1972

The Australian 9 February 1972

Victorian Civil and Administrative Tribunal (2012) "VCAT cuts the ribbon at William Cooper Justice Centre, Jun 6th, 2012", http://www.vcat.vic.gov.au/news/vcat-cuts-ribbon-william-cooper-justice-centre

Victorian Government (2014) *2014 Victorian Aboriginal Honour Roll* https://w.www.vic.gov.au/aboriginalvictoria/community-engagement/leadership-programs/aboriginal-honour-roll/2014-victorian-aboriginal-honour-roll.html

Warren Mills Music (2011) www.splitter.com.au/warrenmillsmusic/shep-shed-2011.php

Wilson-Miller, James "Visionaries of Change," Self-Concept Enhancement and Learning Facilitation Research Centre, University of Western Sydney, Australia http://www.aare.edu.au/05pap/wil05320.pdf P5

Witoslawski, Ashlea (2019) "Cummeragunja walk-off anniversary celebrated."4.2.19 *Shepparton News*

Woorama (2007) *Eugenics and Aborigines, Genetic Science – Its Role in Indigenous Policy, Identity, Genocide* http//suite101.com/article/eugenics-and-aborigines-a22972, P2

DOWNLOAD FREE GIFT NOW

Just to thank you for buying my book, I would like to give you a 14-page PDF of the hidden history of the first contact of Europeans with Australian Aborigines. It is the untold story that is not in your school text books. Hear from Aborigines who have had the story passed down through generations and from the explorers.

For information on my other books go to – www.barbara-miller-books.com

TO DOWNLOAD GO TO

http://eepurl.com/dn69ab

I'd love a review on Amazon and/or Goodreads. Here is the amazon link to this book -
https://www.amazon.com/review/create?asin=B07X1MYCDX/

And the link to my Goodreads page - https://www.goodreads.com/author/show/17901589.Barbara_Miller

You can also email me feedback. I'd love to hear from you –

bmiller-books@bigpond.com or contact me on facebook - https://www.facebook.com/Barbara-Miller-Books-479991872149265/

Will I Survive?
This thought haunted Lena.
With family torn from her in
Warsaw Ghetto and perishing in
Treblinka Death Camp
BARBARA MILLER
IF I SURVIVE
IF I SURVIVE
Her Miraculous story will inspire you
barbara-miller-books.com

An Aboriginal elder told her
you may be white but you have a black heart
In helping the Mapoon Aboriginal people
return to their homeland after removal for
mining, she found her own home
Barbara Miller
finalist
White
Woman
Black
Heart
JOURNEY HOME TO
OLD MAPOON, A MEMOIR
WHITE WOMAN BLACK HEART
The inside story of an Aboriginal community's brave stand
barbara-miller-books.com

Did the deep north of Australia experience racism, discrimination and segregation? How did the Yarrabah community break free of apartheid?

THE DYING DAYS OF SEGREGATION IN AUSTRALIA: CASE STUDY YARRABAH

Meet the Aboriginal leaders who took a stand and won

barbara-miller-books.com

Read about one of Australia's early Indigenous activists who met with Prime Ministers and petitioned Kings & who championed the cause of Jews at Kristallnacht in 1938

WILLIAM COOPER, GENTLE WARRIOR

This book is the history of Indigenous Australia in a nutshell

What stirred the explorers to face hardships to find the elusive South Land between Africa and South America?
How did they treat native peoples of the Pacific along the way?

THE EUROPEAN QUEST TO FIND TERRA AUSTRALIS INCOGNITA: QUIROS, TORRES AND JANSZOON

Who found Australia first and where was the first landing?

 barbara-miller-books.com 

Made in the USA
Columbia, SC
11 September 2020

19966382R00176